I0494780

The Golden Vault Of

Motivational

Quotations

Timeless Words Of Wisdom
From The Greatest Minds &
Most Inspiring Leaders
On The Planet

4,013 - Motivational Quotations
65,763 - Words of Wisdom
1612 - Brilliant Minds
230 - Pages

Compiled by
Richard & Lynn Voigt
I.M. Education Specialist

The Golden Vault of Motivational Quotations
© 2012 by RIVO Inc – All Rights Reserved!

ISBN-13: 978-1468168495

ISBN-10: 1468168495

ALL RIGHTS RESERVED. No part of this report may be reproduced or transmitted in any form whatsoever, known or yet invented, electronic or mechanical, scanning or photocopying, nor through any informational archival, storage, or retrieval system without prior written, dated, signed authorization of rights from RIVO Inc on behalf of the authors. All visual marks, images, and compositions included in this report, either in whole or in part, are governed and protected under International copyright and trademark laws by their rightful owner.

First Printing, 2012

Printed in the United States of America

To Access More Powerful Marketing Tools Visit:

www.ActionHeadlines.com

www.Headlines.me

www.RIVOinc.com

Income Disclaimer

This publication contains educational materials meant to inspire ways to promote personal ideas, products and services that may be appropriate to incorporate or use in or as a business strategy, marketing method or any other related personal or business advice that, regardless of the author's results and experience, may not produce the same results (or any results) for you. The authors make absolutely no guarantee, expressed or implied, that by using or following any of the ideas below that you will make any money or improve current profits, as there are several factors and variables that come into play regarding any level of achievement or success in said personal and/or business venture.

Primarily, results will depend on the nature of the product or business model, the conditions of the marketplace, the experience of the individual, and situations and elements that are beyond your control. As with any business endeavor, you assume all risk related to investment and money based on your own discretion and at your own potential expense. If you intend to quote, copy, or use any content herein, in part or whole, it shall be the sole responsibility of the individual to be mindful of all active and lawfully protected copyrights, trademarks, and/or services-marks, by conducting due diligence prior to said usage.

Liability Disclaimer

This publication is strictly intended for educational purposes only and was intended to inspire the individual to create ideas of their own design. This publication represents the views of the authors as of the date of publication. Due to constant changing conditions facing the information age, the authors reserve the irrevocable right to modify and update their opinions based upon changing conditions. While the authors have made a "good faith" effort to verify the accuracy of information within this book, the authors or their affiliates/partners do not assume any liability or responsibility for inadvertent errors, omissions, or inaccuracies. This publication is not intended to be used as a legal guide or resource, nor are the authors attempting to render any legal, accounting, or other said professional services. If legal consultation or advice is required, the authors recommend the reader immediately seek the services of a competent profes-sional for all legal or accounting advice. It shall be the reader's responsibility to be fully aware of federal, state, local or country laws that govern and affect said business transactions. Any slight of ethnicity, culture, gender, ori-entation, or existing organization as is any reference to persons or businesses, living or dead, is unintentional and purely coincidental.

Terms of Use

All contents of this publication are under exclusive Inter-national copyright © 2012 RIVO Inc. All rights not expressly granted herein are also reserved! Your pur-chase is a non-transferable, "personal use" license to this publication. You cannot distribute it or share it with other individuals. There are no resale rights or private label rights granted when purchasing this publication. In other words, it's for your own personal use only.

Now that all the legal stuff is out of the way, let's begin to have a lifetime of fun by applying, modifying, and custom-izing the following educational materials to help you creatively promote your own original ideas or marketing niche.

The Golden Vault Of
Motivational
Quotations

Timeless Words Of Wisdom
From The Greatest Minds &
Most Inspiring Leaders
On The Planet

4,013 - Motivational Quotations
65,763 - Words of Wisdom
1612 - Brilliant Minds
232 - Pages

Compiled by
Richard & Lynn Voigt
I.M. Education Specialist

The Golden Vault Of
Motivational Quotations

Throughout history people have been looking to Great Leaders as a source of inspiration for achieving dreams and setting goals. Within this collection of over 4,000 motivational quotations from over 1,600 brilliant contributors, you'll find the greatest words of wisdom from the greatest minds on our planet.

Their wisdom has become the true inspiration for many people to reclaim the ability to believe in themselves. To believe that they are capable of achieving anything their mind can believe and obtain a higher purpose in their lives.

This collection of "Inspirational Words" deals with motivational quotes from around the world; from the greatest leaders and thinkers of our society.

Motivational quotes are the greatest source of true inspiration of people searching for personal development and self-improvement.

May this collection of the world's greatest quotes inspire you and your followers, and motivate them to live their lives to their fullest potential.

The Golden Vault
Of Motivational Quotes

Words of Wisdom from Greatest & Most Inspiring Leaders On The Planet

1	"Competition Is The Keen Cutting Edge Of Business, Always Shaving Away At Costs." - Henry Ford
2	"Effective Leadership Is Putting First Things First. Effective Management Is Discipline, Carrying It Out." - Stephen Covey
3	"Time Is Money." - Benjamin Franklin
4	"Don't Agonize, Organize." - Florynce Kennedy
5	"Love Conquers All." - Virgil
6	"Failure Is Impossible." - Susan B. Anthony
7	"Sweat Saves Blood." - Erwin Rommel
8	"Wisdom Begins In Wonder." - Socrates
9	"Reject Hatred Without Hating." - Mary Baker Eddy
10	"Wisdom Outweighs Any Wealth." - Sophocles
11	"Love Is Metaphysical Gravity." - R. Buckminster Fuller
12	"Leave The Atom Alone." - E. Y. Harburg
13	"Love Is Love's Reward." - John Dryden
14	"Everybody's A Filmmaker Today." - John Milius
15	"Nothing Recedes Like Success." - Walter Winchell
16	"Earth Laughs In Flowers." - Ralph Waldo Emerson
17	"Every Winner Has Scars." - Herbert N. Casson
18	"Fans Don't Boo Nobodies." - Reggie Jackson
19	"I Paint With Shapes." - Alexander Calder
20	"Music Is My Religion." - Jimi Hendrix
21	"Wit Is Educated Insolence." - Aristotle
22	"Age Considers; Youth Ventures." - Rabindranath Tagore
23	"All War Is Deception." - Sun Tzu
24	"Do The Next Thing." - John Wanamaker
25	"Happiness Depends Upon Ourselves." - Aristotle
26	"Success Is Never Final." - Winston Churchill
27	"Faith Is Spiritualized Imagination." - Henry Ward Beecher
28	"Historian: An Unsuccessful Novelist." - H. L. Mencken

29	"Imagination Rules The World." - Napoleon Bonaparte
30	"Life Is About Timing." - Carl Lewis
31	"In Dreams Begins Responsibility." - William Butler Yeats
32	"Life Is But Thought." - Sara Teasdale
33	"All Music Is Beautiful." - Billy Strayhorn
34	"Cleverness Is Not Wisdom." - Euripides
35	"Nobody Roots For Goliath." - Wilt Chamberlain
36	"Never Floss With A Stranger." - Joan Rivers
37	"Every Moment Is An Experience." - Jake Roberts
38	"Beware Of Geeks Bearing Formulas." - Warren Buffett
39	"Unbeing Dead Isn't Being Alive." - E. E. Cummings
40	"A Satellite Has No Conscience." - Edward R. Murrow
41	"Wisdom Is A Sacred Communion." - Victor Hugo
42	"Experience Is A Great Teacher." - John Legend
43	"Old Age Is A Shipwreck." - Charles De Gaulle
44	"Everything In Life Is Luck." - Donald Trump
45	"I Am Two With Nature." - Woody Allen
46	"Life...Can Only Be Understood Backwards..." - Soren Kierkegaard
47	"Our Aspirations Are Our Possibilities" - Robert Browning
48	"In Politics Nothing Is Contemptible." - Benjamin Disraeli
49	"I Like Marriage. The Idea." - Toni Morrison
50	"I Like Children - Fried." - W. C. Fields
51	"Peace Is Liberty In Tranquility." - Marcus Tullius Cicero
52	"Music Should Be Your Escape." - Missy Elliot
53	"Polygraph Tests Are 20th-Century Witchcraft." - Sam Ervin
54	"Oh, That Lovely Title, Ex-President." - Dwight D. Eisenhower
55	"Art Is Science Made Clear." - Wilson Mizner
56	"In Imagination, There's No Limitation." - Mark Victor Hansen
57	"Time Is My Greatest Enemy." - Evita Peron
58	"Peace Is A Conscious Choice." - John Denver
59	"Dreams Are Necessary To Life." - Anais Nin
60	"Humor Is Mankind's Greatest Blessing." - Mark Twain
61	"Chance Favors The Prepared Mind." - Louis Pasteur
62	"Humor Is Reason Gone Mad." - Groucho Marx
63	"Simplicity Is The Ultimate Sophistication" - Leonardo de Vinci
64	"Honor Your Commitments With Integrity." - Les Brown
65	"The Computer Is A Moron." - Douglas Engelbart
66	"Wrestling Is Ballet With Violence." - Jesse Ventura
67	"Faith Is A Passionate Intuition." - William Wordsworth
68	"Life Well Spent Is Long." - Karen Horney

69	"Never Fight An Inanimate Object." - P. J. O'Rourke
70	"I Rant, Therefore I Am." - Dennis Miller
71	"Success Is Dependent On Effort." - Sophocles
72	"Who, Being Loved, Is Poor?" - Oscar Wilde
73	"Peace Begins With A Smile." - Mother Teresa
74	"Nothing Is Permanent But Change." - Heraclitus
75	"Fatigue Is The Best Pillow." - Benjamin Franklin
76	"The Journey Is The Reward." - Taoist Proverb
77	"Film Lovers Are Sick People." - Francois Truffaut
78	"Weather Forecast For Tonight: Dark." - George Carlin
79	"While There's Life, There's Hope." - Marcus Tullius Cicero
80	"Film Spectators Are Quiet Vampires." - Jim Morrison
81	"Horse Racing Is Animated Roulette." - Roger Kahn
82	"What We Play Is Life." - Louis Armstrong
83	"Wisdom Begins At The End." - Daniel Webster
84	"Habit Is Stronger Than Reason." - George Santayana
85	"All Sports For All People." - Pierre De Coubertin
86	"Do All Things With Love." - Og Mandino
87	"Anger Is A Short Madness." - Horace
88	"All Mankind Love A Lover." - Ralph Waldo Emerson
89	"Time Is The Wisest Counselor." - Pericles
90	"Turn Your Wounds Into Wisdom." - Oprah Winfrey
91	"Without Forgiveness, There's No Future." - Desmond Tutu
92	"That Great Dust-Heap Called 'History'." - Augustine Birrell
93	"Knowledge Comes, But Wisdom Lingers." - Alfred Lord Tennyson
94	"Intelligence Is Not A Science." - Frank Carlucci
95	"Faith Is Reason Grown Courageous." - Sherwood Eddy
96	"Love Is Being Stupid Together." - Paul Valery
97	"God Is The Perfect Poet." - Robert Browning
98	"Peace Is Its Own Reward." - Mohandas Gandhi
99	"Politics Have No Relation To Morals." - Niccolo Machiavelli
100	"May The Force Be With You." - Yoda
101	"The Groves Were God's First Temples." - William C. Bryant
102	"Nobody Makes Movies Bad On Purpose." - Roland Emmerich
103	"The Most Profound Things Are Inexpressible." - Jenny Holzer
104	"It Is Not A Fragrant World." - Raymond Chandler
105	"There Is No Forgiveness In Nature." - Ugo Betti
106	"Our Favorite Holding Period Is Forever." - Warren Buffet
107	"Lost Time Is Never Found Again." - Benjamin Franklin
108	"Always In Motion The Future Is." - Yoda

109	"Art Is Either Plagiarism Or Revolution." - Paul Gauguin
110	"Every Artist Writes His Own Autobiography." - Henry Ellis
111	"Every Artist Was First An Amateur." - Ralph Waldo Emerson
112	"Fortune And Love Favor The Brave." - Ovid
113	"Education Is The Transmission Of Civilization." - Will Durant
114	"The Unconscious Is Our Best Collaborator." - Mike Nichols
115	"Die, V.: To Stop Sinning Suddenly." - Elbert Hubbard
116	"Wisdom Is Found Only In Truth." - Johann Wolfgang Von Goethe
117	"Without Deviation Progress Is Not Possible." - Frank Zappa
118	"Around The Survivors A Perimeter Create." - Yoda
119	"When Humor Goes, There Goes Civilization." - Erma Bombeck
120	"Life Is Wasted On The Living." - Douglas Adams
121	"There Is No Wealth But Life." - John Ruskin
122	"Democracy Is An Abuse Of Statistics." - Jorge Luis Borges
123	"Conflict Cannot Survive Without Your Participation." - Wayne Dyer
124	"Golf Is A Good Walk Spoiled." - Mark Twain
125	"Change Alone Is Eternal, Perpetual, Immortal." - Arthur Schopenhauer
126	"Who So Loves Believes The Impossible." - Elizabeth Barrett Browning
127	" Boxing Has Become America's Tragic Theater." - Joyce Carol Oates
128	"Life Must Be Lived As Play." - Plato
129	"Imagination Is More Important Than Knowledge." - Albert Einstein
130	"There Are No Gains Without Pains." - Benjamin Franklin
131	"He Who Angers You Conquers You." - Elizabeth Kenny
132	"Get Mad, Then Get Over It." - Colin Powell
133	"Mediocrity Is Self-Inflicted. Genius is Self-Bestowed" - Walter Russell
134	"Intellectuals Solves Problems, Geniuses Prevent Them." - Albert Einstein
135	"Life Is An Adventure In Forgiveness." - Norman Cousins
136	"The World Is Mud-Luscious And Puddle-Wonderful." - E. E. Cummings
137	"Hurry Is Slow." - Latin Proverb
138	"Immature Artists Imitate. Mature Artists Steal." - Lionel Trilling
139	"Pictures Must Not Be Too Picturesque." - Ralph Waldo Emerson
140	"Until You Try You Don't Know." - Henry James
141	"Life Loves The Liver Of It." - Maya Angelou
142	"To Me Faith Means Not Worrying." - John Dewey
143	"Belief Is The Death Of Intelligence." - Robert Anton Wilson

144	"Sports Are A Microcosm Of Society." - Billie Jean King
145	"Love Does Not Dominate; It Cultivates." - Johann Wolfgang Von Goethe
146	"Common Sense Is Not So Common." - Voltaire
147	"Electricity Is Really Just Organized Lightning." - George Carlin
148	"The Superfluous, A Very Necessary Thing." - Voltaire
149	"I Came, I Saw, I Conquered." - Julius Caesar
150	"Music Is The Shorthand Of Emotion." - Leo Tolstoy
151	"When You Believe You Can-You Can!" - Maxwell Maltz
152	"In Music The Passions Enjoy Themselves." - Friedrich Nietzsche
153	"Only The Insecure Strive For Security." - Wayne Dyer
154	"A Stumble May Prevent A Fall." - Thomas Fuller
155	"When Words Leave Off, Music Begins." - Heinrich Heine
156	"Patience Is The Companion Of Wisdom." - Saint Augustine
157	"Television Is Democracy At Its Ugliest." - Paddy Chayefsky
158	"Things Do Not Change; We Change." - Henry David Thoreau
159	"Education Is A Vaccine For Violence." - Edward James Olmos
160	"You Become What You Think About." - Earl Nightingale
161	"The Future Will Be Better Tomorrow." - Dan Quayle
162	"There Are No Shortcuts In Evolution." - Louis D. Brandeis
163	"Beauty Awakens The Soul To Act." - Dante Alighieri
164	"The Bible Is Literature, Not Dogma." - George Santayana
165	"My Inner Child Is Not Wounded." - Shannen Doherty
166	"Spend Some Time Alone Every Day." - The Dalai Lama
167	"Art Is Subject To Arbitrary Fashion." - Kary Mullis
168	"Man Is A Universe Within Himself." - Bob Marley
169	"Great Hopes Make Everything Great Possible." - Benjamin Franklin
170	"To Work Is To Feel Alive." - Tony Bennett
171	"The Poet Doesn't Invent. He Listens." - Jean Cocteau
172	"Nothing Happens Unless First A Dream." - Carl Sandburg
173	"Lesser Artists Borrow, Great Artists Steal." - Igor Stravinsky
174	"History Is More Or Less Bunk." - Henry Ford
175	"Be Courageous! Have Faith! Go Forward!" - Duke Ellington
176	"There's An Electrical Thing About Movies." - Oliver Stone
177	"Perspective Is Worth 80 IQ Points." - Alan Kay
178	"Faith Is Not Contrary To Reason." - Sherwood Eddy
179	"Hell Is Full Of Musical Amateurs." - George Bernard Shaw
180	"Music Is The Soul Of Language." - Max Heindel
181	"Patience Will Achieve More Than Force." - Edmund Burke
182	"No Great Thing Is Created Suddenly." - Epictetus
183	"Chase Your Passion, Not Your Pension." - Denis Waitley

184	"Fiction Reveals Truths That Reality Obscures." - Jessamyn West
185	"Muscles Come And Go; Flab Lasts." - Bill Vaughan
186	"Perpetual Optimism Is A Force Multiplier." - Colin Powell
187	"View Every Problem As An Opportunity..." - Joseph Sugarman
188	"Libraries Are Not Made, They Grow." - Augustine Birrell
189	"Youth Is Wasted On The Young." - George Bernard Shaw
190	"Gray Skies Are Just Clouds Passing Over." - Frank Gifford
191	"Only A Few Things Are Really Important." - Marie Dressler
192	"Technology Has To Be Invented Or Adopted." - Jared Diamond
193	"You Cannot Have Success Without The Failures." - H. G. Hasler
194	"Ultimately, Blind Faith Is The Only Kind." - Mason Cooley
195	"Glory Is Fleeting, But Obscurity Is Forever." - Napoleon Bonaparte
196	"Artists Don't Make Objects. Artists Make Mythologies." - Anish Kapoor
197	"History Is A Vast Early Warning System." - Norman Cousins
198	"Smooth Seas Do Not Make Skillful Sailors." - African Proverb
199	"Forgiveness Is A Gift You Give Yourself." - Suzanne Somers
200	"You Must Unlearn What You Have Learned." - Yoda
201	"To Rule Is Easy, To Govern Difficult." - Johann Wolfgang Von Goethe
202	"Trying To Force Creativity Is Never Good." - Sarah Mclachlan
203	"Nature, To Be Commanded, Must Be Obeyed." - Francis Bacon
204	"Apology Is Only Egotism Wrong Side Out." - Oliver Wendell Holmes
205	"Everyone Is Ignorant, Only On Different Subjects" - Will Rogers
206	"Without Discipline, There's No Life At All." - Katharine Hepburn
207	"He Has Van Gogh's Ear For Music." - Billy Wilder
208	"Carpe Per Diem - Seize The Check." - Robin Williams
209	"Time Is The Wisest Counselor Of All." - Pericles
210	"A Joke Is A Very Serious Thing." - Winston Churchill
211	"TV Is Chewing Gum For The Eyes." - Frank Lloyd Wright
212	"Things Are Beautiful If You Love Them." - Jean Anouilh
213	"Don't Be A Blueprint. Be An Original." - Roy Acuff
214	"Never Wear Anything That Panics The Cat." - P. J. O'Rourke
215	"A Goal Properly Set Is Halfway Reached." - Zig Ziglar
216	"Great Art Picks Up Where Nature Ends." - Marc Chagall
217	"Knowledge Is Power - Knowledge Equals Power" - Francis Bacon
218	"Great Minds Have Purposes, Others Have Wishes." - Washington Irving
219	"Dreams Are The Touchstones Of Our Character." - Henry David Thoreau
220	"Do One Thing Everyday That Scares You" - Eleanor Roosevelt

221	"Art Doesn't Transform. It Just Plain Forms." - Roy Lichtenstein
222	"Difficulty Is The Excuse History Never Accepts." - Edward R. Murrow
223	"All Diseases Run Into One, Old Age." - Ralph Waldo Emerson
224	"When Anger Rises, Think Of The Consequences." - Confucius
225	"Friendship Is One Mind In Two Bodies." - Mencius
226	"Winning Is Habit. Unfortunately, So Is Losing." - Vince Lombardi
227	"I'll Let The Racket Do The Talking." - John Mcenroe
228	"A Prudent Question Is One-Half Of Wisdom." - Francis Bacon
229	"I Think Serial Monogamy Says It All." - Tracey Ullman
230	"Mistakes Are Merely Steps Up The Ladder..." - Paul J. Meyer
231	"Hitting Is Timing. Pitching Is Upsetting Timing." - Warren Spahn
232	"You Can Do Anything, But Not Everything." - David Allen
233	"Nobody Can Bring You Peace But Yourself." - Ralph Waldo Emerson
234	"One Man's Folly Is Another Man's Wife." - Helen Rowland
235	"No Man Was Ever Wise By Chance." - Lucius Annaeus Seneca
236	"Do Not Fear Mistakes. There Are None." - Miles Davis
237	"Always Be A Poet, Even In Prose." - Charles Baudelaire
238	"I Buy When Other People Are Selling." - J. Paul Getty
239	"Our National Flower Is The Concrete Cloverleaf." - Lewis Mumford
240	"Control Your Destiny Or Somebody Else Will." - Jack Welch
241	"Keep Cool; Anger Is Not An Argument." - Daniel Webster
242	"True Friends Stab You In The Front." - Oscar Wilde
243	"The Time I Kill Is Killing Me." - Mason Cooley
244	"Love Is The Beauty Of The Soul." - Saint Augustine
245	"The Integrity Of The Game Is Everything." - Peter Ueberroth
246	"Real Riches Are The Riches Possessed Inside." - B. C. Forbes
247	"We Tend To Get What We Expect." - Norman Vincent Peale
248	"Action Is The Real Measure Of Intelligence." - Napoleon Hill
249	"Wit Is The Lowest Form Of Humor." - Alexander Pope
250	"I Rate Enthusiasm Even Above Professional Skill." - Edward Appleton
251	"So Little Done, So Much To Do." - Cecil Rhodes
252	"Your Faithfulness Makes You Trustworthy To God." - Edwin Louis Cole
253	"Wisdom Is Always An Overmatch For Strength." - Phil Jackson
254	"Time Is A Dressmaker Specializing In Alterations." - Faith Baldwin
255	"Power Is Dangerous Unless You Have Humility." - Richard J. Daley
256	"A Ruffled Mind Makes A Restless Pillow." - Charlotte Brontë
257	"Forgiveness Is The Final Form Of Love." - Reinhold Niebuhr
258	"A Poem Is Never Finished, Only Abandoned." - Paul Valery
259	"Winners Never Quit And Quitters Never Win." - Vince Lombardi
260	"There Is Always Room At The Top." - Daniel Webster

261	"A Nickel Ain't Worth A Dime Anymore." - Yogi Berra
262	"Success Is A Journey, Not A Destination." - Ben Sweetland
263	"Whatever You Are, Be A Good One." - Abraham Lincoln
264	"Every Calling Is Great When Greatly Pursued." - Oliver Wendell Holmes
265	"Humor Is The Affectionate Communication Of Insight." - Leo Rosten
266	"Experience Is The Teacher Of All Things." - Julius Caesar
267	"I Make Movies I Want To See." - Neil Labute
268	"By The Work One Knows The Workman." - Jean De La Fontaine
269	"In Life, As In Chess, Forethought Wins." - Charles Buxton
270	"Be Smart, Be Intelligent And Be Informed." - Tony Alessandra
271	"Wisdom Is The Supreme Part Of Happiness." - Sophocles
272	"Poetry Is What Gets Lost In Translation." - Robert Frost
273	"Reality Is Wrong. Dreams Are For Real." - Tupac Shakur
274	"I Have Not Yet Begun To Fight!" - John Paul Jones
275	"Motivation Will Almost Always Beat Mere Talent." - Norman R. Augustine
276	"I Don't Design Clothes, I Design Dreams." - Ralph Lauren
277	"Dreams Are Today's Answers To Tomorrow's Questions." - Edgar Cayce
278	"I Am Realistic - I Expect Miracles." - Wayne Dyer
279	"That Government Is Best Which Governs Least." - Thomas Paine
280	"Give Me Liberty Or Give Me Death." - Patrick Henry
281	"Some Stories Are True That Never Happened." - Elie Wiesel
282	"Every Good Painter Paints What He Is." - Jackson Pollock
283	"God Will Forgive Me. It's His Job." - Heinrich Heine
284	"Patriotism Is The Virtue Of The Vicious." - Oscar Wilde
285	"There Are Never Enough I Love You's." - Lenny Bruce
286	"The Only Source Of Knowledge Is Experience." - Albert Einstein
287	"Just Play. Have Fun. Enjoy The Game." - Michael Jordan
288	"Old Age Is No Place For Sissies." - Bette Davis
289	"Cannibals Prefer Those Who Have No Spines." - Stanislaw Lem
290	"Art Is The Proper Task Of Life." - Friedrich Nietzsche
291	"If You Have To Forecast, Forecast Often." - Edgar R. Fiedler
292	"Success Is Doing Ordinary Things Extraordinarily Well." - Jim Rohn
293	"All Bad Poetry Springs From Genuine Feeling." - Oscar Wilde
294	"The Truest Wisdom Is A Resolute Determination." - Napoleon Bonaparte
295	"Most Ball Games Are Lost, Not Won." - Casey Stengel
296	"Poetry Heals The Wounds Inflicted By Reason." - Novalis
297	"All Glory Comes From Daring To Begin." - William Shakespeare

298	"All Art Is But Imitation Of Nature." - Lucius Annaeus Seneca
299	"You Cannot Feed The Hungry On Statistics." - Heinrich Heine
300	"When You're Dead, You're Dead. That's It." - Marlene Dietrich
301	"Rules Are Not Necessarily Sacred, Principles Are." - Franklin Delano Roosevelt
302	"You May Delay, But Time Will Not." - Benjamin Franklin
303	"It's Always Fun To Do The Impossible." - Walt Disney
304	"I Never Enjoyed Working In A Film." - Marlene Dietrich
305	"Love Is Often The Fruit Of Marriage." - Moliere
306	"Life Is A Long Lesson In Humility." - James M. Barrie
307	"All Lasting Business Is Built On Friendship." - Alfred A. Montapert
308	"In Art The Best Is Good Enough." - Johann Wolfgang Von Goethe
309	"A Picture Is A Poem Without Words." - Horace
310	"Derivatives Are Financial Weapons Of Mass Destruction." - Warren Buffett
311	"The Doors Of Wisdom Are Never Shut." - Benjamin Franklin
312	"Success Is Where Preparation And Opportunity Meet." - Bobby Unser
313	"Forgiveness Is A Virtue Of The Brave." - Indira Gandhi
314	"Forgiveness Means Letting Go Of The Past." - Gerald Jampolsky
315	"Fashions Have Done More Harm Than Revolutions." - Victor Hugo
316	"The Present Is A Point Just Passed." - David Russell
317	"LOVE: A Temporary Insanity Curable By Marriage." - Ambrose Bierce
318	"Rules And Models Destroy Genius And Art." - William Hazlitt
319	"You Exist Only In What You Do." - Federico Fellini
320	"To Understand Is To Forgive, Even Oneself." - Alexander Chase
321	"A Picture Is Worth A Thousand Words." - Napoleon Bonaparte
322	"Where There Is Love There Is Life." - Mohandas Gandhi
323	"Without Music, Life Would Be A Mistake." - Friedrich Nietzsche
324	"Some Defeats Are Only Installments To Victory." - Jacob A. Riis
325	"Winning Isn't Everything, It's The Only Thing." - Vince Lombardi
326	"Every Man Over Forty Is A Scoundrel." - George Bernard Shaw
327	"Any Good Music Must Be An Innovation." - Les Baxter
328	"To Be Loved, You Must Be Lovable." - Italian Proverb
329	"Love Is The Poetry Of The Senses." - Honore De Balzac
330	"Don't Be "Consistent" But Be Simple True." - Oliver Wendell Holmes
331	"Memory Is The Mother Of All Wisdom." - Aeschylus
332	"To Err Is Human; To Forgive, Divine." - Alexander Pope
333	"What Is History But A Fable Agreed Upon?" - Napoleon Bonaparte
334	"You Are The Music While The Music Lasts." - T. S. Eliot

335	"I Bought Some Batteries, But They Weren't Included." - Steven Wright
336	"Listen Or Your Tongue Will Make You Deaf." - Mike Nichols
337	"There Is Only One Terminal Dignity - Love." - Helen Hayes
338	"There's Always A Way - If You're Committed." - Anthony Robbins
339	"Climb The Mountains And Get Their Good Tidings." - John Muir
340	"Champions Keep Playing Until They Get It Right." - Billie Jean King
341	"Life's Tough. It's Even Tougher If You're Stupid." - John Wayne
342	"Every True Genius Is Bound To Be Naive." - Friedrich Schiller
343	"When You Become Senile, You Won't Know It." - Bill Cosby
344	"Control Your Own Destiny Or Someone Else Will." - Jack Welch
345	"Information's Pretty Thin Stuff Unless Mixed With Experience." - Clarence Day
346	"Ignorance Is No Excuse, It's The Real Thing." - Irene Peter
347	"Games Are The Most Elevated Form Of Investigation" - Albert Einstein
348	"Without Enough Sleep, We All Become Tall Two-Year-Olds." - Jojo Jensen
349	"A Public-Opinion Poll Is No Substitute For Thought." - Warren Buffett
350	"You Will Find Only What You Bring In." - Yoda
351	"Trifles Make Perfection, And Perfection Is No Trifle." - Michelangelo
352	"Life Itself Still Remains A Very Effective Therapist." - Karen Horney
353	"The Poetry Of The Earth Is Never Dead." - John Keats
354	"All Adventures, Especially Into New Territory, Are Scary." - Sally Ride
355	"Men Have Become The Tools Of Their Tools." - Henry David Thoreau
356	"I Am Become Death, The Destroyer Of Worlds." - J. Robert Oppenheimer
357	"Love Is What You've Been Through With Somebody." - James Thurber
358	"Anger Dwells Only In The Bosom Of Fools." - Albert Einstein
359	"Humor Is Just Another Defense Against The Universe." - Mel Brooks
360	"There Is No Revenge So Complete As Forgiveness." - Josh Billings
361	"Maturity Is Only A Short Break In Adolescence." - Jules Feiffer
362	"Live Out Of Your Imagination, Not Your History." - Stephen Covey
363	"Love Is The Triumph Of Imagination Over Intelligence." - H. L. Mencken
364	"I Love Life Because What More Is There." - Anthony Hopkins
365	"Poetry Is Nearer To Vital Truth Than History." - Plato
366	"Spring Is Nature's Way Of Saying, Let's Party!" - Robin Williams
367	"The Fewer The Facts, The Stronger The Opinion." - Arnold H. Glasow

368	"The Internet Is The Viagra Of Big Business." - Jack Welch
369	"Tennis And Golf Are Best Played, Not Watched." - Roger Kahn
370	"The Wise Man Avoids Evil By Anticipating It." - Publilius Syrus
371	"The Russians Feared Ike. They Didn't Fear Me." - Lyndon B. Johnson
372	"Expressing Anger Is A Form Of Public Littering." - Willard Gaylin
373	"Whatever Is Begun In Anger Ends In Shame." - Benjamin Franklin
374	"A Lifetime Of Training For Just Ten Seconds." - Jesse Owens
375	"I've Written Some Poetry I Don't Understand Myself." - Carl Sandburg
376	"Fall Down Seven Times; Stand Up Eight Times." - Japanese Proverb
377	"The Real Art Of Conducting Consists In Transitions." - Gustav Mahler
378	"Politics Doesn't Make Strange Bedfellows - Marriage Does." - Groucho Marx
379	"When Evil Men Plot, Good Men Must Plan." - Martin Luther King, Jr.
380	"One Man's Theology Is Another Man's Belly Laugh." - Robert A. Heinlein
381	"Failure Is Success If We Learn From It." - Malcolm Forbes
382	"If You Drink Don't Drive. Don't Even Putt." - Dean Martin
383	"You're Only As Good As Your Last Haircut." - Fran Lebowitz
384	"Poets Are The Unacknowledged Legislators Of The World." - Percy Bysshe Shelley
385	"To Win...You've Got To Stay In The Game..." - Claude M. Bristol
386	"Action Is The Foundational Key To All Success." - Pablo Picasso
387	"A Film Is A Petrified Fountain Of Thought." - Jean Cocteau
388	"Marriage Is An Adventure, Like Going To War." - Gilbert K. Chesterton
389	"Truly Wonderful The Mind Of A Child Is." - Yoda
390	"Intelligence Without Ambition Is A Bird Without Wings." - Salvador Dali
391	"Marriage Is A Mistake Every Man Should Make." - George Jessel
392	"Without A Struggle, There Can Be No Progress." - Frederick Douglass
393	"Time Is The Longest Distance Between Two Places." - Tennessee Williams
394	"Music Is Love In Search Of A Word." - Sidney Lanier
395	"People Living Deeply Have No Fear Of Death." - Anais Nin
396	"God's Gifts Put Man's Best Dreams To Shame." - Elizabeth Barrett Browning
397	"Faith: Not Wanting To Know What Is True." - Friedrich Nietzsche
398	"In Art As In Love, Instinct Is Enough." - Anatole France
399	"Forgive Many Things In Others; Nothing In Yourself." - Ausonius

400	"Life Is Never Easy For Those Who Dream." - Robert James Waller
401	"The Future Has A Way Of Arriving Unannounced." - George Will
402	"Whatever You're Ready For Is Ready For You." - Mark Victor Hansen
403	"Great Warrior, Hmm? Wars Not Make One Great." - Yoda
404	"Hell Hath No Fury Like A Bureaucrat Scorned." - Milton Friedman
405	"Time Moves In One Direction, Memory In Another." - William Gibson
406	"Those Who Believe In Telekinetics, Raise My Hand." - Kurt Vonnegut
407	"Every Really New Idea Looks Crazy At First." - Abraham H. Maslow
408	"Science Does Not Know Its Debt To Imagination." - Ralph Waldo Emerson
409	"One's Ships Come In Over A Calm Sea." - Florence Scovill Shinn
410	"What We Love We Shall Grow To Resemble." - Bernard Of Clairvaux
411	"Sports Do Not Build Character. They Reveal It." - Heywood Broun
412	"Forgive Your Enemies, But Never Forget Their Names." - John F. Kennedy
413	"Give Me A Museum And I'll Fill It." - Pablo Picasso
414	"You'll Have Time To Rest When You're Dead." - Robert De Niro
415	"The Bluebird Carries The Sky On His Back." - Henry David Thoreau
416	"Writing About Music Is Like Dancing About Architecture." - Laurie Anderson
417	"May You Live Every Day Of Your Life." - Jonathan Swift
418	"You Affect The World By What You Browse." - Tim Berners-Lee
419	"One Forgives To The Degree That One Loves." - Francois De La Rochefoucauld
420	"I Was The Kid Next Door's Imaginary Friend." - Emo Philips
421	"Have You Ever Noticed What Golf Spells Backwards?" - Al Boliska
422	"You Don't Pay Taxes - They Take Taxes." - Chris Rock
423	"Humor Is The Instinct For Taking Pain Playfully." - Max Eastman
424	"Olympism Is The Marriage Of Sport And Culture." - Juan Antonio Samaranch
425	"Strength Is A Matter Of The Made-Up Mind." - John Beecher
426	"Innovation Distinguishes Between A Leader And A Follower." - Steve Jobs
427	"Music Is A Performance And Needs The Audience." - Michael Tippett
428	"Nine-Tenths Of Wisdom Is Being Wise In Time." - Theodore Roosevelt
429	"Poetry Is The Synthesis Of Hyacinths And Biscuits." - Carl Sandburg
430	"Dawn: When Men Of Reason Go To Bed." - Ambrose Bierce
431	"Vitality Is Radiated From Exceptional Art And Architecture." - Arthur Erickson

432	"Nature Always Wears The Colors Of The Spirit." - Ralph Waldo Emerson
433	"Everything Makes Me Nervous - Except Making Films." - Elizabeth Taylor
434	"Cleanliness Becomes More Important When Godliness Is Unlikely." - P. J. O'Rourke
435	"The Pessimist Borrows Trouble; The Optimist Lends Encouragement." - William Arthur Ward
436	"Any Sufficiently Advanced Technology Is Indistinguishable From Magic." - Arthur C. Clarke
437	"This Is Slavery, Not To Speak One's Thought." - Euripides
438	"Touch A Scientist And You Touch A Child." - Ray Bradbury
439	"Goals Help You Channel Your Energy Into Action." - Les Brown
440	"A Goal Is A Dream With A Deadline." - Napoleon Hill
441	"Sleeplessness Is A Desert Without Vegetation Or Inhabitants." - Jessamyn West
442	"Poetry: The Best Words In The Best Order." - Samuel Taylor Coleridge
443	"Those Who Stand For Nothing Fall For Anything." - Alexander Hamilton
444	"Genuine Poetry Can Communicate Before It Is Understood." - T. S. Eliot
445	"To Conquer Fear Is The Beginning Of Wisdom." - Bertrand Russell
446	"The Only Abnormality Is The Incapacity To Love." - Anais Nin
447	"Somewhere, Something Incredible Is Waiting To Be Known." - Blaise Pascal
448	"Do Or Do Not; There Is No Try." - Yoda
449	"The Perfection Of Art Is To Conceal Art." - Marcus Fabius Quintilian
450	"Happy People Plan Actions, They Don't Plan Results." - Denis Waitley
451	"Our Work Is The Presentation Of Our Capabilities." - Edward Gibbon
452	"Vision Is The Art Of Seeing The Invisible." - Jonathan Swift
453	"God Cannot Alter The Past, Though Historians Can." - Samuel Butler
454	"Some Folks Are Wise And Some Are Otherwise." - Tobias Smollett
455	"Wrinkles Should Merely Indicate Where Smiles Have Been." - Mark Twain
456	"Grave Danger You Are in. Impatient You Are." - Yoda
457	"Your Life Is What Your Thoughts Make It." - Marcus Aurelius
458	"If You Want To Be Loved, Be Lovable." - Ovid
459	"Life Is Either A Great Adventure Or Nothing." - Helen Keller
460	"You Can't Shake Hands With A Clenched Fist." - Indira Gandhi

461	"Every Flower Is A Soul Blossoming In Nature." - Gerard De Nerval
462	"We Have, I Fear, Confused Power With Greatness." - Stewart Udall
463	"If Voting Changed Anything, They'd Make It Illegal." - Emma Goldman
464	"Life Is Hard. After All, It Kills You." - Katharine Hepburn
465	"The First Casualty When War Comes Is Truth." - Hiram Johnson
466	"Who Looks Outside, Dreams; Who Looks Inside, Awakes." - Carl Jung
467	"Have No Fear Of Perfection--You'll Never Reach It." - Salvador Dali
468	"Marriage: A Word Which Should Be Pronounced Mirage." - Herbert Spencer
469	"Forgiveness Is The Key To Action And Freedom." - Hannah Arendt
470	"Can't Believe It. That Is Why You Fail." - Yoda
471	"Myths Are Public Dreams, Dreams Are Private Myths." - Joseph Campbell
472	"We'll Either Find A Way, Or Make One." - Hannibal
473	"When You Are Through Changing, You Are Through." - Bruce Barton
474	"We Cannot Command Nature Except By Obeying Her." - Francis Bacon
475	"So Vast Is Art, So Narrow Human Wit." - Alexander Pope
476	"It Takes A Long Time To Become Young." - Pablo Picasso
477	"Genius Always Finds Itself A Century Too Early." - Ralph Waldo Emerson
478	"A Poet Can Survive Everything But A Misprint." - Oscar Wilde
479	"Genius Ain't Anything More Than Elegant Common Sense." - Josh Billings
480	"Intense Love Does Not Measure, It Just Gives." - Mother Teresa
481	"Business Is A Combination Of War And Sport." - Andre Maurois
482	"Bulls Do Not Win Bull Fights. People Do." - Norman Ralph Augustine
483	"You Wouldn't Have Won If We'd Beaten You." - Yogi Berra
484	"Winter Is Nature's Way Of Saying, Up Yours." - Robert Byrne
485	"Chaos Often Breeds Life, When Order Breeds Habit." - Henry B. Adams
486	"Most Misfortunes Are The Results Of Misused Time." - Napoleon Hill
487	"Information Is The Oxygen Of The Modern Age." - Ronald Reagan
488	"Use Your Feeling And Find Him You Will." - Yoda
489	"Self-Confidence Is The First Requisite To Great Undertakings" - Samuel Johnson
490	"Every Man Dies. Not Every Man Really Lives." - William Wallace
491	"You Win Some, Lose Some, And Wreck Some." - Dale Earnhardt
492	"A Loving Heart Is The Beginning Of All Knowledge." - Thomas Carlyle

493	"The Finest Eloquence Is That Which Gets Things Done." - David Lloyd George
494	"Winning Is Not Everything, But Wanting To Win Is." - Vince Lombardi
495	"You Can't Win Unless You Learn How To Lose." - Kareem Abdul-Jabbar
496	"Procrastination Is The Art Of Keeping Up With Yesterday." - Don Marquis
497	"Anger Is One Of The Sinews Of The Soul." - Thomas Fuller
498	"Never Have More Children Than You Have Car Windows." - Erma Bombeck
499	"Who Hears Music Feels His Solitude Peopled At Once." - Robert Browning
500	"Old Age Is Fifteen Years Older Than I Am." - Oliver Wendell Holmes
501	"If There Is No Struggle, There Is No Progress." - Frederick Douglass
502	"Love Means Not Ever Having To Say You're Sorry." - Erich Segal
503	"Don't Look Back. Something Might Be Gaining On You." - Satchel Paige
504	"When Angry, Count To Four; When Very Angry, Swear." - Mark Twain
505	"I Dream My Painting And Then Paint My Dream." - Vincent Van Gogh
506	"Fair Peace Becomes Men; Ferocious Anger Belongs To Beasts." - Ovid
507	"The iPod Completely Changed The Way People Approach Music." - Karl Lagerfeld
508	"Fear Makes Strangers Of People Who Would Be Friends." - Shirley Maclaine
509	"Art, Like Morality, Consists In Drawing The Line Somewhere." - Gilbert K. Chesterton
510	"To The Uneducated, An A Is Just Three Sticks." - A. A. Milne
511	"Food Is An Important Part Of A Balanced Diet." - Fran Lebowitz
512	"We Are Punished By Our Sins, Not For Them." - Elbert Hubbard
513	"Anger And Intolerance Are The Enemies Of Correct Understanding." - Mohandas Gandhi
514	"When Love Is Not Madness, It Is Not Love." - Pedro Calderon De La Barca
515	"Don't Let Other People Tell You What You Want." - Pat Riley
516	"Inventories Can Be Managed, But People Must Be Led." - H. Ross Perot
517	"Did I Live, Did I Love, Did I Matter?" - Brendon Burchard
518	"Color In A Picture Is Like Enthusiasm In Life." - Vincent Van Gogh
519	"Half The Lies They Tell About Me Aren't True." - Yogi Berra

520	"If You Don't Have A Competitive Advantage, Don't Compete." - Jack Welch
521	"To Avoid Criticism, Do Nothing, Say Nothing, Be Nothing." - Elbert Hubbard
522	"Talk Is Cheap - Except When Congress Does It." - Cullen Hightower
523	"The Science Of Today Is The Technology Of Tomorrow." - Edward Teller
524	"Cinema Is The Most Beautiful Fraud In The World." - Jean-Luc Godard
525	"Whenever Anyone Says, 'Theoretically,' They Really Mean, 'Not Really.'" - Dave Parnas
526	"Life Has No Limitations, Except The Ones You Make." - Les Brown
527	"Excellence Is Not A Skill. It Is An Attitude." - Ralph Marston
528	"If Everyone Is Thinking Alike, Then Somebody Isn't Thinking." - George S. Patton
529	"I Intend To Live Forever. So Far, So Good." - Steven Wright
530	"He Is A Self-Made Man And Worships His Creator." - John Bright
531	"We Are The Movies And The Movies Are Us." - David Ansen
532	"The Years Teach Much Which The Days Never Know." - Ralph Waldo Emerson
533	"The Only Limits Are, As Always, Those Of Vision." - James Broughton
534	"Most Of Us Do Not Consciously Look At Movies." - Roger Ebert
535	"The Purpose Of Life Is A Life Of Purpose." - Robert Byrne
536	"Small Opportunities Are Often The Beginning Of Great Enterprises." - Demosthenes
537	"Friendship Is A Single Soul Dwelling In Two Bodies." - Aristotle
538	"Genius Is Nothing But A Great Aptitude For Patience." - Georges Louis Leclerc
539	"Experience Is One Thing You Can't Get For Nothing." - Oscar Wilde
540	"An Unjust Peace Is Better Than A Just War." - Marcus Tullius Cicero
541	"Profanity Is The Common Crutch Of The Conversational Cripple." - David Keuck
542	"Only The Wisest And Stupidest Of Men Never Change." - Confucius
543	"Education Is A Progressive Discovery Of Our Own Ignorance." - Will Durant
544	"It's Not The Voting That's Democracy; It's The Counting." - Tom Stoppard
545	"I Don't Use Drugs, My Dreams Are Frightening Enough." - M. C. Escher
546	"You Can Never Plan The Future By The Past." - Edmund Burke
547	"Poetry Is An Echo, Asking A Shadow To Dance." - Carl Sandburg

548	"Poetry Is The Rhythmical Creation Of Beauty In Words." - Edgar Allan Poe
549	"The First And Best Victory Is To Conquer Self." - Plato
550	"A War For A Great Principle Ennobles A Nation." - Albert Pike
551	"Life Is The Art Of Drawing Without An Eraser." - John W. Gardner
552	"A Mistake Is Simply Another Way Of Doing Things." - Katharine Graham
553	"Mind What You Have Learned. Save You It Can." - Yoda
554	"Any Experience Can Be Transformed Into Something Of Value." - Vash Young
555	"A Man Of Courage Is Also Full Of Faith." - Marcus Tullius Cicero
556	"This World Is But A Canvas To Our Imagination." - Henry David Thoreau
557	"Real Programmers Can Write Assembly Code In Any Language." - Larry Wall
558	"We Build Too Many Walls And Not Enough Bridges." - Isaac Newton
559	"The First Step To Becoming Is To Will It." - Mother Teresa
560	"Happiness Is A Conscious Choice, Not An Automatic Response." - Michael Bartel
561	"Fears Are Nothing More Than A State Of Mind." - Napoleon Hill
562	"Never Confuse A Single Defeat With A Final Defeat." - F. Scott Fitzgerald
563	"Poetry Is All That Is Worth Remembering In Life." - William Hazlitt
564	"If You Don't Like My Movies, Don't Watch Them." - Dario Argento
565	"Poetry Is The Art Of Uniting Pleasure With Truth." - Samuel Johnson
566	"The Man Who Has No Imagination Has No Wings." - Muhammad Ali
567	"Beauty In Art Is Often Nothing But Ugliness Subdued." - Jean Rostand
568	"I Perhaps Owe Having Become A Painter To Flowers." - Claude Monet
569	"Formula For Success: Rise Early, Work Hard, Strike Oil." - J. Paul Getty
570	"Success Is The One Unpardonable Sin Against Our Fellows." - Ambrose Bierce
571	"Day - A Period Of Twenty-Four Hours, Mostly Misspent." - Ambrose Bierce
572	"Life Is Painting A Picture, Not Doing A Sum." - Oliver Wendell Holmes
573	"The Glory Of Christianity Is To Conquer By Forgiveness." - William Blake

574	"Change Is Inevitable - Except From A Vending Machine." - Robert C. Gallagher
575	"The Awareness Of Our Own Strength Makes Us Modest." - Paul Cezanne
576	"Comedy Is Simply A Funny Way Of Being Serious." - Peter Ustinov
577	"Sometime They'll Give A War And Nobody Will Come." - Carl Sandburg
578	"A New Untruth Is Better Than An Old Truth." - Oliver Wendell Holmes
579	"Even A True Artist Does Not Always Produce Art." - Carroll O'connor
580	"In Politics The Middle Way Is None At All." - John Adams
581	"Have Faith In God; God Has Faith In You." - Edwin Louis Cole
582	"Life Imitates Art Far More Than Art Imitates Life." - Oscar Wilde
583	"Reason Is Our Soul's Left Hand, Faith Her Right." - John Donne
584	"He That Walketh With Wise Men Shall Be Wise..." - Bible, Proverbs 13:20
585	"The Art Of Being Wise Knows What To Overlook." - William James
586	"The Perfect Normal Person Is Rare In Our Civilization." - Karen Horney
587	"Don't Wait. The Time Will Never Be Just Right." - Napoleon Hill
588	"Computers Are Useless. They Can Only Give You Answers." - Pablo Picasso
589	"Life Without Liberty Is Like A Body Without Spirit." - Kahlil Gibran
590	"Gravitation Is Not Responsible For People Falling In Love." - Albert Einstein
591	"The Language Of Friendship Is Not Words But Meanings." - Henry David Thoreau
592	"Ideologies Separate Us. Dreams And Anguish Bring Us Together." - Eugene Ionesco
593	"The Most Powerful In The Universe Is Compound Interest." - Albert Einstein
594	"The Secret Of A Happy Marriage Remains A Secret." - Henny Youngman
595	"A People Free To Choose Will Always Choose Peace." - Ronald Reagan
596	"Wonder Rather Than Doubt Is The Root Of Knowledge." - Abraham Hershel
597	"I've Had A Perfectly Wonderful Evening. But This Wasn't It." - Groucho Marx
598	"Alimony Is Like Buying Hay For A Dead Horse." - Groucho Marx
599	"Failure Is, In A Sense, The Highway To Success..." - John Keats

600	"Success Is Never Permanent, And Failure Is Never Final." - Mike Ditka
601	"Tis Very Certain The Desire Of Life Prolongs It." - Lord Byron
602	"Don't Let Yesterday Use Up Too Much Of Today." - Will Rogers
603	"Ads Are The Cave Art Of The Twentieth Century." - Marshall Mcluhan
604	"In A Democracy, Dissent Is An Act Of Faith." - J. William Fulbright
605	"If Two Wrongs Don't Make A Right, Try Three." - Laurence J. Peter
606	"We Make War That We May Live In Peace." - Aristotle
607	"Science Never Solves A Problem Without Creating Ten More." - George Bernard Shaw
608	"Learning - The Kind Of Ignorance Distinguishing The Studious." - Ambrose Bierce
609	"If Winning Isn't Everything, Why Do They Keep Score?" - Vince Lombardi
610	"The Secret To Film Is That It's An Illusion." - George Lucas
611	"The Most Important Thing About Goals Is Having One." - Geoffry F. Abert
612	"There Is No Sadder Sight Than A Young Pessimist." - Mark Twain
613	"Adopt The Pace Of Nature: Her Secret Is Patience." - Ralph Waldo Emerson
614	"Not If Anything To Say About It I Have." - Yoda
615	"There Is More To Life Than Increasing Its Speed." - Mohandas Gandhi
616	"The Best Weapon Against An Enemy Is Another Enemy." - Friedrich Nietzsche
617	"Art Is Man's Expression Of His Joy In Labor." - Henry A. Kissinger
618	"If We Don't End War, War Will End Us." - H. G. Wells
619	"At The Touch Of Love Everyone Becomes A Poet." - Plato
620	"Restlessness And Discontent Are The First Necessities Of Progress." - Thomas A. Edison
621	"A Pint Of Sweat, Saves A Gallon Of Blood." - George S. Patton
622	"Whenever Anyone Says, 'Theoretically,' They Really Mean, 'Not Really.'" - Dave Parnas
623	"If Passion Drives You, Let Reason Hold The Reins." - Benjamin Franklin
624	"Solitary Trees, If They Grow At All, Grow Strong." - Winston Churchill
625	"Foreplay, Cuddling - A Jedi Craves Not These Things." - Yoda
626	"The History Of Art Is The History Of Revivals." - Samuel Butler
627	"Conservatives Define Themselves In Terms Of What They Oppose." - George Will
628	"The Consumer Isn't A Moron; She Is Your Wife." - David Ogilvy

629	"I Spent A Year In That Town, One Sunday." - George Burns
630	"I Never Said Most Of The Things I Said." - Yogi Berra
631	"The Internet Is A Telephone System That's Gotten Uppity." - Clifford Stoll
632	"In Cyberspace, The First Amendment Is A Local Ordinance." - John Perry Barlow
633	"Power Tends To Corrupt And Absolute Power Corrupts Absolutely." - Lord Acton
634	"When It Comes To Luck, You Make Your Own." - Bruce Springsteen
635	"The Hand Cannot Reach Higher Than Does The Heart." - Orison Swett Marden
636	"Art Is Not A Thing; It Is A Way." - Elbert Hubbard
637	"One Touch Of Nature Makes The Whole World Kin." - William Shakespeare
638	"How Glorious A Greeting The Sun Gives The Mountains!" - John Muir
639	"You Want A Friend In Washington? Get A Dog." - Harry S. Truman
640	"No Man Is Ever Old Enough To Know Better." - Holbrook Jackson
641	"Man Can Alter His Life By Altering His Thinking" - William James
642	"If Music Be The Food Of Love, Play On." - William Shakespeare
643	"Do What You Fear Most And You Control Fear." - Tom Hopkins
644	"Music Is Moonlight In The Gloomy Night Of Life." - Jean Paul
645	"Despise The Enemy Strategically, But Take Him Seriously Tactically." - Mao Tse-Tung
646	"Most People Have To Talk So They Won't Hear." - May Sarton
647	"Intellectual Property Has The Shelf Life Of A Banana." - Bill Gates
648	"To Have Great Poets, There Must Be Great Audiences." - Walt Whitman
649	"When The Going Gets Weird, The Weird Turn Pro." - Hunter S. Thompson
650	"The One Without Dreams Is The One Without Wings." - Muhammad Ali
651	"Never Go To Bed Mad. Stay Up And Fight." - Phyllis Diller
652	"Love Is An Irresistible Desire To Be Irresistibly Desired." - Robert Frost
653	"The Violets In The Mountains Have Broken The Rocks." - Tennessee Williams
654	"We Pay When Old For The Excesses Of Youth." - J. B. Priestley
655	"...Society Honors Its Living Conformists And Its Dead Troublemakers." - Mignon Mclaughlin
656	"Our Greatest Battles Are That With Our Own Minds." - Jameson Frank

657	"Never Does Nature Say One Thing And Wisdom Another." - Juvenal
658	"A Poem Begins In Delight And Ends In Wisdom." - Robert Frost
659	"The Principle Of Art Is To Pause, Not Bypass." - Jerzy Kosinski
660	"The Mass Of Men Lead Lives Of Quiet Desperation." - Henry David Thoreau
661	"Always Keep An Open Mind And A Compassionate Heart." - Phil Jackson
662	"Therefore Is A Word The Poet Must Not Know." - Andre Gide
663	"Do Not Trust People. They Are Capable Of Greatness." - Stanislaw Lem
664	"Reason And Judgment Are The Qualities Of A Leader." - Tacitus
665	"We Are Time's Subjects, And Time Bids Be Gone." - William Shakespeare
666	"What The Country Needs Are A Few Labor-Making Inventions." - Arnold H. Glasow
667	"Good Teaching Is One-Fourth Preparation And Three-Fourths Pure Theatre." - Gail Godwin
668	"Time Is But The Stream I Go A-Fishing In." - Henry David Thoreau
669	"Business, That's Easily Defined - It's Other People's Money." - Peter Drucker
670	"I Believe In God, Only I Spell It Nature." - Frank Lloyd Wright
671	"Love Is The Flower You've Got To Let Grow." - John Lennon
672	"Inside Every Working Anarchy, There's An Old Boy Network." - Mitchell Kapor
673	"I Want To Put A Ding In The Universe." - Steve Jobs
674	"Poetry Is Thoughts That Breathe, And Words That Burn." - Thomas Gray
675	"It's The Unhappy People Who Most Fear Change." - Mignon Mclaughlin
676	"Make Everything As Simple As Possible, But Not Simpler" - Albert Einstein
677	"Always Forgive Your Enemies; Nothing Annoys Them So Much." - Oscar Wilde
678	"Where There Is Great Love, There Are Always Wishes." - Willa Cather
679	"He Who Opens A School Door, Closes A Prison." - Victor Hugo
680	"Everything Has Been Figured Out, Except How To Live." - Jean-Paul Sartre
681	"I Used To Be Snow White, But I Drifted." - Mae West
682	"As I Get Older, I Just Prefer To Knit." - Tracey Ullman

683	"Your Attitude, Not Your Aptitude, Will Determine Your Altitude." - Zig Ziglar
684	"The Only Thing A Golfer Needs Is More Daylight." - Ben Hogan
685	"If Men Were Angels, No Government Would Be Necessary." - James Madison
686	"Never Be Afraid To Sit A While And Think." - Lorraine Hansberry
687	"Time Ripens All Things; No Man Is Born Wise." - Miguel De Cervantes
688	"Experience Is Simply The Name We Give Our Mistakes." - Oscar Wilde
689	"Drank Some Boiling Water Because I Wanted To Whistle." - Mitch Hedberg
690	"All Of Us Need To Grow Continuously In Our Lives." - Les Brown
691	"It Takes A Long Time To Grow An Old Friend." - John Leonard
692	"Real Knowledge Is To Know The Extent Of One's Ignorance." - Confucius
693	"To Be A Poet Is A Condition, Not A Profession." - Robert Frost
694	"For Your Information, I Would Like To Ask A Question." - Samuel Goldwyn
695	"Goals Are New, Forward-Moving Objectives. They Magnetize You Towards Them." - Mark Victor Hansen
696	"Music Is A Higher Revelation Than All Wisdom And Philosophy." - Ludwig Van Beethoven
697	"Go To Heaven For The Climate, Hell For The Company." - Mark Twain
698	"Success Is That Old ABC - Ability, Breaks, And Courage." - Charles Luckman
699	"A Poet Must Leave Traces Of His Passage, Not Proof." - Rene Char
700	"Forgiveness Means Giving Up All Hope For A Better Past." - Lily Tomlin
701	"Nature And Books Belong To The Eyes That See Them." - Ralph Waldo Emerson
702	"Movement Without Direction Will Create A Hole In The Ground." - Sophia Bedford-Pierce
703	"After Thirty, A Body Has A Mind Of Its Own." - Bette Midler
704	"Science Without Religion Is Lame, Religion Without Science Is Blind." - Albert Einstein
705	"Before Everything Else, Getting Ready Is The Secret Of Success." - Henry Ford
706	"The Object Of Art Is To Give Life A Shape." - William Shakespeare

707	"Yesterday I Dared To Struggle. Today I Dare To Win." - Bernadette Devlin
708	"Never Doubt That You Can Change History. You Already Have." - Marge Piercy
709	"Mad - Affected With A High Degree Of Intellectual Independence." - Ambrose Bierce
710	"None Are So Old As Those Who Have Outlived Enthusiasm." - Henry David Thoreau
711	"The Poet Is A Liar Who Always Speaks The Truth." - Jean Cocteau
712	"Politics Is Not A Game. It Is An Earnest Business." - Winston Churchill
713	"Look At Life Through The Windshield, Not The Rear-View Mirror." - Byrd Baggett
714	"Don't Simply Retire From Something; Have Something To Retire To." - Harry Emerson Fosdick
715	"Music Can Change The World Because It Can Change People." - Bono
716	"Religion Is What Keeps The Poor From Murdering The Rich." - Napoleon Bonaparte
717	"A Champion Is Someone Who Gets Up When He Can't." - Jack Dempsey
718	"O Lord, Help Me To Be Pure, But Not Yet." - Saint Augustine
719	"Movies Are Like An Expensive Form Of Therapy For Me." - Tim Burton
720	"Boxing Is Smoky Halls And Kidneys Battered Until They Bleed." - Roger Kahn
721	"Love Is My Religion - I Could Die For It." - John Keats
722	"Age Is A Very High Price To Pay For Maturity." - Tom Stoppard
723	"If Not You, Then Who? If Not Now, Then When? " - Hillel
724	"Beware How You Take Away Hope From Another Human Being." - Oliver Wendell Holmes
725	"You Cannot Believe In God Until You Believe In Yourself." - Swami Vivekananda
726	"Love Is A Smoke Made With The Fume Of Sighs." - William Shakespeare
727	"Legend: A Lie That Has Attained The Dignity Of Age." - H. L. Mencken
728	"Music Is The Best Means We Have Of Digesting Time." - W. H. Auden
729	"The Mediator Of The Inexpressible Is The Work Of Art." - Johann Wolfgang Von Goethe
730	"All Hockey Players Are Bilingual. They Know English And Profanity." - Gordie Howe

731	"There Was Never A Genius Without A Tincture Of Madness." - Aristotle
732	"Never Interrupt Your Enemy When He Is Making A Mistake." - Napoleon Bonaparte
733	"I Believe In Equality For Everyone, Except Reporters And Photographers." - Mohandas Gandhi
734	"Marriage, A Market Which Has Nothing Free But The Entrance." - Michel De Montaigne
735	"Always Write Angry Letters To Your Enemies. Never Mail Them." - James Fallows
736	"Everywhere Is Within Walking Distance If You Have The Time." - Steven Wright
737	"The Harder You Work, The Harder It Is To Surrender." - Vince Lombardi
738	"Love Is The Delusion That One Woman Differs From Another." - H. L. Mencken
739	"I Think We Are A Product Of All Our Experiences." - Sanford I. Weill
740	"Always Forgive Your Enemies - Nothing Annoys Them So Much." - Oscar Wilde
741	"Be Less Curious About People And More Curious About Ideas." - Marie Curie
742	"The More You Can Dream The More You Can Do." - Michael Korda
743	"A Man Masters Nature Not By Force But By Understanding." - Jacob Bronowski
744	"The Buck Stops With The Guy Who Signs The Checks." - Rupert Murdoch
745	"Culture Is The Arts Elevated To A Set Of Beliefs." - Tom Wolfe
746	"Success Is Determined By Those Whom Prove The Impossible, Possible." - James W. Pence
747	"Music In The Soul Can Be Heard By The Universe." - Lao Tzu
748	"It Is Not The Answer That Enlightens, But The Question." - Eugene Ionesco
749	"Middle Age Is Youth Without Levity, And Age Without Decay." - Doris Day
750	"Not Life, But Good Life, Is To Be Chiefly Valued." - Socrates
751	"The Future Depends Of What We Do In The Present." - Mahatma Gandhi
752	"Only The Dead Have Seen The End Of The War." - Plato
753	"He Is So Old That His Blood Type Was Discontinued." - George William Curtis

754	"Television Is A Medium Because Anything Well Done Is Rare." - Fred Allen
755	"Love Makes Your Soul Crawl Out From Its Hiding Place." - Zora Neale Hurston
756	"If You've Broken The Eggs, You Should Make The Omelet." - Anthony Eden
757	"Don't Be A Spectator, Don't Let Life Pass You By." - Lou Holtz
758	"We Cannot Defend Freedom Abroad By Deserting It At Home." - Edward R. Murrow
759	"Turn On To Politics, Or Politics Will Turn On You." - Ralph Nader
760	"Price Is What You Pay. Value Is What You Get." - Warren Buffett
761	"Patience, Persistence And Perspiration Make An Unbeatable Combination For Success." - Napoleon Hill
762	"If You Believe Everything You Read, You Better Not Read." - Japanese Proverb
763	"You Can Never Get Silence Anywhere Nowadays, Have You Noticed?" - Bryan Ferry
764	"Adapt Or Perish, Now As Ever, Is Nature's Inexorable Imperative." - H. G. Wells
765	"Money Is Better Than Poverty, If Only For Financial Reasons." - Woody Allen
766	"Life Is Too Short To Sleep On Low Thread-Count Sheets." - Leah Stussy
767	"I Deserve Respect For The Things I Did Not Do." - Dan Quayle
768	"The Bird A Nest, The Spider A Web, Man Friendship." - William Blake
769	"The Idea Is To Die Young As Late As Possible." - Ashley Montagu
770	"Hope Is The Only Bee That Makes Honey Without Flowers." - Robert Green Ingersoll
771	"Music Is Well Said To Be The Speech Of Angels." - Thomas Carlyle
772	"The Only True Wisdom Is In Knowing You Know Nothing." - Socrates
773	"Success Is How High You Bounce When You Hit Bottom." - George S. Patton
774	"People Always Make War When They Say They Love Peace." - David Herbert Lawrence
775	"Let Us Become The Change We Seek In This World." - Mohandas Gandhi
776	"The Waking Mind Is The Least Serviceable In The Arts." - Henry Miller
777	"When The Rich Wage War, It's The Poor Who Die." - Jean-Paul Sartre
778	"There Are Three Constants In Life... Change, Choice And Principles." - Stephen Covey

779	"It's A Poor Sort Of Memory That Only Works Backwards." - Lewis Carroll
780	"The Art Of Living Is More Like Wrestling Than Dancing." - Marcus Aurelius
781	"The True Sign Of Intelligence Is Not Knowledge But Imagination." - Albert Einstein
782	"Dream Manfully And Nobly, And Thy Dreams Shall Be Prophets." - Robert Bulwer-Lytton
783	"Poetry Is Language At Its Most Distilled And Most Powerful." - Rita Dove
784	"All That I Know I Learned After I Was Thirty." - Georges Clemenceau
785	"It's Always Worthwhile To Make Others Aware Of Their Worth." - Malcolm Forbes
786	"Painting Is Silent Poetry, And Poetry Is Painting That Speaks." - Plutarch
787	"The Public Is Wonderfully Tolerant. It Forgives Everything Except Genius." - Oscar Wilde
788	"Nationalism Is A Silly Cock Crowing On His Own Dunghill." - Richard Aldington
789	"I Regard Golf As An Expensive Way Of Playing Marbles." - Gilbert K. Chesterton
790	"People Will Buy Anything That Is 'One To A Customer." - Sinclair Lewis
791	"What's On Your Mind, If You Will Allow The Overstatement?" - Fred Allen
792	"I Do Not Pray For Success, I Ask For Faithfulness." - Mother Teresa
793	"Microsoft Isn't Evil, They Just Make Really Crappy Operating Systems." - Linus Torvalds
794	"Help Others Achieve Their Dreams And You Will Achieve Yours." - Les Brown
795	"Great Spirits Have Always Faced Violent Protest From Mediocre Minds." - Albert Einstein
796	"I've Just Learned About His Illness. Let's Hope It's Nothing Trivial." - Irvin S. Cobb
797	"The Key To Wisdom Is Knowing All The Right Questions." - John A. Simone Jr.
798	"Never Leave That Till Tomorrow Which You Can Do Today." - Benjamin Franklin
799	"Voters Don't Decide Issues, They Decide Who Will Decide Issues." - George Will

800	"No Man Can Think Clearly When His Fists Are Clenched." - George Jean Nathan
801	"He Who Looks Outside Dreams, He Who Looks Inside Awakens." - Carl Gustav Jung
802	"Life Is Half Spent Before We Know What It Is." - George Herbert
803	"The Only Thing We Have To Fear Is Fear Itself." - Franklin D. Roosevelt
804	"Principles Have No Real Force Except When One Is Well-Fed." - Mark Twain
805	"We Loved With A Love That Was More Than Love." - Edgar Allan Poe
806	"Just Because Everything Is Different Doesn't Mean Anything Has Changed." - Irene Peter
807	"You Know They're Not Going To Lose 162 Consecutive Games." - Harry Caray
808	"Honesty Is The First Chapter In The Book Of Wisdom." - Thomas Jefferson
809	"I Never Learned From A Man Who Agreed With Me." - Robert A. Heinlein
810	"A Nation Of Sheep Will Beget A Government Of Wolves" - Edward R. Murrow
811	"Peace Hath Higher Tests Of Manhood, Than Battle Ever Knew." - John Greenleaf Whittier
812	"I'd Just As Soon Play Tennis With The Net Down." - Robert Frost
813	"Forgiveness Is The Giving, And So The Receiving, Of Life." - George Macdonald
814	"The Counterfeit And Counterpart Of Nature Is Reproduced In Art." - Henry Wadsworth Longfellow
815	"History Is A Vision Of God's Creation On The Move." - Arnold J. Toynbee
816	"The More Bombers, The Less Room For Doves Of Peace." - Nikita Khrushchev
817	"First-Rate People Hire First-Rate People; Second-Rate People Hire Third-Rate People." - Leo Rosten
818	"Don't Let Someone Else's Opinion Of You Become Your Reality." - Les Brown
819	"Education Is Not Preparation For Life; Education Is Life Itself." - John Dewey
820	"Love Is Composed Of A Single Soul Inhabiting Two Bodies." - Aristotle
821	"Our Self Image, Strongly Held, Essentially Determines What We Become." - Maxwell Maltz

822	"What The Mind Can Conceive And Believe, It Can Achieve." - Napoleon Hill
823	"Big Pay And Little Responsibility Are Circumstances Seldom Found Together." - Napoleon Hill
824	"Men Talk Of Killing Time, While Time Quietly Kills Them." - Dion Boucicault
825	"Never Trust A Computer You Can't Throw Out A Window." - Steve Wozniak
826	"You Miss 100 Percent Of The Shots You Never Take." - Wayne Gretzky
827	"Reality Is Merely An Illusion, Albeit A Very Persistent One." - Albert Einstein
828	"I Expect Nothing. I Fear No One. I Am Free." - Nikos Kazantzakis
829	"We Can Lick Gravity, But Sometimes The Paperwork Is Overwhelming." - Wernher Von Braun
830	"To Imagine Is Everything, To Know Is Nothing At All." - Anatole France
831	"Fatherhood Is Pretending The Present You Love Most Is Soap-On-A-Rope." - Bill Cosby
832	"Music Happens To Be An Art Form That Transcends Language." - Herbie Hancock
833	"No Person Has The Right To Rain On Your Dreams." - Marian Wright Edelman
834	"Some People Walk In The Rain, Others Just Get Wet." - Roger Miller
835	"Great Spirits Have Always Encountered Violent Opposition From Mediocre Minds." - Albert Einstein
836	"Adversity Causes Some Men To Break; Others To Break Records." - William A. Ward
837	"The Greatest Enemy Of Individual Freedom Is The Individual Himself." - Anonymous
838	"It Is Not Length Of Life, But Depth Of Life." - Ralph Waldo Emerson
839	"Forewarned, Forearmed, Is To Be Prepared Is Half The Victory." - Miguel De Cervantes
840	"Laws Too Gentle Are Seldom Obeyed; Too Severe, Seldom Executed." - Benjamin Franklin
841	"Art For Art's Sake Is A Philosophy Of The Well-Fed." - Frank Lloyd Wright
842	"Easier To Resist At The Beginning Than At The End" - Leonardo da Vinci
843	"God Did Not Intend Religion To Be An Exercise Club." - Naguib Mahfouz

844	"So, Where's The Cannes Film Festival Being Held This Year?" - Christina Aguilera
845	"All Wars Are Civil Wars, Because All Men Are Brothers." - Francois Fenelon
846	"Peace And Justice Are Two Sides Of The Same Coin." - Dwight D. Eisenhower
847	"Art Is Magic Delivered From The Lie Of Being Truth." - Theodor Adorno
848	"To Command Is To Serve, Nothing More And Nothing Less." - Andre Malraux
849	"The Brighter You Are, The More You Have To Learn." - Don Herold
850	"Life Is The Flower For Which Love Is The Honey." - Victor Hugo
851	"A Baby Is God's Opinion That Life Should Go On." - Carl Sandburg
852	"Honor Is Not The Exclusive Property Of Any Political Party." - Herbert Hoover
853	"Do Not Try To Live Forever. You Will Not Succeed." - George Bernard Shaw
854	"What's Going On In The Inside Shows On The Outside." - Earl Nightingale
855	"Patience Accomplishes Its Object, While Hurry Speeds To Its Ruin." - Saadi
856	"Parrots Make Great Pets. They Have More Personality Than Goldfish." - Chevy Chase
857	"Even Peace May Be Purchased At Too High A Price." - Benjamin Franklin
858	"All Right Everyone, Line Up Alphabetically According To Your Height." - Casey Stengel
859	"Like Many Women My Age, I Am 28 Years Old." - Mary Schmich
860	"Poetry Is A Way Of Taking Life By The Throat." - Robert Frost
861	"Named Must Your Fear Be Before Banish It You Can." - Yoda
862	"Success Is Simply A Matter Of Luck. Ask Any Failure." - Earl Wilson
863	"Some Cause Happiness Wherever They Go; Others, Whenever They Go." - Oscar Wilde
864	"Intelligence Is Really A Kind Of Taste: Taste In Ideas." - Susan Sontag
865	"Virtues Are Acquired Through Endeavor, Which Rests Wholly Upon Yourself." - Sidney Lanier
866	"One Doesn't Have A Sense Of Humor. It Has You." - Larry Gelbart
867	"The Beginning Is The Most Important Part Of The Work." - Plato
868	"It Is Sad To Grow Old But Nice To Ripen." - Brigitte Bardot
869	"I Would Talk In Iambic Pentameter If It Were Easier." - Howard Nemerov

870	"Hell, I Never Vote For Anybody, I Always Vote Against." - W. C. Fields
871	"What We Have Learned From Other Becomes Our Own Reflection." - Ralph Waldo Emerson
872	"Corporation: An Ingenious Device For Obtaining Profit Without Individual Responsibility." - Ambrose Bierce
873	"Our Truest Life Is When We Are In Dreams Awake." - Henry David Thoreau
874	"When A Marriage Works, Nothing On Earth Can Take Its Place." - Helen Gahagan
875	"Fate Is For Those Too Weak To Determine Their Own Destiny." - Kamran Hamid
876	"The Whole Purpose Of Education Is To Turn Mirrors Into Windows." - Sydney J. Harris
877	"Art Washes Away From The Soul The Dust Of Everyday Life." - Pablo Picasso
878	"I'm Glad I Brought This Course, This Monster, To Its Knees." - Ben Hogan
879	"Peace Is Not Only Better Than War, But Infinitely More Arduous." - George Bernard Shaw
880	"Anger Is Never Without A Reason, But Seldom A Good One." - Benjamin Franklin
881	"The Poem Is The Point At Which Our Strength Gave Out." - Richard Rosen
882	"People Need Dreams, There's As Much Nourishment In 'Em As Food." - Dorothy Gilman
883	"Civilization Is Unbearable, But It Is Less Unbearable At The Top." - Timothy Leary
884	"I Have Long Believed That Sacrifice Is The Pinnacle Of Patriotism." - Bob Riley
885	"Do A Little More Each Day Than You Think You Can." - Lowell Thomas
886	"You Can Kill A Man But You Can't Kill An Idea." - Medgar Evers
887	"The Greater The Difficulty, The More The Glory In Surmounting It." - Epicurus
888	"The Worst Thing In This World, Next To Anarchy, Is Government." - Henry Ward Beecher
889	"Nurture Great Thoughts For You Cannot Go Higher Than Your Thoughts." - Benjamin Disraeli
890	"An Advertising Agency Is 85 Percent Confusion And 15 Percent Commission." - Fred Allen

891	"Old Age Comes On Suddenly, And Not Gradually As Is Thought." - Emily Dickinson
892	"A Conservative Is One Who Admires Radicals Centuries After They're Dead." - Leo Rosten
893	"No Free Man Shall Ever Be Debarred The Use Of Arms." - Thomas Jefferson
894	"The Essence Of All Beautiful Art, All Great Art, Is Gratitude." - Friedrich Nietzsche
895	"He Who Knows How To Flatter Also Knows How To Slander." - Napoleon Bonaparte
896	"Life Is Something That Happens When You Can't Get To Sleep." - Fran Lebowitz
897	"A Problem Is A Chance For You To Do Your Best." - Duke Ellington
898	"The Key To Why Things Change Is The Key To Everything." - James Burke
899	"Life Must Be Understood Backwards; But... It Must Be Lived Forward." - Soren Kierkegaard
900	"If Love Is The Answer, Could You Please Rephrase The Question?" - Lily Tomlin
901	"Learn What Is True In Order To Do What Is Right." - Thomas Henry Huxley
902	"We Have Art In Order Not To Die Of The Truth." - Friedrich Nietzsche
903	"Education Is An Ornament In Prosperity And A Refuge In Adversity." - Aristotle
904	"Every Failure Brings With It The Seed Of An Equivalent Success." - Napoleon Hill
905	"Love Is A Game That Two Can Play And Both Win." - Eva Gabor
906	"We Have A System That Increasingly Taxes Work And Subsidizes Non-work." - Milton Friedman
907	"There Is No Instance Of A Nation Benefiting From Prolonged Warfare." - Sun Tzu
908	"All Men Who Have Achieved Great Things Have Been Great Dreamers." - Orison Swett Marden
909	"I Have Never Been Hurt By What I Have Not Said." - Calvin Coolidge
910	"It Is Madness For Sheep To Talk Peace With A Wolf." - Thomas Fuller
911	"I've Been Cushioned Against Having To Work, With Rocky's Continual Bounty." - Knut Hamsun
912	"All Change Is Not Growth, As All Movement Is Not Forward." - Ellen Glasgow
913	"Technology Is Making Gestures Precise And Brutal, And With Them Men." - Theodor Adorno

914	"One Must Ask Children And Birds How Cherries And Strawberries Taste." - Johann Wolfgang Von Goethe
915	"What's Right Is What's Left After Everything Else Has Been Wronged." - Robin Williams
916	"I Couldn't Wait For Success, So I Went Ahead Without It." - Jonathan Winters
917	"You Need To Have Creative Vision And The Desire To Succeed." - Coco Chanel
918	"Economics Is Extremely Useful As A Form Of Employment For Economists." - John Kenneth Galbraith
919	"Friendship Often Ends In Love; But Love In Friendship - Never." - Charles Caleb Colton
920	"The Freedom Of Man I Contend Is The Freedom To Eat." - Eleanor Roosevelt
921	"We Do Not Consider Patriotism Desirable If It Contradicts Civilized Behavior." - Friedrich Durrenmatt
922	"A Day Without A Nap Is Like A Cupcake Without Frosting." - Terri Guillemets
923	"He Too Serves A Certain Purpose Who Only Stands And Cheers." - Henry B. Adams
924	"I Can't Even Get Three Weeks Off To Have Cosmetic Surgery." - Paul Lynde
925	"Good Judgment Comes From Experience And Experience Comes From Bad Judgment." - Fred Brooks
926	"Art Is The Only Way To Run Away Without Leaving Home." - Twyla Tharp
927	"English Spelling Is Weird...Or Is It Wierd?" – Irwin Hill
928	"Coming Generations Will Learn Equality From Poverty, And Love From Woes." - Kahlil Gibran
929	"I Think An Artist's Responsibility Is More Complex Than People Realize." - Jodie Foster
930	"All Things Are Artificial, For Nature Is The Art Of God." - Thomas Browne
931	"I Don't Believe In God But I'm Very Interested In Her." - Arthur C. Clarke
932	"The Most Beautiful Adventures Are Not Those We Go To Seek." - Eleanor Roosevelt
933	"I Don't Care Much About Music. What I Like Is Sounds." - Dizzy Gillespie
934	"In Comic Strips, The Person On The Left Always Speaks First." - George Carlin

935	"A Man Paints With His Brains And Not With His Hands." - Michelangelo
936	"An Artist Cannot Fail; It Is A Success To Be One." - Charles Horton Cooley
937	"He Loves Nature In Spite Of What It Did To Him." - Forrest Tucker
938	"If At First You Don't Succeed, Failure May Be Your Style." - Quentin Crisp
939	"History Is A Tool Used By Politicians To Justify Their Intentions." - Ted Koppel
940	"Experience Is A Good Teacher, But She Sends In Terrific Bills." - Minna Antrim
941	"The Purpose Of Business Is To Create And Keep A Customer." - Peter Drucker
942	"In The Absence Of Justice, What Is Sovereignty But Organized Robbery?" - Saint Augustine
943	"Where There's Marriage Without Love, There Will Be Love Without Marriage." - Benjamin Franklin
944	"Do What You Can, With What You Have, Where You Are." - Theodore Roosevelt
945	"The Clearest Way Into The Universe Is Through A Forest Wilderness." - John Muir
946	"Marriage Is Not About Age; It's About Finding The Right Person." - Sophia Bush
947	"The Best Way To Predict The Future Is To Create It." - Peter Drucker
948	"An Artist Never Really Finishes His Work, He Merely Abandons It." - Andre Gide
949	"Composers Shouldn't Think Too Much – It Interferes With Their Plagiarism." - Howard Dietz
950	"The Way Taxes Are, You Might As Well Marry For Love." - Henry A. Kissinger
951	"Time Management Is A Misnomer... The Challenge Is To Manage Ourselves" - Steven Covy
952	"When I Was A Boy The Dead Sea Was Only Sick." - George Burns
953	"Computing Is Not About Computers Any More. It Is About Living." - Nicholas Negroponte
954	"Vision Is The Art Of Seeing What Is Invisible To Others." - Jonathan Swift
955	"Whoever Wants To Reach A Distant Goal Must Take Small Steps." - Saul Bellow

956	"Conservatives Are Not Necessarily Stupid, But Most Stupid People Are Conservatives." - John Stuart Mill
957	"The Internet Is A Great Way To Get On The Net." - Bob Dole
958	"You Have Not Converted A Man Because You Have Silenced Him." - John Morley
959	"The Only Place Success Comes Before Work Is In The Dictionary." - Vince Lombardi
960	"We Learn From Experience That Men Never Learn Anything From Experience." - George Bernard Shaw
961	"Love Of Beauty Is Taste. The Creation Of Beauty Is Art." - Ralph Waldo Emerson
962	"Autumn Is A Second Spring When Every Leaf Is A Flower." - Albert Camus
963	"In The Field Of Observation, Chance Favors Only The Prepared Mind." - Louis Pasteur
964	"The Man Who Makes No Mistakes Does Not Usually Make Anything." - William Connor Magee
965	"Low Self-Esteem Is Like Driving Through Life With Your Hand-Break On." - Maxwell Maltz
966	"God Made Everything Out Of Nothing, But The Nothingness Shows Through." - Paul Valery
967	"Life Is Something To Do When You Can't Get To Sleep." - Fran Lebowitz
968	"It Is A Characteristic Of Wisdom Not To Do Desperate Things." - Henry David Thoreau
969	"Today Knowledge Has Power. It Controls Access To Opportunity And Advancement." - Peter Drucker
970	"History Never Looks Like History When You Are Living Through It." - John W. Gardner
971	"Skiing Combines Outdoor Fun With Knocking Down Trees With Your Face." - Dave Barry
972	"Learn To Pause.... Or Nothing Worthwhile Will Catch Up To You." - Doug King
973	"Ten Soldiers Wisely Led Will Beat A Hundred Without A Head." - Euripides
974	"People Are Trapped In History And History Is Trapped In Them." - James A. Baldwin
975	"Love Is The Child Of Illusion And The Parent Of Disillusion." - Miguel De Unamuno
976	"A Hen Is Only An Egg's Way Of Making Another Egg." - Samuel Butler

977	"I Don't Paint Things. I Only Paint The Difference Between Things." - Henri Matisse
978	"Let The People Think They Govern And They Will Be Governed." - William Penn
979	"If You Make Friends With Yourself You Will Never Be Alone." - Maxwell Maltz
980	"Rank Does Not Confer Privilege Or Give Power. It Imposes Responsibility." - Peter Drucker
981	"Poetry Is Plucking At The Heartstrings, And Making Music With Them." - Dennis Gabor
982	"I'd Luv To Kiss Ya, But I Just Washed My Hair." - Bette Davis
983	"He Has No Enemies, But Is Intensely Disliked By His Friends." - Oscar Wilde
984	"Don't Play Too Much Golf. Two Rounds A Day Are Plenty." - Harry Vardon
985	"A Friend Doesn't Go On A Diet Because You Are Fat." - Erma Bombeck
986	"I Have Been No More Than A Medium, As It Were." - Henri Matisse
987	"Football Is Violence And Cold Weather And Sex And College Rye." - Roger Kahn
988	"How Many Good Books Suffer Neglect Through The Ineddiciency Of Their Beginnings." – Edgar Allan Poe
989	"The Meek Shall Inherit The Earth, But Not Its Mineral Rights." - J. Paul Getty
990	"What's A Good Tournament For Him? Winning It. He's Good Enough." - Greg Norman
991	"A Business That Makes Nothing But Money Is A Poor Business." - Henry Ford
992	"Management Is Doing Things Right; Leadership Is Doing The Right Things." - Peter Drucker
993	"Look Deep Into Nature, And Then You Will Understand Everything Better." - Albert Einstein
994	"Never Ascribe To Malice, That Which Can Be Explained By Incompetence." - Napoleon (Hanlon's Razor)
995	"The Best Way To Predict The Future Is To Invent It." - Alan Kay
996	"I'd Rather Live With A Good Question Than A Bad Answer." - Aryeh Frimer
997	"Nothing Is Particularly Hard If You Divide It Into Small Jobs." - Henry Ford
998	"I Went Through Baseball As A Player To Be Named Later." - Joe Garagiola

999	"Golf Is A Day Spent In A Round Of Strenuous Idleness." - William Wordsworth
1000	"The Revolution Is A Dictatorship Of The Exploited Against The Exploiters." - Fidel Castro
1001	"I Am Free Of All Prejudices. I Hate Every One Equally." - W. C. Fields
1002	"I'm Married To The Theater But My Mistress Is The Films." - Oskar Werner
1003	"Think? Why Think! We Have Computers To Do That For Us." - Jean Rostand
1004	"Wisdom Is Knowing What To Do Next; Virtue Is Doing It." - David Starr Jordan
1005	"A Lost Battle Is A Battle One Thinks One Has Lost." - Jean-Paul Sartre
1006	"In Hollywood A Marriage Is A Success If It Outlasts Milk." - Rita Rudner
1007	"His Mother Should Have Thrown Him Away And Kept The Stork." - Mae West
1008	"Democracy Gives Every Man The Right To Be His Own Oppressor." - James Russell Lowell
1009	"Much To Learn You Still Have... This Is Just The Beginning!" - Yoda
1010	"Republicans Have Nothing But Bad Ideas And Democrats Have No Ideas." - Lewis Black
1011	"The Roots Of Education Are Bitter, But The Fruit Is Sweet." - Aristotle
1012	"Sometimes I Worry About Being A Success In A Mediocre World." - Lily Tomlin
1013	"The Dark Side Clouds Everything. Impossible To See The Future Is." - Yoda
1014	"Every Great Film Should Seem New Every Time You See It." - Roger Ebert
1015	"We Didn't Lose The Game; We Just Ran Out Of Time." - Vince Lombardi
1016	"The Successful Revolutionary Is A Statesman, The Unsuccessful One A Criminal." - Erich Fromm
1017	"Baseball Is Drama With An Endless Run And An Ever-Changing Cast." - Joe Garagiola
1018	"Love Is Life. And If You Miss Love, You Miss Life." - Leo Buscaglia
1019	"Always Remember That The Future Comes One Day At A Time." - Dean Acheson
1020	"Whatever Sentence Woll Bear To Be Read Twice, We May Be Sure Was Thought Twice." Henry David Thoreau
1021	"There Are Always Flowers For Those Who Want To See Them." - Henri Matisse

1022	"I Don't Want To Be Interesting. I Want To Be Good." - Ludwig Mies Van Der Rohe
1023	"We'll Love You Just The Way You Are If You're Perfect." - Alanis Morissette
1024	"Show Me A Good Loser, And I'll Show You A Loser." - Vince Lombardi
1025	"The Most Important Political Office Is That Of The Private Citizen." - Louis D. Brandeis
1026	"Wisdom Is Knowledge Which Has Become A Part Of One's Being…" - Orison Swett Marden
1027	"Nobody Ever Went Broke Underestimating The Taste Of The American Public." - H. L. Mencken
1028	"Football Is An Incredible Game. Sometimes It's So Incredible, It's Unbelievable." - Tom Landry
1029	"Heaven Is Under Our Feet As Well As Over Our Heads." - Henry David Thoreau
1030	"Education Is A Better Safeguard Of Liberty Than A Standing Army." - Edward Everett
1031	"Don't Stay In Bed, Unless You Can Make Money In Bed." - Robert Benchley
1032	"I Have Never Advocated War Except As A Means Of Peace." - Ulysses S. Grant
1033	"Music Washes Away From The Soul The Dust Of Everyday Life." - Berthold Auerbach
1034	"Without Art, The Crudeness Of Reality Would Make The World Unbearable." - George Bernard Shaw
1035	"Your Future Is Created By What You Do Today, Not Tomorrow" - Robert Kiyosaki
1036	"In All Things Of Nature There Is Something Of The Marvelous." - Aristotle
1037	"The Thermometer Of Success Is Merely The Jealousy Of The Malcontents." - Salvador Dali
1038	"Throw Your Heart Over The Fence And The Rest Will Follow." - Norman Vincent Peale
1039	"Wisdom Is Not Wisdom When It Is Derived From Books Alone." - Horace
1040	"Time Is What We Want Most, But What We Use Worst." - William Penn
1041	"But Friendship Is The Breathing Rose, With Sweets In Every Fold." - Oliver Wendell Holmes
1042	"The Herd Instinct Among Forecasters Makes Sheep Look Like Independent Thinkers." - Edgar R. Fiedler

1043	"Nationalism Is An Infantile Disease. It Is The Measles Of Mankind." - Albert Einstein
1044	"Love Is A Canvas Furnished By Nature And Embroidered By Imagination." - Voltaire
1045	"If You Can Build A Business Up Big Enough, It's Respectable." - Will Rogers
1046	"Expect The Best. Prepare For The Worst. Capitalize On What Comes." - Zig Ziglar
1047	"A Good Plan Today Is Better Than A Great Plan Tomorrow." - General George S. Patton
1048	"Airplanes May Kill You, But They Ain't Likely To Hurt You." - Satchel Paige
1049	"Those Who Make Peaceful Revolution Impossible Will Make Violent Revolution Inevitable." - John F. Kennedy
1050	"By Trying We Can Easily Endure Adversity. Another Man's, I Mean." - Mark Twain
1051	"The Only Way To Have A Friend Is To Be One." - Ralph Waldo Emerson
1052	"The Fear Of Loss Is A Path To The Dark Side." - Yoda
1053	"Poetry Is The Art Of Creating Imaginary Gardens With Real Toads." - Marianne Moore
1054	"I Failed To Make The Chess Team Because Of My Height." - Woody Allen
1055	"Politics Is War Without Bloodshed, While War Is Politics With Bloodshed." - Mao Tse-Tung
1056	"Marriage Is Nature's Way Of Keeping Us From Fighting With Strangers." - Alan King
1057	"The Poets Have Been Mysteriously Silent On The Subject Of Cheese." - Gilbert K. Chesterton
1058	"As You Make Your Bed, So You Must Lie In It." - Daniel J. Boorstin
1059	"I Believe In Getting Into Hot Water; It Keeps You Clean." - Gilbert Keith Chesterton
1060	"Time Goes, You Say? Ah, No! Alas, Time Stays, We Go." - Henry Austin Dobson
1061	"Everything I've Ever Done Was Out Of Fear Of Being Mediocre." - Chet Atkins
1062	"It Is Only As We Develop Others That We Permanently Succeed." - Harvey S. Firestone
1063	"Art In Nature Is Rhythmic And Has A Horror Of Constraint." - Robert Delaunay

1064	"Life Without Love Is Like A Tree Without Blossoms Or Fruit." - Kahlil Gibran
1065	"He Taught Me Housekeeping; When I Divorce I Keep The House." - Zsa Zsa Gabor
1066	"The Internet Treats Censorship As A Malfunction And Routes Around It." - John Perry Barlow
1067	"If A Man's Wit Be Wandering, Let Him Study The Mathematics." - Francis Bacon
1068	"I Was Sleeping The Other Night, Alone, Thanks To The Exterminator." - Emo Philips
1069	"The Butterfly Counts Not Months But Moments, And Has Time Enough." - Rabindranath Tagore
1070	"When We Direct Our Thoughts Properly, We Can Control Our Emotions..." - W. Clement Stone
1071	"If You Judge People, You Have No Time To Love Them." - Mother Teresa
1072	"I Am The Literary Equivalent Of A Big Mac And Fries." - Stephen King
1073	"Baseball Has The Great Advantage Over Cricket Of Being Sooner Ended." - George Bernard Shaw
1074	"All Achievements, All Earned Riches, Have Their Beginning In An Idea." - Napoleon Hill
1075	"Man Should Forget His Anger Before He Lies Down To Sleep." - Mohandas Gandhi
1076	"Bride: A Woman With A Fine Prospect Of Happiness Behind Her." - Ambrose Bierce
1077	"When The Rich Think About The Poor, They Have Poor Ideas." - Evita Peron
1078	"All The Things One Has Forgotten Scream For Help In Dreams." - Elias Canetti
1079	"Education Is The Key To Unlock The Golden Door Of Freedom." - George Washington Carver
1080	"There Are No Passengers On Spaceship Earth. We Are All Crew." - Marshall Mcluhan
1081	"To See Clearly Is Poetry, Prophecy And Religion All In One." - John Ruskin
1082	"A Wide Screen Just Makes A Bad Film Twice As Bad." - Samuel Goldwyn
1083	"Following The Light Of The Sun, We Left The Old World." - Christopher Columbus
1084	"Education Is Learning What You Didn't Even Know You Didn't Know." - Daniel J. Boorstin

1085	"The Distance Between Insanity And Genius Is Measured Only By Success." - Bruce Feirstein
1086	"I'll Be Floating Like A Butterfly And Stinging Like A Bee." - Muhammad Ali
1087	"High Achievement Always Takes Place In The Framework Of High Expectation." - Charles F. Kettering
1088	"Truth Lies Not Only In A Dream, But In Many Dreams." - Pier Paolo Pasolini
1089	"A Sense Of Humor Is A Major Defense Against Minor Troubles." - Mignon Mclaughlin
1090	"Poetry Is A Mirror Which Makes Beautiful That Which Is Distorted." - Percy Bysshe Shelley
1091	"Forgive Yourself For Your Faults And Your Mistakes And Move On." - Les Brown
1092	"The Actions Of Men Are The Best Interpreters Of Their Thoughts." - John Locke
1093	"If You Want To Be Found Stand Where The Seeker Seeks." - Sidney Lanier
1094	"I Cry Out For Order And Find It Only In Art." - Helen Hayes
1095	"World War Ii Was The Last Government Program That Really Worked." - George Will
1096	"Patriotism Is Often An Arbitrary Veneration Of Real Estate Above Principles." - George Jean Nathan
1097	"Military Justice Is To Justice What Military Music Is To Music." - Groucho Marx
1098	"No Act Of Kindness, No Matter How Small, Is Ever Wasted." - Aesop
1099	"A Great Artist Is Always Before His Time Or Behind It." - George Edward Moore
1100	"I Do Not Fear Computers. I Fear The Lack Of Them." - Isaac Asimov
1101	"You Miss A 100 Percent Of The Shots You Don't Take." - Wayne Gretzky
1102	"He Has The Finest, Fundamentally Sound Golf Swing I've Ever Seen." - Jack Nicklaus
1103	"A Manager Is Responsible For The Application And Performance Of Knowledge." - Peter Drucker
1104	"The Future Has Already Arrived. It's Just Not Evenly Distributed Yet." - William Gibson
1105	"Whether In Chains Or In Laurels, Liberty Knows Nothing But Victories." - Douglas Macarthur
1106	"Men Love To Wonder, And That Is The Seed Of Science." - Ralph Waldo Emerson

1107	"Politics Is For The Present, But An Equation Is For Eternity." - Albert Einstein
1108	"It's Not Enough That I Should Succeed - Others Should Fail." - David Merrick
1109	"The More Horrifying This World Becomes, The More Art Becomes Abstract." - Ellen Key
1110	"Success Is The Maximum Utilization Of The Ability That You Have." - Zig Ziglar
1111	"We Live In A World In Which Politics Has Replaced Philosophy." - Martin L. Gross
1112	"The Task Of Art Today Is To Bring Chaos Into Order." - Theodor Adorno
1113	"Every Single Art Form Is Involved In Film, In A Way." - Sydney Pollack
1114	"Prayer Does Not Change God, But It Changes Him Who Prays." - Soren Kierkegaard
1115	"A Hospital Bed Is A Parked Taxi With The Meter Running." - Groucho Marx
1116	"What One Has Not Experienced, One Will Never Understand In Print." - Isadora Duncan
1117	"You Grow Up The Day You Have Your First Real Laugh--At Yourself." - Ethel Barrymore
1118	"Cinema Is A Matter Of What's In The Frame And What's Out." - Martin Scorsese
1119	"Most People Would Rather Die Than Think; In Fact, They Do So." - Bertrand Arthur William Russell
1120	"Art Is Parasitic On Life, Just As Criticism Is Parasitic On Art." - Harry S. Truman
1121	"The Incestuous Relationship Between Government And Big Business Thrives In The Dark." - Jack Anderson
1122	"True Art Is Characterized By An Irresistible Urge In The Creative Artist." - Albert Einstein
1123	"There Cannot Be A Crisis Next Week. My Schedule Is Already Full." - Henry A. Kissinger
1124	"Experience Keeps A Dear School, But Fools Will Learn In No Other." - Benjamin Franklin
1125	"I'm Like Bush, I See The World More Like Checkers Than Chess." - Dennis Miller
1126	"Works Of Art Make Rules; Rules Do Not Make Works Of Art." - Claude Debussy

1127	"Democracy Is Being Allowed To Vote For The Candidate You Dislike Least." - Robert Byrne
1128	"Drawing On My Fine Command Of The English Language, I Said Nothing." - Robert Benchley
1129	"Everybody Knows How To Raise Children, Except The People Who Have Them." - P. J. O'Rourke
1130	"A Single Rose Can Be My Garden... A Single Friend, My World." - Leo Buscaglia
1131	"Definition Of Statistics: The Science Of Producing Unreliable Facts From Reliable Figures." - Evan Esar
1132	"A Conservative Is A Man Who Just Sits And Thinks, Mostly Sits." - Woodrow Wilson
1133	"Better Than A Thousand Hollow Words, Is One Word That Brings Peace." - The Buddha
1134	"It Is The Soothing Thing About History That It Does Repeat Itself." - Gertrude Stein
1135	"When I Work, And In My Art, I Hold Hands With God." - Robert Mapplethorpe
1136	"I Am Not A Scientist. I Am, Rather, An Impresario Of Scientists." - Jacques Yves Cousteau
1137	"Humanity Is Acquiring All The Right Technology For All The Wrong Reasons." - R. Buckminster Fuller
1138	"We Don't Have A Monopoly. We Have Market Share. There's A Difference." - Steve Ballmer
1139	"A Teacher Affects Eternity; He Can Never Tell Where His Influence Stops." - Henry B. Adams
1140	"Success Doesn't Happen." It Is Organized, Preempted, Captured, By Consecrated Common Sense." - Anonymous
1141	"When Nobody Around You Measures Up, It's Time To Check Your Yardstick." - Bill Lemly
1142	"I Don't Think Anyone Should Write Their Autobiography Until After They're Dead." - Samuel Goldwyn
1143	"First Love Is Only A Little Foolishness And A Lot Of Curiosity." - George Bernard Shaw
1144	"A Friend Is Someone Who Gives You Total Freedom To Be Yourself." - James Douglas Morrison
1145	"Success Consists Of Going From Failure To Failure Without Loss Of Enthusiasm." - Winston Churchill
1146	"There Are No Rules Of Architecture For A Castle In The Clouds." - Gilbert K. Chesterton

1147	"You Can't Help Getting Older, But You Don't Have To Get Old." - George Burns
1148	"Bashfulness Is An Ornament To Youth, But A Reproach To Old Age." - Aristotle
1149	"A Poet's Autobiography Is His Poetry. Anything Else Is Just A Footnote." - Yevgeny Yevtushenko
1150	"He Is Simply A Shiver Looking For A Spine To Run Up." - Paul Keating
1151	"Whatever Our Souls Are Made Of, His And Mine Are The Same." - Emily Bronte
1152	"For All Life Is A Dream, And Dreams Themselves Are Only Dreams." - Pedro Calderon De La Barca
1153	"Curiosity Killed The Cat, But For A While I Was A Suspect." - Steven Wright
1154	"Loneliness And The Feeling Of Being Unwanted Is The Most Terrible Poverty." - Mother Teresa
1155	"Education's Purpose Is To Replace An Empty Mind With An Open One." - Malcolm Forbes
1156	"You Must Be The Change You Wish To See In The World." - Gandhi
1157	"Humor Is Merely Tragedy Standing On Its Head With Its Pants Torn." - Irvin S. Cobb
1158	"An Eye For Eye Only Ends Up Making The Whole World Blind." - Mohandas Gandhi
1159	"Politics Is Too Serious A Matter To Be Left To The Politicians." - Charles De Gaulle
1160	"The Past Actually Happened But History Is Only What Someone Wrote Down." - A. Whitney Brown
1161	"Republicans Are Men Of Narrow Vision, Who Are Afraid Of The Future." - Jimmy Carter
1162	"Poets Are Soldiers That Liberate Words From The Steadfast Possession Of Definition." - Eli Khamarov
1163	"Leaders Have To Act More Quickly Today. The Pressure Comes Much Faster." - Andy Grove
1164	"A Woman Uses Her Intelligence To Find Reasons To Support Her Intuition." - Gilbert K. Chesterton
1165	"The Real Problem Is Not Whether Machines Think But Whether Men Do." - B. F. Skinner
1166	"You Are Where You Are Today Because You've Chosen To Be There." - Harry Browne
1167	"I Have Always Imagined That Paradise Will Be A Kind Of Library" - Jorge Luis Borges

1168	"Good Judgment Comes From Experience, And Often Experience Comes From Bad Judgment." - Rita Mae Brown
1169	"In Order To Become The Master, The Politician Poses As The Servant." - Charles De Gaulle
1170	"Vote For The Man Who Promises Least; He'll Be The Least Disappointing." - Bernard Baruch
1171	"It Is Never To Late To Be What You Might Have Been." - George Eliot
1172	"History Will Be Kind To Me For I Intend To Write It." - Winston Churchill
1173	"If You Can Count Your Money, You Don't Have A Billion Dollars." - J. Paul Getty
1174	"Knowledge Has To Be Improved, Challenged, And Increased Constantly, Or It Vanishes." - Peter Drucker
1175	"My Fake Plants Died Because I Did Not Pretend To Water Them." - Mitch Hedberg
1176	"Television Has Brought Back Murder Into The Home – Where It Belongs." - Alfred Hitchcock
1177	"Let A Hundred Flowers Bloom, Let A Hundred Schools Of Thought Contend." - Mao Tse-Tung
1178	"Be Nice To Nerds. Chances Are You'll End Up Working For One." - Bill Gates
1179	"I Never Knew How To Worship Until I Knew How To Love." - Henry Ward Beecher
1180	"It Has Become Appallingly Obvious That Our Technology Has Exceeded Our Humanity." - Albert Einstein
1181	"An Economist's Guess Is Liable To Be As Good As Anybody Else's." - Will Rogers
1182	"I Cook With Wine, Sometimes I Even Add It To The Food." - W. C. Fields
1183	"Marriage Is A Great Institution, But I'm Not Ready For An Institution." - Mae West
1184	"A Kiss Makes The Heart Young Again And Wipes Out The Years." - Rupert Brooke
1185	"You Don't Play Against Opponents, You Play Against The Game Of Basketball." - Bobby Knight
1186	"More Countries Have Understood That Women's Equality Is A Prerequisite For Development." - Kofi Annan
1187	"You Cannot Be Lonely If You Like The Person You're Alone With." - Wayne Dyer
1188	"Every Politician Should Have Been Born An Orphan And Remain A Bachelor." - Lady Bird Johnson

1189	"The Nineteenth Century Believed In Science But The Twentieth Century Does Not." - Gertrude Stein
1190	"A Work Of Art Is The Unique Result Of A Unique Temperament." - Oscar Wilde
1191	"Start Every Day Off With A Smile And Get It Over With." - W. C. Fields
1192	"It All Started When My Dog Began Getting Free Roll Over Minutes." - Jay London
1193	"Education Is What Survives When What Has Been Learned Has Been Forgotten." - B. F. Skinner
1194	"As We Advance In Life We Learn The Limits Of Our Abilities." - Henry Ford
1195	"In Peace, Sons Bury Their Fathers. In War, Fathers Bury Their Sons." - Herodotus
1196	"Drawing Is Like Making An Expressive Gesture With The Advantage Of Permanence." - Henri Matisse
1197	"Why Is It Drug Addicts And Computer Aficionados Are Both Called Users?" - Clifford Stoll
1198	"Play Is The Only Way The Highest Intelligence Of Humankind Can Unfold." - Joseph Chilton Pearce
1199	"Believe Those Who Are Seeking The Truth. Doubt Those Who Find It." - André Gide
1200	"He Who Has A Why To Live Can Bear Almost Any How." - Richard Bach
1201	"There Is Poetry As Soon As We Realize That We Possess Nothing." - John Cage
1202	"There's Only One Thing That Can Kill The Movies, And That's Education." - Will Rogers
1203	"As A Small Businessperson, You Have No Greater Leverage Than The Truth." - John Greenleaf Whittier
1204	"I Feel So Miserable Without You; It's Almost Like Having You Here." - Stephen Bishop
1205	"As Equality Increases, So Does The Number Of People Struggling For Predominance." - Mason Cooley
1206	"In Business Or In Life, Don't Follow The Wagon Tracks Too Closely." - H. Jackson Brown
1207	"It's Not Your Salary That Makes You Rich, It's Your Spending Habits." - Charles A. Jaffe
1208	"The End Move In Politics Is Always To Pick Up A Gun." - R. Buckminster Fuller

1209	"Anyone Who Says He Can See Through Women Is Missing A Lot." - Groucho Marx
1210	"Sooner Or Later, Those Who Win Are Those Who Think They Can." - Paul Tournier
1211	"If You Do Not Conquer Self, You Will Be Conquered By Self." - Napoleon Hill
1212	"The Best Bridge Between Despair And Hope Is A Good Night's Sleep." - E. Joseph Cossman
1213	"The Politicians Were Talking Themselves Red, White And Blue In The Face." - Clare Boothe Luce
1214	"All The People Like Us Are We, And Everyone Else Is They." - Rudyard Kipling
1215	"Forgiveness Does Not Change The Past, But It Does Enlarge The Future." - Paul Boese
1216	"Keep Your Eyes On The Stars And Your Feet On The Ground." - Theodore Roosevelt
1217	"Success Doesn't Happen." It Is Organized, Preempted, Captured, By Consecrated Common Sense." - F. E. Willard
1218	"Success...My Nomination For The Single Most Important Ingredient Is Energy Well Directed." - Louis Lundborg
1219	"Honesty Is The Best Policy - When There Is Money In It." - Mark Twain
1220	"Hell, There Are No Rules Here - We're Trying To Accomplish Something." - Thomas A. Edison
1221	"A Judge Is A Law Student Who Marks His Own Examination Papers." - H. L. Mencken
1222	"Cross Country Skiing Is Great If You Live In A Small Country." - Steven Wright
1223	"Here Is My First Principle Of Foreign Policy: Good Government At Home." - William E. Gladstone
1224	"Pro Football Is Like Nuclear Warfare. There Are No Winners, Only Survivors." - Frank Gifford
1225	"Marriage, Like Money, Is Still With Us; And, Like Money, Progressively Devalued." - Robert Graves
1226	"Life Is A Moderately Good Play With A Badly Written Third Act." - Truman Capote
1227	"Anger Is A Wind Which Blows Out The Lamp Of The Mind." - Robert Green Ingersoll
1228	"Everyone's A Pacifist Between Wars. It's Like Being A Vegetarian Between Meals." - Colman Mccarthy

1229	"Everything Happens To Everybody Sooner Or Later If There Is Time Enough." - George Bernard Shaw
1230	"It Is Easier To Forgive An Enemy Than To Forgive A Friend." - William Blake
1231	"Computer Science Is No More About Computers Than Astronomy Is About Telescopes." - Edsger Dijkstra
1232	"Love Is The Magician That Pulls Man Out Of His Own Hat." - Ben Hecht
1233	"A People That Values Its Privileges Above Its Principles Soon Loses Both." - Dwight D. Eisenhower
1234	"I Love Mickey Mouse More Than Any Woman I Have Ever Known." - Walt Disney
1235	"There Are No Rules For Good Photographs, There Are Only Good Photographs." - Ansel Adams
1236	"Americans Love To Fight. All Real Americans Love The Sting Of Battle." - George S. Patton
1237	"One Should Believe In Marriage As In The Immortality Of The Soul." - Honore De Balzac
1238	"The Weak Can Never Forgive. Forgiveness Is The Attribute Of The Strong." - Mohandas Gandhi
1239	"Politics Is The Art Of Choosing Between The Disastrous And The Unpalatable." - John Kenneth Galbraith
1240	"If At First You Do Succeed Try Not To Look Too Surprised." - Anonymous
1241	"One Can Have No Smaller Or Greater Mastery Than Mastery Of Oneself." - Leonardo Da Vinci
1242	"If Nominated, I Will Not Run; If Elected, I Will Not Serve." - William Tecumseh Sherman
1243	"You Must Be The Change You Wish To See In The World." - Mohandas Gandhi
1244	"Sites Need To Be Able To Interact In One Single, Universal Space." - Tim Berners-Lee
1245	"Roses Are Red, Violets Are Blue, I'm Schizophrenic, And So Am I." - Oscar Levant
1246	"Success Is Never Final And Failure Never Fatal. It's Courage That Counts." - George F. Tilton
1247	"Success Is Going From Failure To Failure Without A Loss Of Enthusiasm." - Winston Churchill
1248	"Sleep Is The Golden Chain That Ties Health And Our Bodies Together." - Thomas Dekker

1249	"Much Unhappiness Has Come Into This World Because Of Things Left Unsaid." - Fyodor Dostoevsky
1250	"Facts Are The Air Of Scientists. Without Them You Can Never Fly." - Linus Pauling
1251	"When A Subject Becomes Totally Obsolete We Make It A Required Course " - Peter Drucker
1252	"History Is The Sum Total Of Things That Could Have Been Avoided." - Konrad Adenauer
1253	"There Is Nothing Worse Than A Sharp Image Of A Fuzzy Concept." - Ansel Adams
1254	"Marriage Is A Bribe To Make The Housekeeper Think She's A Householder." - Thornton Wilder
1255	"Music Is Nothing Else But Wild Sounds Civilized Into Time And Tune." - Thomas Fuller
1256	"Positive Thinking Will Let You Do Everything Better Than Negative Thinking Will." - Zig Ziglar
1257	"Our Thoughts And Imaginations Are The Only Real Limits To Our Possibilities." - Ralph Waldo Trine
1258	"Failure Is Simply The Opportunity To Begin Again, This Time More Intelligently." - Henry Ford
1259	"Emancipate Yourself From Mental Slavery, None But Ourselves Can Free Our Mind." - Bob Marley
1260	"The Meeting Of Preparation With Opportunity Generates The Offspring We Call Luck." - Anthony Robbins
1261	"Alas, After A Certain Age Every Man Is Responsible For His Face." - Albert Camus
1262	"He Who Enjoys Good Health Is Rich, Though He Knows It Not." - Italian Proverb
1263	"Advertisements Contain The Only Truths To Be Relied On In A Newspaper." - Mark Twain
1264	"Don't Let What You Cannot Do Interfere With What You Can Do." - John Wooden
1265	"When Your Self-Worth Goes Up, Your Net Worth Goes Up With It." - Mark Victor Hansen
1266	"It's Not Whether You Get Knocked Down, It's Whether You Get Up." - Vince Lombardi
1267	"I Think It's A Terrible Shame That Politics Has Become Show Business." - Sydney Pollack
1268	"Everything You See Happening Is The Consequence Of That Which You Are." - David R. Hawkins

1269	"Middle Age Is When Your Age Starts To Show Around Your Middle." - Bob Hope
1270	"A Man Who Won't Die For Something Is Not Fit To Live." - Martin Luther King, Jr.
1271	"Whenever You See A Successful Business, Someone Once Made A Courageous Decision." - Peter Drucker
1272	"Judge Of Your Natural Character By What You Do In Your Dreams." - Ralph Waldo Emerson
1273	"Other People's Opinion Of You Does Not Have To Become Your Reality." - Les Brown
1274	"It's Not What You Look At That Matters, It's What You See." - Henry David Thoreau
1275	"It Is In Your Moments Of Decision That Your Destiny Is Shaped." - Anthony Robbins
1276	"A Man's Growth Is Seen In The Successive Choirs Of His Friends." - Ralph Waldo Emerson
1277	"Effort Only Fully Releases Its Reward After A Person Refuses To Quit." - Napoleon Hill
1278	"The Hardest Thing To Understand In The World Is The Income Tax." - Albert Einstein
1279	"The Secret Of Business Is To Know Something That Nobody Else Knows." - Aristotle Onassis
1280	"Common Sense In An Uncommon Degree Is What The World Calls Wisdom." - Samuel Taylor Coleridge
1281	"Movies Are An Art Form That Is Very Available To The Masses." - Richard King
1282	"In Order To Avoid Being Called A Flirt, She Always Yielded Easily." - Charles Count Talleyrand
1283	"Scientific Theory Is A Contrived Foothold In The Chaos Of Living Phenomena." - Wilhelm Reich
1284	"If You Meet The Buddha In The Lane, Feed Him The Ball." - Phil Jackson
1285	"I Paint Objects As I Think Them, Not As I See Them." - Pablo Picasso
1286	"In Every Walk With Nature One Receives Far More Than He Seeks." - John Muir
1287	"My Father Had A Profound Influence On Me, He Was A Lunatic." - Spike Milligan
1288	"Remember, God Provides The Best Camouflage Several Hours Out Of Every 24." - David M. Shoup
1289	"Nothing Is A Waste Of Time If You Use The Experience Wisely." - Auguste Rodin

1290	"The Function Of Leadership Is To Produce More Leaders, Not More Followers." - Ralph Nader
1291	"The Fear Of Life Is The Favorite Disease Of The 20th Century." - William Lyon Phelps
1292	"What The World Really Needs Is More Love And Less Paper Work." - Pearl Bailey
1293	"Dreams Are Illustrations... From The Book Your Soul Is Writing About You." - Marsha Norman
1294	"The Great Difficulty In Education Is To Get Experience Out Of Ideas." - George Santayana
1295	"The Principles Of True Art Is Not To Portray, But To Evoke." - Jerzy Kosinski
1296	"An Idealist Is A Person Who Helps Other People To Be Prosperous." - Henry Ford
1297	"Wrong Is Wrong, No Matter Who Does It Or Who Says It." - Malcolm X
1298	"No One Can Confidently Say That He Will Still Be Living Tomorrow." - Euripides
1299	"Your Theory Is Crazy, But It's Not Crazy Enough To Be True." - Niels Bohr
1300	"The Journey Of A Thousand Miles Must Begin With A Single Step." - Lao Tzu
1301	"The Artist Who Aims At Perfection In Everything Achieves It In Nothing." - Eugene Delacroix
1302	"When In Doubt, Mumble; When In Trouble, Delegate; When In Charge, Ponder." - James H. Boren
1303	"They Must Often Change, Who Would Be Constant In Happiness Or Wisdom." - Confucius
1304	"Doubt Is Part Of All Religion. All The Religious Thinkers Were Doubters." - Isaac Bashevis Singer
1305	"Freedom Of The Press Is Guaranteed Only To Those Who Own One." - A. J. Liebling
1306	"I Would Never Die For My Beliefs Because I Might Be Wrong." - Bertrand Russell
1307	"Concentrate: Put All Your Eggs In One Basket, And Watch That Basket." - Andrew Carnegie
1308	"Success Is The Prize For Those Who Stand True To Their Ideas!" - Josh S. Hinds
1309	"Get Your Facts First, Then You Can Distort Them As You Please." - Mark Twain

1310	"To Live Is So Startling It Leaves Little Time For Anything Else." - Emily Dickinson
1311	"I Play Golf With Friends Sometimes, But There Are Never Friendly Games." - Ben Hogan
1312	"He Has A Profound Respect For Old Age. Especially When It's Bottled." - Gene Fowler
1313	"The Only Real Mistake Is The One From Which We Learn Nothing." - John Powell
1314	"This One Step, Choosing A Goal And Sticking To It, Changes Everything." - Scott Reed
1315	"If Into The Security Recordings You Go, Only Pain Will You Find." - Yoda
1316	"Bad Politicians Are Sent To Washington By Good People Who Don't Vote." - William E. Simon
1317	"The Future Is Not In The Hands Of Fate, But In Ours." - Jules Jusseran
1318	"Doing The Right Thing Is More Important Than Doing The Thing Right" - Peter Drucker
1319	"Women Are Wiser Than Men Because They Know Less And Understand More." - James Thurber
1320	"How Strange That Nature Does Not Knock, And Yet Does Not Intrude!" - Emily Dickinson
1321	"A Book Must Be The Ax For The Frozen Sea Within Us" - Kafka
1322	"Trees Are The Earth's Endless Effort To Speak To The Listening Heaven." - Rabindranath Tagore
1323	"True Patriotism Hates Injustice In Its Own Land More Than Anywhere Else." - Clarence Darrow
1324	"Controversy Equalizes Fools And Wise Men - And The Fools Know It." - Oliver Wendell Holmes
1325	"After Silence, That Which Comes Nearest To Expressing The Inexpressible Is Music." - Aldous Huxley
1326	"A Mind Troubled By Doubt Cannot Focus On The Course To Victory." - Arthur Golden
1327	"One Man Practicing Sportsmanship Is Far Better Than A Hundred Teaching It." - Knute Rockne
1328	"The Cure For Boredom Is Curiosity. There Is No Cure For Curiosity." - Ellen Parr
1329	"Between Two Evils, I Always Pick The One I Never Tried Before." - Bette Davis
1330	"All Life Is An Experiment. The More Experiments You Make The Better." - Ralph Waldo Emerson

1331	"Airline Travel Is Hours Of Boredom Interrupted By Moments Of Stark Terror." - Al Boliska
1332	"The Lunatic, The Lover, And The Poet, Are Of Imagination All Compact." - William Shakespeare
1333	"The Very Ink With Which History Is Written Is Merely Fluid Prejudice." - Mark Twain
1334	"God Made Me Fast. And When I Run, I Feel His Pleasure." - Eric Liddell
1335	"Come Forth Into The Light Of Things, Let Nature Be Your Teacher." - William Wordsworth
1336	"The Essence Of All Art Is To Have Pleasure In Giving Pleasure." - Dale Carnegie
1337	"Success Is Getting What You Want. Happiness Is Wanting What You Get." - Dale Carnegie
1338	"Cannot Possibly Attend First Night, Will Attend Second.... If There Is One." - Winston Churchill
1339	"The Difficult Can Be Done Immediately, The Impossible Takes A Little Longer." - Army Corp Of Engineers
1340	"Human History Becomes More And More A Race Between Education And Catastrophe." - H. G. Wells
1341	"The Artist Belongs To His Work, Not The Work To The Artist." - Novalis
1342	"Happiness Is Having A Large, Loving, Caring, Close-Knit Family In Another City." - George Burns
1343	"Research Is What I'm Doing When I Don't Know What I'm Doing." - Wernher Von Braun
1344	"Love Is Like War: Easy To Begin But Very Hard To Stop." - H. L. Mencken
1345	"Art, In Itself, Is An Attempt To Bring Order Out Of Chaos." - Stephen Sondheim
1346	"Wanted: A Needle Swift Enough To Sew This Poem Into A Blanket." - Charles Simic
1347	"You Must Pay The Price If You Wish To Secure The Blessing." - Andrew Jackson
1348	"A Man Is Not Old Until Regrets Take The Place Of Dreams." - John Barrymore
1349	"If I Had Been The Virgin Mary, I Would Have Said No." - Margaret Smith
1350	"When You Judge Another, You Do Not Define Them, You Define Yourself." - Wayne Dyer

1351	"Any Fool Can Criticize, Condemn, And Complain – And Most Fools Do." - Dale Carnegie
1352	"The Wisdom Of The Wise Is An Uncommon Degree Of Common Sense." - Dean Inge
1353	"People Who Are Really Serious About Software Should Make Their Own Hardware." - Alan Kay
1354	"Science Is The Great Antidote To The Poison Of Enthusiasm And Superstition." - Adam Smith
1355	"No Man Is Smart, Except By Comparison To Those Who Know Less" - Edgar Watson Howe
1356	"I'm Not A Member Of Any Organized Political Party, I'm A Democrat!" - Will Rogers
1357	"Parents Are The Last People On Earth Who Ought To Have Children." - Samuel Butler
1358	"You Don't Have To Have Fought In A War To Love Peace." - Geraldine Ferraro
1359	"Intelligence Is The Wife, Imagination Is The Mistress, Memory Is The Servant." - Victor Hugo
1360	"The First Thing I Remember Liking That Liked Me Back Was Food." - Rhoda Morgenstern
1361	"It's The Friends You Can Call Up At 4 A.M. That Matter." - Marlene Dietrich
1362	"The Main Thing Is To Keep The Main Thing The Main Thing." - Stephen Covey
1363	"Patriotism Is The Willingness To Kill And Be Killed For Trivial Reasons." - Bertrand Russell
1364	"An Artist Is A Dreamer Consenting To Dream Of The Actual World." - George Santayana
1365	"For Every Talent That Poverty Has Stimulated It Has Blighted A Hundred." - John W. Gardner
1366	"Those Who Do Not Remember The Past Are Condemned To Repeat It." - George Santayana
1367	"I Want For Myself What I Want For Other Women, Absolute Equality." - Agnes Macphail
1368	"Coming Together Is A Beginning; Keeping Together Is Progress; Working Together Is Success." - Henry Ford
1369	"The Process Of Scientific Discovery Is, In Effect, A Continual Flight From Wonder." - Albert Einstein
1370	"The Best Way To Make Your Dreams Come True Is To Wake Up." - Paul Valery

1371	"A Hug Is Like A Boomerang - You Get It Back Right Away." - Bil Keane
1372	" Too Many People Overvalue What They Are Not And Undervalue What They Are." - Malcolm Forbes
1373	"Youth Is The Gift Of Nature, But Age Is A Work Of Art." - Stanislaw Lec
1374	"Marriage Is A Feast Where The Grace Is Sometimes Better Than The Dinner." - Charles Caleb Colton
1375	"An Inventor Is Simply A Fellow Who Doesn't Take His Education Too Seriously." - Charles F. Kettering
1376	"The Most Imaginative People Are The Most Credulous, For Them Everything Is Possible." - Alexander Chase
1377	"If 'Pro' Is The Opposite Of 'Con' What Is The Opposite Of 'Progress'?" - Paul Harvey
1378	"Success Is Simple. Do What's Right, The Right Way, At The Right Time." - Arnold H. Glasow
1379	"It's Far Easier To Forgive An Enemy After You've Got Even With Him." - Olin Miller
1380	"A Good Marriage Would Be Between A Blind Wife And A Deaf Husband." - Michel De Montaigne
1381	"A Psychiatrist Asks A Lot Of Expensive Questions Your Wife Asks For Nothing." - Joey Adams
1382	"In The Business World, The Rearview Mirror Is Always Clearer Than The Windshield." - Warren Buffett
1383	"How Old Would You Be If You Didn't Know How Old You Are?" - Satchel Paige
1384	"Love Can Sometimes Be Magic. But Magic Can Sometimes... Just Be An Illusion." - Javan
1385	"All This Worldly Wisdom Was Once The Unamiable Heresy Of Some Wise Man." - Henry David Thoreau
1386	"Ah, Summer, What Power You Have To Make Us Suffer And Like It." - Russell Baker
1387	"History Is A Cyclic Poem Written By Time Upon The Memories Of Man." - Percy Bysshe Shelley
1388	"I Have Noticed That Nothing I Never Said Ever Did Me Any Harm." - Calvin Coolidge
1389	"Marriage Is A Wonderful Institution, But Who Wants To Live In An Institution?" - Groucho Marx
1390	"If You Have Ten Thousand Regulations You Destroy All Respect For The Law." - Winston Churchill

1391	"If God Wanted Us To Bend Over He'd Put Diamonds On The Floor." - Joan Rivers
1392	"Those Who Are At War With Others Are Not At Peace With Themselves." - William Hazlitt
1393	"Shoot For The Moon. Even If You Miss, You'll Land Among The Stars." - Les Brown
1394	"Technological Progress Has Merely Provided Us With More Efficient Means For Going Backwards." - Aldous Huxley
1395	"Ninety Percent Of The Politicians Give The Other Ten Percent A Bad Reputation." - Henry A. Kissinger
1396	"Forgiveness Is A Funny Thing, It Warms The Hearts And Cools The Sting." - Peter Allen
1397	"If They Want Peace, Nations Should Avoid The Pin-Pricks That Precede Cannon Shots." - Napoleon Bonaparte
1398	"There's No Money In Poetry, But Then There's No Poetry In Money, Either." - Robert Graves
1399	"Art Enables Us To Find Ourselves And Lose Ourselves At The Same Time." - Thomas Merton
1400	"To Make An Apple Pie From Scratch, You Must First Invent The Universe." - Carl Sagan
1401	"In Youth We Run Into Difficulties. In Old Age Difficulties Run Into Us." - Beverly Sills
1402	"Peace Cannot Be Achieved Through Violence, It Can Only Be Attained Through Understanding." - Ralph Waldo Emerson
1403	"If You Don't Drive Your Business, You Will Be Driven Out Of Business." - B. C. Forbes
1404	"If My Films Don't Show A Profit, I Know I'm Doing Something Right." - Woody Allen
1405	"Humor Distorts Nothing, And Only False Gods Are Laughed Off Their Earthly Pedestals." - Agnes Repplier
1406	"What Art Offers Is Space - A Certain Breathing Room For The Spirit." - John Updike
1407	"When A Thought Takes One's Breath Away, A Grammar Lesson Seems An Impertinence." - Thomas W. Higginson
1408	"If You Ask Me Anything I Don't Know, I'm Not Going To Answer." - Yogi Berra
1409	"90 Percent Of My Time Is Spent On 10 Percent Of The World." - Colin Powell
1410	"It's Not The Load That Breaks You Down...It's The Way You Carry It." - Lena Horn

1411	"I Have A Fine Sense Of The Ridiculous, But No Sense Of Humor." - Edward Albee
1412	"Wisdom, Compassion, And Courage Are The Three Universally Recognized Moral Qualities Of Men." - Confucius
1413	"We Can't Plan Life. All We Can Do Is Be Available For It." - Lauryn Hill
1414	"A Man In Love Is Incomplete Until He Has Married. Then He's Finished." - Zsa Zsa Gabor
1415	"Success Has A Simple Formula: Do Your Best, And People May Like It." - Sam Ewing
1416	"The Future Belongs To Those Who Believe In The Beauty Of Their Dreams." - Eleanor Roosevelt
1417	"My Theory Is That All Of Scottish Cuisine Is Based On A Dare." - Mike Myers
1418	"Education Comes From Within; You Get It By Struggle And Effort And Thought." - Napoleon Hill
1419	"The Only Time My Prayers Are Never Answered Is On The Golf Course." - Billy Graham
1420	"Marriage Is Good For Those Who Are Afraid To Sleep Alone At Night." - St. Jerome
1421	"Success Is A Science; If You Have The Conditions, You Get The Result." - Oscar Wilde
1422	"The Future Belongs To Those Who Believe In The Beauty Of The Dream." - Eleanor Roosevelt
1423	"The Way To Love Anything Is To Realize That It May Be Lost." - Gilbert K. Chesterton
1424	"The Four Building Blocks Of The Universe Are Fire, Water, Gravel And Vinyl." - Dave Barry
1425	"Great Men Are Rarely Isolated Mountain Peaks; They Are The Summits Of Ranges." - Thomas W. Higginson
1426	"The Bell That Tolls For All In Boxing Belongs To A Cash Register." - Bob Verdi
1427	"Successful People Ask Better Questions, And As A Result, They Get Better Answers." - Anthony Robbins
1428	"The Bible Looks Like It Started Out As A Game Of Mad Libs." - Bill Maher
1429	"The Time For Action Is Now. It's Never Too Late To Do Something." - Carl Sandburg
1430	"Forty Is The Old Age Of Youth; Fifty The Youth Of Old Age." - Victor Hugo

1431	"The Real And Lasting Victories Are Those Of Peace, And Not Of War." - Ralph Waldo Emerson
1432	"All Wrong-Doing Arises Because Of Mind. If Mind Is Transformed Can Wrong-Doing Remain?" - The Buddha
1433	"Laws Are Like Sausages, It Is Better Not To See Them Being Made." - Otto Von Bismarck
1434	"About The Time We Can Make The Ends Meet, Somebody Moves The Ends." - Herbert Hoover
1435	"It Takes An Endless Amount Of History To Make Even A Little Tradition." - Henry James
1436	"As A Man Grows Older It Is Harder And Harder To Frighten Him." - Jean Paul Richter
1437	"Imagination And Fiction Make Up More Than Three Quarters Of Our Real Life." - Simone Weil
1438	"Show Me A Thoroughly Satisfied Man And I Will Show You A Failure." - Thomas Alva Edison
1439	" Greatness Lies Not In Being Strong, But In The Right Use Of Strength." - Henry Ward Beecher
1440	"This Is One Small Step For A Man, One Giant Leap For Mankind." - Neil Armstrong
1441	"Don't Confuse Fame With Success. Madonna Is One; Helen Keller Is The Other." - Erma Bombeck
1442	"It Takes A Lot Of Courage To Show Your Dreams To Someone Else." - Erma Bombeck
1443	"He Hits The Ball A Long Way And He Knows How To Win." - Gary Mccord
1444	"The Bonds Of Matrimony Are Like Any Other Bonds – They Mature Slowly." - Peter De Vries
1445	"Great Work Is Done By People Who Are Not Afraid To Be Great." - Fernando Flores
1446	"Everyone Enjoys Doing The Kind Of Work For Which He Is Best Suited." - Napoleon Hill
1447	"Science Has Made Us Gods Even Before We Are Worthy Of Being Men." - Jean Rostand
1448	"There's So Much Comedy On Television. Does That Cause Comedy In The Streets?" - Dick Cavett
1449	"Health Is The Greatest Gift, Contentment The Greatest Wealth, Faithfulness The Best Relationship." - The Buddha
1450	"The Most I Can Do For My Friend Is Simply Be His Friend." - Henry David Thoreau

1451	"I Was Married By A Judge. I Should Have Asked For A Jury." - Groucho Marx
1452	"A Morning-Glory At My Window Satisfies Me More Than The Metaphysics Of Books." - Walt Whitman
1453	"The Trouble With Jogging Is That The Ice Falls Out Of Your Glass." - Martin Mull
1454	"An Artist Is Somebody Who Produces Things That People Don't Need To Have." - Andre Gide
1455	"Rationalism Is The Enemy Of Art, Though Necessary As A Basis For Architecture." - Arthur Erickson
1456	"The Less You Open Your Heart To Others, The More Your Heart Suffers." - Deepak Chopra
1457	"The 1st Amendment Protects The Right To Speak, Not The Right To Spend." - Byron White
1458	"Freedom Means The Opportunity To Be What We Never Thought We Would Be." - Daniel J. Boorstin
1459	"The Government Solution To A Problem Is Usually As Bad As The Problem." - Milton Friedman
1460	"The Art Of Being Wise Is The Art Of Knowing What To Overlook." - William James
1461	"Our Character Is What We Do When We Think No One Is Looking." - H. Jackson Brown Jr.
1462	"Success Is Often The Result Of Taking A Misstep In The Right Direction." - Al Bernstein
1463	"Always Two There Are, No More, No Less: A Master And An Apprentice." - Yoda
1464	"I See Great Things In Baseball. It's Our Game - The American Game." - Walt Whitman
1465	"I Gave It My Body And Mind, But I Have Kept My Soul." - Phil Jackson
1466	"A Thought Is Often Original, Though You Have Uttered It A Hundred Times." - Oliver Wendell Holmes
1467	"A Guilty Conscience Needs To Confess. A Work Of Art Is A Confession." - Albert Camus
1468	"Success Isn't A Result Of Spontaneous Combustion. You Must Set Yourself On Fire." - Arnold H. Glasow
1469	"The Door To Wisdom Swings On Hinges Of Common Sense And Uncommon Thoughts." Anonymous
1470	"The Wheel That Squeaks The Loudest Is The One That Gets The Grease." - Josh Billings

1471	"There Is No Love Without Forgiveness, And There Is No Forgiveness Without Love." - Bryant H. Mcgill
1472	"Experience Is The Child Of Thought, And Thought Is The Child Of Action." - Benjamin Disraeli
1473	"You Will Find Poetry Nowhere Unless You Bring Some Of It With You." - Joseph Joubert
1474	"He Uses Statistics As A Drunken Man Uses Lamp-Posts – For Support Rather Than Illumination." - Andrew Lang
1475	"The Bad News Is Time Flies. The Good News Is You're The Pilot." - Michael Althsuler
1476	"How We Spend Our Days Is, Of Course, How We Spend Our Lives." - Anne Dillard
1477	"Morality Is Of The Highest Importance - But For Us, Not For God." - Albert Einstein
1478	"Dreams Have Only One Owner At A Time. That's Why Dreamers Are Lonely." - Erma Bombeck
1479	"In Modern War... You Will Die Like A Dog For No Good Reason." - Ernest Hemingway
1480	"Each Nation Feels Superior To Other Nations. That Breeds Patriotism - And Wars." - Dale Carnegie
1481	"Do The Hard Jobs First. The Easy Jobs Will Take Care Of Themselves." - Dale Carnegie
1482	"It Seems A Long Time Since The Morning Mail Could Be Called Correspondence." - Jacques Barzun
1483	"The Only Way To Prove That You're A Good Sport Is To Lose." - Ernie Banks
1484	"It's Called A Pen. It's Like A Printer, Hooked Straight To My Brain." - Dale Dauten
1485	"I Refuse To Join Any Club That Would Have Me As A Member." - Groucho Marx
1486	"A Gentle Answer Turns Away Wrath, But A Harsh Word Stirs Up Anger." - Bible, Proverbs 15:1
1487	"I Don't Know Anything About Music. In My Line You Don't Have To." - Elvis Presley
1488	"Few Men Have The Natural Strength To Honor A Friend's Success Without Envy." - Aeschylus
1489	"Marriage Is A Wonderful Invention: Then Again, So Is A Bicycle Repair Kit." - Billy Connolly
1490	"I Looked Up My Family Tree And Found Out I Was The Sap." - Rodney Dangerfield

1491	"What Do We Want Our Kids To Do? Sweep Up Around Japanese Computers?" - Walter F. Mondale
1492	"There Are Twelve Hours In The Day, And Above Fifty In The Night." - Marie De Rabutin-Chantal
1493	"Dreams Are True While They Last, And Do We Not Live In Dreams?" - Alfred Lord Tennyson
1494	"A Friend Is One Who Knows You And Loves You Just The Same." - Elbert Hubbard
1495	"Leisure Time Is That Five Or Six Hours When You Sleep At Night." - George Allen
1496	"The Bookfull Blockhead, Ignorantly Read With Loads Of Learned Lumber In His Head." - Alexander Pope
1497	"We Should Not Let Our Fears Hold Us Back From Pursuing Our Hopes." - John F. Kennedy
1498	"The Amount Of Sleep Required By The Average Person Is Five Minutes More." - Wilson Mizener
1499	"The Two Basic Items Necessary To Sustain Life Are Sunshine And Coconut Milk." - Dustin Hoffman
1500	"There Are Two Theories On Hitting The Knuckleball. Unfortunately, Neither Of Them Works." - Charley Lau
1501	"Never Raise Your Hand To Your Children - It Leaves Your Midsection Unprotected." - Robert Orben
1502	"Flowers Are Without Hope. Because Hope Is Tomorrow And Flowers Have No Tomorrow." - Antonio Porchia
1503	"Everyone Needs To Be Valued. Everyone Has The Potential To Give Something Back." - Princess Diana
1504	"He Who Has A Why To Live For Can Bear Almost Any How." - Friedrich Nietzsche
1505	"Success Is Never Final And Failure Never Fatal. It Is Courage That Counts." - George F. Tilton
1506	"When You Make A Film You Usually Make A Film About An Idea." - Sydney Pollack
1507	"One Good Thing About Music, When It Hits You, You Feel No Pain." - Bob Marley
1508	"You Can Preach A Better Sermon With Your Life Than With Your Lips." - Oliver Goldsmith
1509	"I Shall Not Die Of A Cold. I Shall Die Of Having Lived." - Willa Cather
1510	"That Government Is Best Which Governs The Least, Because Its People Discipline Themselves." - Thomas Jefferson
1511	"I Don't Make Jokes. I Just Watch The Government And Report The Facts." - Will Rogers

1512	"Whenever You Do A Thing, Act As If All The World Were Watching." - Thomas Jefferson
1513	"I Believe In The Religion Of Islam. I Believe In Allah And Peace." - Muhammad Ali
1514	"I Like To Pretend That My Art Has Nothing To Do With Me." - Roy Lichtenstein
1515	"That's The Motivation Of An Artist - To Seek Attention Of Some Kind." - James Taylor
1516	"Most Of Us Have Far More Courage Than We Ever Dreamed We Possessed." - Dale Carnegie
1517	"Some People Are So Afraid Do Die That They Never Begin To Live." - Henry Van Dyke
1518	"Art Is The Most Intense Mode Of Individualism That The World Has Known." - Oscar Wilde
1519	"You Can No More Win A War Than You Can Win An Earthquake." - Jeannette Rankin
1520	"Those Who Have Succeeded At Anything And Don't Mention Luck Are Kidding Themselves." - Larry King
1521	"The Young Man Knows The Rules, But The Old Man Knows The Exceptions." - Oliver Wendell Holmes
1522	"If You Want The Rainbow, You've Got To Put Up With The Rain." - Jimmy Durante
1523	"I Choose A Block Of Marble And Chop Off Whatever I Don't Need." - Auguste Rodin
1524	"Music Is Everybody's Possession. It's Only Publishers Who Think That People Own It." - John Lennon
1525	"I've Learned That Mistakes Can Often Be As Good A Teacher As Success." - Jack Welch
1526	"A Soldier Will Fight Long And Hard For A Bit Of Colored Ribbon." - Napoleon Bonaparte
1527	"Youth Is A Wonderful Thing. What A Crime To Waste It On Children." - George Bernard Shaw
1528	"It Takes One Person To Forgive, It Takes Two People To Be Reunited." - Lewis B. Smedes
1529	"If You Do What You've Always Done, You'll Get What You've Always Gotten." - Anthony Robbins
1530	"When Nine Hundred Years Old You Reach, Look As Good, You Will Not." - Yoda
1531	"When I Look Into The Future, It's So Bright It Burns My Eyes." - Oprah Winfrey

1532	"Their Very Conservatism Is Secondhand, And They Don't Know What They Are Conserving." - Robertson Davies
1533	"Leaders Keep Their Eyes On The Horizon, Not Just On The Bottom Line." - Warren G. Bennis
1534	"There Is A Wisdom Of The Head, And A Wisdom Of The Heart." - Charles Dickens
1535	"A Friendship Founded On Business Is Better Than A Business Founded On Friendship." - John D. Rockefeller
1536	"Let Him Who Would Enjoy A Good Future Waste None Of His Present." - Roger Babson
1537	"The Man Who Is Swimming Against The Stream Knows The Strength Of It." - Woodrow Wilson
1538	"I Am Extraordinarily Patient, Provided I Get My Own Way In The End." - Margaret Thatcher
1539	"As We Are Liberated From Our Own Fear, Our Presence Automatically Liberates Others." - Nelson Mandela
1540	"I Am Not Discouraged, Because Every Wrong Attempt Discarded Is Another Step Forward." - Thomas A. Edison
1541	"No Man Is Good Enough To Govern Another Man Without That Other's Consent." - Abraham Lincoln
1542	"Laziness Is Nothing More Than The Habit Of Resting Before You Get Tired." - Jules Renard
1543	"What An Immense Power Over Life Is The Power Of Possessing Distinct Aims." - Elizabeth Stuart Phelps
1544	"Everyone Told Me To Pass On Speed Because It Was A 'Bus Movie.'" - Sandra Bullock
1545	"My Computer Beat Me At Checkers, But I Sure Beat It At Kickboxing." - Emo Philips
1546	"Classical Music Is The Kind We Keep Thinking Will Turn Into A Tune." - Kin Hubbard
1547	"Without Change, Something Sleeps Inside Us, And Seldom Awakens. The Sleeper Must Awaken." - Frank Herbert
1548	"I Think That I Shall Never See A Poem Lovely As A Tree." - Joyce Kilmer
1549	"The Best Argument Against Democracy Is A Five-Minute Conversation With The Average Voter." - Winston Churchill
1550	"It Is Often Easier To Ask For Forgiveness Than To Ask For Permission." - Grace Hopper
1551	"To Affect The Quality Of The Day, That Is The Highest Of Arts." - Henry David Thoreau

1552	"The Price Of Anything Is The Amount Of Life You Exchange For It." - Henry David Thoreau
1553	"Shoot For The Moon. Even If You Miss, You'll Land Among The Stars." - Les Brown
1554	"A Man Content To Go To Heaven Alone Will Never Go To Heaven." - Boethius
1555	"He Who Lives By The Crystal Ball Soon Learns To Eat Ground Glass." - Edgar R. Fiedler
1556	"To Me - Old Age Is Always Ten Years Older Than I Am." - John Burroughs
1557	"Every Great Advance In Science Has Issued From A New Audacity Of Imagination." - John Dewey
1558	"The Only Way You Can Beat The Lawyers Is To Die With Nothing." - Will Rogers
1559	"Faith, To My Mind, Is A Stiffening Process, A Sort Of Mental Starch." - E. M. Forster
1560	"Forgiveness Is A Funny Thing. It Warms The Heart And Cools The Sting." - William A. Ward
1561	"True Love Is Like Ghosts, Which Everyone Talks About And Few Have Seen." - Francois De La Rochefoucauld
1562	"The True Work Of Art Is But A Shadow Of The Divine Perfection." - Michelangelo
1563	"Humor Brings Insight And Tolerance. Irony Brings A Deeper And Less Friendly Understanding." - Agnes Repplier
1564	"You Can't Depend On Your Eyes When Your Imagination Is Out Of Focus." - Mark Twain
1565	"I Am Patient With Stupidity But Not With Those Who Are Proud Of It." - Edith Sitwell
1566	"Wisdom Doesn't Necessarily Come With Age. Sometimes Age Just Shows Up All By Itself." - Tom Wilson
1567	"Older People Shouldn't Eat Health Food, They Need All The Preservatives They Can Get." - Robert Orben
1568	"Satisfaction Lies In The Effort, Not In The Attainment. Full Effort Is Full Victory." - Mohandas Gandhi
1569	"What Sculpture Is To A Block Of Marble, Education Is To A Human Soul." - Joseph Addison
1570	"Learn To See Things As They Really Are, Not As We Imagine They Are." - Vernon Howard
1571	"He Is Not Only Dull Himself; He Is The Cause Of Dullness In Others." - Samuel Johnson

1572	"Truly Great Friends Are Hard To Find, Difficult To Leave, And Impossible To Forget." - G. Randolf
1573	"We Waste Time Looking For The Perfect Lover, Instead Of Creating The Perfect Love." - Tom Robbins
1574	"Recession Is When A Neighbor Loses His Job. Depression Is When You Lose Yours." - Ronald Reagan
1575	"Faith Consists In Believing When It Is Beyond The Power Of Reason To Believe." - Voltaire
1576	"There Is No Greater Evidence Of Superior Intelligence Than To Be Surprised At Nothing." - Josh Billings
1577	"Movies Are A Complicated Collision Of Literature, Theatre, Music And All The Visual Arts." - Yahoo Serious
1578	"In This World Nothing Can Be Said To Be Certain, Except Death And Taxes." - Benjamin Franklin
1579	"The Day Which We Fear As Our Last Is But The Birthday Of Eternity." - Lucius Annaeus Seneca
1580	"I Have No Ambition To Govern Men; It Is A Painful And Thankless Office." - Thomas Jefferson
1581	"Confidence Comes Not From Always Being Right But From Not Fearing To Be Wrong." - Peter T. Mcintyre
1582	"Only In Growth, Reform And Change, Paradoxically Enough, Is True Security To Be Found." - Anne Morrow Lindbergh
1583	"All Our Dreams Can Come True, If We Have The Courage To Pursue Them." - Walt Disney
1584	"Golf Is Not A Game Of Good Shots. It's A Game Of Bad Shots." - Ben Hogan
1585	"He Has All The Virtues I Dislike And None Of The Vices I Admire." - Winston Churchill
1586	" Some People Dream Of Success... While Others Wake Up And Work Hard At It." - Anonymous
1587	"If We Could But Paint With The Hand What We See With The Eye." - Honore De Balzac
1588	"Do You Realize If It Weren't For Edison We'd Be Watching TV By Candlelight?" - Al Boliska
1589	"Genius Is More Often Found In A Cracked Pot Than In A Whole One." - E. B. White
1590	"I Have Never Killed A Man, But I Have Read Many Obituaries With Great Pleasure." - Clarence Darrow
1591	"In Art, The Hand Can Never Execute Anything Higher Than The Heart Can Imagine." - Ralph Waldo Emerson

1592	"It's Easy To Make A Buck. It's A Lot Tougher To Make A Difference." - Tom Brokaw
1593	"There Comes A Time In Every Man's Life, And I've Had Plenty Of Them." - Casey Stengel
1594	"Our Lives Begin To End The Day We Become Silent About Things That Matter." - Dr. Martin Luther King Jr.
1595	"I Went To A Fight The Other Night, And A Hockey Game Broke Out." - Rodney Dangerfield
1596	"I Have A Love Interest In Every One Of My Films - A Gun." - Arnold Schwarzenegger
1597	"Born Again?! No, I'm Not. Excuse Me For Getting It Right The First Time." - Dennis Miller
1598	"Anyone Who Thinks There's Safety In Numbers Hasn't Looked At The Stock Market Pages." - Irene Peter
1599	"Creativity Is Allowing Yourself To Make Mistakes. Art Is Knowing Which Ones To Keep." - Scott Adams
1600	"You Can't Wait For Inspiration. You Have To Go After It With A Club." - Jack London
1601	"Having Family Responsibilities And Concerns Just Has To Make You A More Understanding Person." - Sandra Day O'Connor
1602	"The Only Thing We Know About The Future Is That It Will Be Different." - Peter Drucker
1603	"I Saw The Angel In The Marble And Carved Until I Set Him Free." - Michelangelo
1604	"I Like Not Only To Be Loved, But To Be Told I Am Loved." - George Eliot
1605	"I Like Long Walks, Especially When They Are Taken By People Who Annoy Me." - Fred Allen
1606	"A Dress That Zips Up The Back Will Bring A Husband And Wife Together." - James H. Boren
1607	"I Haven't Spoken To My Wife In Years. I Didn't Want To Interrupt Her." - Rodney Dangerfield
1608	"It Is Neither Wealth Nor Splendor; But Tranquility And Occupation Which Give You Happiness." - Thomas Jefferson
1609	"Who Would Give A Law To Lovers? Love Is Unto Itself A Higher Law." - Boethius
1610	"Making The Simple Complicated Is Commonplace; Making The Complicated Simple, Awesomely Simple, That's Creative." - Charles Mingus
1611	"Anytime You Suffer A Setback Or Disappointment, Put Your Head Down And Plow Ahead." - Les Brown

1612	"Climb High; Climb Far. Your Goal Is The Sky; Your Aim Is The Star." - Inscription At Williams College
1613	"I Know I Am Getting Better At Golf Because I Am Hitting Fewer Spectators." - Gerald R.Ford
1614	"A Man's Accomplishments In Life Are The Cumulative Effect Of His Attention To Detail." - John Foster Dulles
1615	"You Don't Have To Go Looking For Love When It's Where You Come From." - Werner Erhard
1616	"And In Movies You Must Be A Gambler. To Produce Films Is To Gamble." - Douglas Sirk
1617	"The Superior Man Understands What Is Right; The Inferior Man Understands What Will Sell." - Confucius
1618	"I Like The Dreams Of The Future Better Than The History Of The Past." - Thomas Jefferson
1619	"Blessed Is He Who Has Found His Work; Let Him Ask No Other Blessedness." - Thomas Carlyle
1620	" Your Ability To Learn Faster Than Your Competition Is Your Only Sustainable Competitive Advantage." - Arie De Gues
1621	"If It Keeps Up, Man Will Atrophy All His Limbs But The Push-Button Finger." - Frank Lloyd Wright
1622	"The Purpose Of Art Is Washing The Dust Of Daily Life Off Our Souls." - Pablo Picasso
1623	"No Poems Can Please For Long Or Live That Are Written By Water Drinkers." - Horace
1624	"The Artist Is Nothing Without The Gift, But The Gift Is Nothing Without Work." - Emile Zola
1625	"Only A Monopolist Could Study A Business And Ruin It By Giving Away Products." - Scott Mcnealy
1626	"Democracy Is The Art And Science Of Running The Circus From The Monkey Cage." - H. L. Mencken
1627	"Democracy Is When The Indigent, And Not The Men Of Property, Are The Rulers." - Aristotle
1628	"Coming Together Is A Beginning, Staying Together Is Progress, And Working Together Is Success." - Henry Ford
1629	"The Majority Of Husbands Remind Me Of An Orangutan Trying To Play The Violin." - Honore De Balzac
1630	"I See Nothing In Space As Promising As The View From A Ferris Wheel." - E. B. White
1631	"It's Not What You Pay A Man, But What He Costs You That Counts." - Will Rogers

1632	"Make No Small Plans For They Have Not The Power To Stir Men's Blood." - Niccolo Machiavelli
1633	"I Used To Jog But The Ice Cubes Kept Falling Out Of My Glass." - David Lee Roth
1634	"The Friend Is The Man Who Knows All About You, And Still Likes You." - Elbert Hubbard
1635	"Getting Information Off The Internet Is Like Taking A Drink From A Fire Hydrant." - Mitchell Kapor
1636	"All You Need Is Love. But A Little Chocolate Now And Then Doesn't Hurt." - Charles M. Schulz
1637	"Patience And Perseverance Have A Magical Effect Before Which Difficulties Disappear And Obstacles Vanish." - John Quincy Adams
1638	"Wishing To Be Friends Is Quick Work, But Friendship Is A Slow Ripening Fruit." - Aristotle
1639	"A James Cagney Love Scene Is One Where He Lets The Other Guy Live." - Bob Hope
1640	"O Bed! O Bed! Delicious Bed! That Heaven Upon Earth To The Weary Head." - Thomas Hood
1641	"It's Going To Be A Bummer If Mars Turns Out To Be Like Us." - Newt Gingrich
1642	"Just Living Is Not Enough... One Must Have Sunshine, Freedom, And A Little Flower." - Hans Christian Anderson
1643	"Learning Sleeps And Snores In Libraries, But Wisdom Is Everywhere, Wide Awake, On Tiptoe." - Josh Billings
1644	"Faith Is Taking The First Step Even When You Don't See The Whole Staircase." - Martin Luther King, Jr.
1645	"Whenever An Individual Or A Business Decides That Success Has Been Attained, Progress Stops." - Thomas J. Watson
1646	"Jim Bakker Spells His Name With Two K's Because Three Would Be Too Obvious." - Bill Maher
1647	"Living In Dreams Of Yesterday, We Find Ourselves Still Dreaming Of Impossible Future Conquests." - Charles Lindbergh
1648	"A Poet Looks At The World The Way A Man Looks At A Woman." - Wallace Stevens
1649	"Love Is A Gross Exaggeration Of The Difference Between One Person And Everybody Else." - George Bernard Shaw
1650	"The Worst Thing In The World Is To Try To Sleep And Not To." - F. Scott Fitzgerald
1651	"My Father Would Take Me To The Playground, And Put Me On Mood Swings." - Jay London

1652	"Why Do You Sit There Looking Like An Envelope Without Any Address On It?" - Mark Twain
1653	"Adding Sound To Movies Would Be Like Putting Lipstick On The Venus De Milo." - Mary Pickford
1654	"Six Hour For A Man, Seven For A Woman, And Eight For A Fool." - English Proverb
1655	"To Me, It Seems A Dreadful Indignity To Have A Soul Controlled By Geography." - George Santayana
1656	"I've Had A Lot Of Worries In My Life, Most Of Which Never Happened." - Mark Twain
1657	"If You Do Not Hope You Will Not Find What Is Beyond Your Hopes." - St. Clement Of Alexandra
1658	"I Just Invent, Then Wait Until Man Comes Around To Needing What I've Invented." - R. Buckminster Fuller
1659	"I Only Regret That I Have But One Life To Lose For My Country." - Nathan Hale
1660	"Do Your Work With Your Whole Heart And You Will Succeed - There's So Little Competition." - Elbert Hubbard
1661	"Almost All Quality Improvement Comes Via Simplification Of Design, Manufacturing... Layout, Processes, And Procedures." - Tom Peters
1662	"The Box Was A Universe, A Poem, Frozen On The Boundaries Of Human Experience." - William Gibson
1663	"A Writer Should Write With His Eyes And A Painter Paint With His Ears." - Gertrude Stein
1664	"Excellence Is In The Details. Give Attention To The Details And Excellence Will Come." - Perry Paxton
1665	"A Lot Of People Are Afraid Of Heights. Not Me, I'm Afraid Of Widths." - Steven Wright
1666	"Love Consists In This, That Two Solitudes Protect And Touch And Greet Each Other." - Rainer Maria Rilke
1667	"I Distrust Camels, And Anyone Else Who Can Go A Week Without A Drink." - Joe E. Lewis
1668	"I'm An Idealist. I Don't Know Where I'm Going, But I'm On My Way." - Carl Sandburg
1669	"To Do Great Work A Man Must Be Very Idle As Well As Very Industrious." - Samuel Butler
1670	"You Know You Are Getting Old When The Candles Cost More Than The Cake." - Bob Hope
1671	"Maybe All One Can Do Is Hope To End Up With The Right Regrets." - Arthur Miller

1672	"A Year Spent In Artificial Intelligence Is Enough To Make One Believe In God." - Alan Perlis
1673	"Frankly, I Don't Mind Not Being President. I Just Mind That Someone Else Is." - Edward Kennedy
1674	"Wine Is Constant Proof That God Loves Us And Loves To See Us Happy." - Benjamin Franklin
1675	" What Comes Out Of You When You Are Squeezed Is What Is Inside You." - Wayne Dyer
1676	"You Can't Wait For Inspiration. You Have To Go After It With A Club." - Jack London
1677	"The Basic Problems Facing The World Today Are Not Susceptible To A Military Solution." - John F. Kennedy
1678	"All Marriages Are Happy. It's The Living Together Afterward That Causes All The Trouble." - Raymond Hull
1679	"When We Remember We Are All Mad, The Mysteries Disappear And Life Stands Explained." - Mark Twain
1680	"Knowing That You Have Complete Control Of Your Thinking You Will Recognize The Power…" - Mikhail Strabo
1681	"Be Able To Go Shopping For A Bathing Suit And Not Become Depressed Afterward." - Marilyn Vos Savant
1682	"I Am Not An Athenian Or A Greek, But A Citizen Of The World." - Diogenes
1683	"If I Had No Sense Of Humor, I Would Long Ago Have Committed Suicide." - Mohandas Gandhi
1684	"What An Immense Power Over The Life Is The Power Of Possessing Distinct Aims." - Elizabeth Stuart Phelps
1685	"The Farther Backward You Can Look, The Farther Forward You Are Likely To See." - Winston Churchill
1686	"Civilization Is A Movement And Not A Condition, A Voyage And Not A Harbor." - Arnold J. Toynbee
1687	"Other Sports Play Once A Week But This Sport Is With Us Every Day." - Peter Ueberroth
1688	"You Never Know What Is Enough Unless You Know What Is More Than Enough." - William Blake
1689	"My Pessimism Extends To The Point Of Even Suspecting The Sincerity Of The Pessimists." - Jean Rostand
1690	"It Usually Takes Me More Than Three Weeks To Prepare A Good Impromptu Speech." - Mark Twain
1691	"Science And Technology Revolutionize Our Lives, But Memory, Tradition And Myth Frame Our Response." - Arthur M. Schlesinger

1692	"If It Doesn't Matter Who Wins Or Loses, Then Why Do They Keep Score?" - Vince Lombardi
1693	"Success Is A Lousy Teacher. It Seduces Smart People Into Thinking They Can't Lose." - Bill Gates
1694	"If We Desire Respect For The Law, We Must First Make The Law Respectable." - Louis D. Brandeis
1695	"Some Men Are Alive Simply Because It Is Against The Law To Kill Them." - Edward W. Howe
1696	"Believe That Life Is Worth Living And Your Belief Will Help Create The Fact." - William James
1697	"Seek Freedom And Become Captive Of Your Desires. Seek Discipline And Find Your Liberty." - Frank Herbert
1698	" Anger Makes You Smaller, While Forgiveness Forces You To Grow Beyond What You Were." - Cherie Carter-Scott
1699	"I Quit Therapy Because My Analyst Was Trying To Help Me Behind My Back." - Richard Lewis
1700	"The Quality Of A Leader Is Reflected In The Standards They Set For Themselves." - Ray Kroc
1701	"For Here We Are Not Afraid To Follow The Truth Wherever It May Lead..." - Thomas Jefferson
1702	"The World Hates Change, Yet It Is The Only Thing That Has Brought Progress." - Charles F. Kettering
1703	"Big Goals Get Big Results. No Goals Get No Results Or Somebody Else's Results.." - Mark Victor Hansen
1704	"One Important Key To Success Is Self-Confidence. An Important Key To Self-Confidence Is Preparation." - Arthur Ashe
1705	"The Two Most Important Things In Life Are Good Friends And A Strong Bullpen." - Bob Lemon
1706	"Pleasant Words Are A Honeycomb, Sweet To The Soul And Healing To The Bones." - Bible, Proverbs 16:24
1707	"Knowing Trees, I Understand The Meaning Of Patience. Knowing Grass, I Can Appreciate Persistence." - Hal Borland
1708	"The Construction Of Europe Is An Art. It Is The Art Of The Possible." - Jacques Chirac
1709	"Artists Who Seek Perfection In Everything Are Those Who Cannot Attain It In Anything." - Gustave Flaubert
1710	"Smoking Kills. If You're Killed, You've Lost A Very Important Part Of Your Life." - Brooke Shields
1711	"Older Men Declare War. But It Is The Youth That Must Fight And Die." - Herbert Hoover

1712	"Love Is All We Have, The Only Way That Each Can Help The Other." - Euripides
1713	"If All The Economists Were Laid End To End, They'd Never Reach A Conclusion." - George Bernard Shaw
1714	"Failure Doesn't Mean You Are A Failure It Just Means You Haven't Succeeded Yet." - Robert H. Schuller
1715	"Humanity Is Never So Beautiful As When Praying For Forgiveness, Or Else Forgiving Another." - Jean Paul
1716	"If There Is Something To Pardon In Everything, There Is Also Something To Condemn." - Friedrich Nietzsche
1717	"Education Is Not The Filling Of A Pail, But The Lighting Of A Fire." - William Butler Yeats
1718	"How Much More Grievous Are The Consequences Of Anger Than The Causes Of It." - Marcus Aurelius
1719	"The Ladder Of Success Is Best Climbed By Stepping On The Rungs Of Opportunity." - Ayn Rand
1720	"Let Your Religion Be Less Of A Theory And More Of A Love Affair." - Gilbert K. Chesterton
1721	"There Is A Muscular Energy In Sunlight Corresponding To The Spiritual Energy Of Wind." - Annie Dillard
1722	"I Can't Do It Never Yet Accomplished Anything; I Will Try Has Performed Wonders." - George P. Burnham
1723	"Observe Good Faith And Justice Toward All Nations. Cultivate Peace And Harmony With All." - George Washington
1724	"Suicide Is Man's Way Of Telling God, You Can't Fire Me - I Quit." - Bill Maher
1725	"Spring Is When You Feel Like Whistling Even With A Shoe Full Of Slush." - Doug Larson
1726	"Life Consists Not In Holding Good Cards But In Playing Those You Hold Well." - Josh Billings
1727	"It's Not That I'm So Smart, It's Just That I Stay With Problems Longer." - Albert Einstein
1728	"To Overcome Evil With Good Is Good, To Resist Evil By Evil Is Evil." - The Prophet Mohammad
1729	"Moderation Is A Virtue Only In Those Who Are Thought To Have An Alternative." - Henry A. Kissinger
1730	"Life Belongs To The Living, And He Who Lives Must Be Prepared For Changes." - Johann Wolfgang Von Goethe
1731	"Mankind Must Put An End To War Before War Puts An End To Mankind." - John F. Kennedy

1732	"Fashion Is Only The Attempt To Realize Art In Living Forms And Social Intercourse." - Francis Bacon
1733	"A Soft Refusal Is Not Always Taken, But A Rude One Is Immediately Believed." - Alexander Chase
1734	"Every Creator Painfully Experiences The Chasm Between His Inner Vision And Its Ultimate Expression." - Isaac Bashevis Singer
1735	"Everybody Gets So Much Information All Day Long That They Lose Their Common Sense." - Gertrude Stein
1736	"I Love To Go To Washington - If Only To Be Near My Money." - Bob Hope
1737	"The Flood Of Money That Gushes Into Politics Today Is A Pollution Of Democracy." - Theodore White
1738	"In Feature Films The Director Is God; In Documentary Films God Is The Director." - Alfred Hitchcock
1739	"History Is The Version Of Past Events That People Have Decided To Agree Upon." - Napoleon Bonaparte
1740	"Be Faithful In Small Things Because It Is In Them That Your Strength Lies." - Mother Teresa
1741	"Nothing But Heaven Itself Is Better Than A Friend Who Is Really A Friend." - Plautus
1742	"A Lot Of Movies Are About Life, Mine Are Like A Slice Of Cake." - Alfred Hitchcock
1743	"The Clock Talked Loud. I Threw It Away, It Scared Me What It Talked." - Tillie Olsen
1744	"Sleeping Is No Mean Art: For Its Sake One Must Stay Awake All Day." - Friedrich Nietzsche
1745	"Love Is An Act Of Endless Forgiveness, A Tender Look Which Becomes A Habit." - Peter Ustinov
1746	"Equality Is The Soul Of Liberty; There Is, In Fact, No Liberty Without It." - Frances Wright
1747	"To Change A Habit, Make A Conscious Decision, Then Act Out The New Behavior." - Maxwell Maltz
1748	"Democracy Does Not Guarantee Equality Of Conditions – It Only Guarantees Equality Of Opportunity." - Irving Kristol
1749	"Art Consists Of Limitation. The Most Beautiful Part Of Every Picture Is The Frame." - Gilbert K. Chesterton
1750	"A Successful Marriage Requires Falling In Love Many Times, Always With The Same Person." - Mignon Mclaughlin
1751	"The 'Net Is A Waste Of Time, And That's Exactly What's Right About It." - William Gibson

1752	"Doubt Is A Pain Too Lonely To Know That Faith Is His Twin Brother." - Kahlil Gibran
1753	"What Does It Mean To Pre-Board? Do You Get On Before You Get On?" - George Carlin
1754	"I Don't Have A Bank Account Because I Don't Know My Mother's Maiden Name." - Paula Poundstone
1755	"The More I Live, The More I Think That Humor Is The Saving Sense." - Jacob August Riis
1756	"The Best Thing One Can Do When It's Raining Is To Let It Rain." - Henry Wadsworth Longfellow
1757	"Personally, I Would Sooner Have Written Alice In Wonderland Than The Whole Encyclopedia Britannica." - Stephen Leacock
1758	"It Destroys One's Nerves To Be Amiable Every Day To The Same Human Being." - Benjamin Disraeli
1759	"The Moment You Cheat For The Sake Of Beauty, You Know You're An Artist." - David Hockney
1760	"A Man's Own Self Is His Friend, A Man's Own Self Is His Foe." - Bhagavad-Gita
1761	"Religion Is The Idol Of The Mob; It Adores Everything It Does Not Understand." - Frederick II
1762	"Experience: That Most Brutal Of Teachers. But You Learn; My God, Do You Learn!" - Clive Staples Lewis
1763	"When Nature Has Work To Be Done, She Creates A Genius To Do It." - Ralph Waldo Emerson
1764	"Treat A Work Of Art Like A Prince. Let It Speak To You First." - Arthur Schopenhauer
1765	"I Never Drink Water Because Of The Disgusting Things That Fish Do In It." - W. C. Fields
1766	"Never Discourage Anyone...Who Continually Makes Progress, No Matter How Slow." - Plato
1767	"I Wonder If Other Dogs Think Poodles Are Members Of A Weird Religious Cult." - Rita Rudner
1768	"A Very Small Degree Of Hope Is Sufficient To Cause The Birth Of Love." - Henri B. Stendhal
1769	"Friendship Needs No Words - It Is Solitude Delivered From The Anguish Of Loneliness." - Dag Hammarskjold
1770	"Give Me A Couple Of Years, And I'll Make That Actress An Overnight Success." - Samuel Goldwyn
1771	"You Can't Set A Hen In One Morning And Have Chicken Salad For Lunch." - George M. Humphrey

1772	"We Are Going To Have Peace Even If We Have To Fight For It." - Dwight D. Eisenhower
1773	"In Love The Paradox Occurs That Two Beings Become One And Yet Remain Two." - Erich Fromm
1774	"The Discipline Of Writing Something Down Is The First Step Toward Making It Happen." - Lee Iacocca
1775	"It's A Cruel Season That Makes You Get Ready For Bed While It's Light Out." - Bill Watterson
1776	"Life Beats Down And Crushes The Soul And Art Reminds You That You Have One." - Stella Adler
1777	"Never Think That War, No Matter How Necessary, Nor How Justified, Is Not A Crime." - Ernest Hemingway
1778	"Love Is The Self-Delusion We Manufacture To Justify The Trouble We Take To Have Sex." - Daniel S. Greenberg
1779	"Anger And Jealousy Can No More Bear To Lose Sight Of Their Objects Than Love." - George Eliot
1780	"A Baby Is Born With A Need To Be Loved - And Never Outgrows It." - Frank A. Clark
1781	"A True Friend Never Gets In Your Way Unless You Happen To Be Going Down." - Arnold H. Glasow
1782	"Early To Rise And Early To Bed Makes A Man Healthy And Wealthy And Dead." - James Thurber
1783	"Once A Woman Has Forgiven Her Man, She Must Not Reheat His Sins For Breakfast." - Marlene Dietrich
1784	"Perhaps In Time The So-Called Dark Ages Will Be Thought Of As Including Our Own." - Georg C. Lichtenberg
1785	"A Good Laugh And A Long Sleep Are The Best Cures In The Doctor's Book." - Irish Proverb
1786	"Because Things Are The Way They Are, Things Will Not Stay The Way They Are." - Bertolt Brecht
1787	"The World Could Use More Vision And Less Television." - Anonymous
1788	"I Never See What Has Been Done; I Only See What Remains To Be Done." - The Buddha
1789	"It Is Error Alone Which Needs The Support Of Government. Truth Can Stand By Itself." - Thomas Jefferson
1790	"Every Production Of An Artist Should Be The Expression Of An Adventure Of His Soul." - W. Somerset Maugham
1791	"No! No Different. Only Different In Your Mind. You Must Unlearn What You Have Learned." - Yoda

1792	"And When Is There Time To Remember, To Sift, To Weigh, To Estimate, To Total?" - Tillie Olsen
1793	"If One Does Not Know To Which Port One Is Sailing, No Wind Is Favorable." - Lucius Annaeus Seneca
1794	"I Don't Take The Movies Seriously, And Anyone Who Does Is In For A Headache." - Bette Davis
1795	"The Gambling Known As Business Looks With Austere Disfavor Upon The Business Known As Gambling." - Ambrose Bierce
1796	"I Don't Know If I Should Care About A Man Who Made Life Easy; I Should Want Someone Who Made It Interesting." - Edith Wharton
1797	"Green Is The Prime Color Of The World, And That From Which Its Loveliness Arises." - Pedro Calderon De La Barca
1798	"Defeat Is Not The Worst Of Failures. Not To Have Tried Is The True Failure." - George Edward Woodberry
1799	"In The Power To Change Yourself Is The Power To Change The World Around You." - Anwar Sadat
1800	"You Must Be Single Minded. Drive For The One Thing On Which You Have Decided." - General George S. Patton
1801	"People Are Stunned To Hear That One Company Has Data Files On 185 Million Americans." - Ralph Nader
1802	"The Entrepreneur Always Searches For Change, Responds To It, And Exploits It As An Opportunity." - Peter Drucker
1803	"If You Don't Like Something, Change It. If You Can't Change It, Change Your Attitude." - Maya Angelou
1804	"I'm Kidding About Having Only A Few Dollars. I Might Have A Few Dollars More." - James Brown
1805	"I Don't Think There's Any Artist Of Any Value Who Doesn't Doubt What They're Doing." - Francis Ford Coppola
1806	"Understanding The Laws Of Nature Does Not Mean That We Are Immune To Their Operations." - David Gerrold
1807	"Education Is More Than A Luxury; It Is A Responsibility That Society Owes To Itself." - Robin Cook
1808	"Each Memorable Verse Of A True Poet Has Two Or Three Times The Written Content." - Alfred De Musset
1809	"Tell The FBI That The Kidnappers Should Pick Out A Judge That Nixon Wants Back." - William O. Douglas
1810	"The Person Who Seeks All Their Applause From Outside Has Their Happiness In Another's Keeping." - Dale Carnegie
1811	"If One Way Be Better Than Another, That You May Be Sure Is Nature's Way." - Aristotle

1812	"We Do Not See Nature With Our Eyes, But With Our Understandings And Our Hearts." - William Hazlitt
1813	"Golf Is A Game In Which You Yell Fore, Shoot Six, And Write Down Five." - Paul Harvey
1814	"Hatred Does Not Cease By Hatred, But Only By Love; This Is The Eternal Rule." - The Buddha
1815	"It Is Only An Auctioneer Who Can Equally And Impartially Admire All Schools Of Art." - Oscar Wilde
1816	"The Sky Above The Port Was The Color Of Television, Tuned To A Dead Station." - William Gibson
1817	"Politicians Are Like Socks; If You Don't Change Them Often Enough They Start To Stink." - Anonymous
1818	"One's Friends Are That Part Of The Human Race With Which One Can Be Human." - George Santayana
1819	"It Is Horrifying That We Have To Fight Our Own Government To Save The Environment." - Ansel Adams
1820	"Punctuality Is One Of The Cardinal Business Virtues: Always Insist On It In Your Subordinates." - Don Marquis
1821	"Forgiveness Is The Fragrance That The Violet Sheds On The Heel That Has Crushed It." - Mark Twain
1822	"Great Achievement Is Usually Born Of Great Sacrifice, And Is Never The Result Of Selfishness." - Napoleon Hill
1823	"I Have A New Philosophy. I'm Only Going To Dread One Day At A Time." - Charles M. Schulz
1824	"The Death Of One Man Is A Tragedy. The Death Of Millions Is A Statistic." - Joseph Stalin
1825	"The Hunger For Love Is Much More Difficult To Remove Than The Hunger For Bread." - Mother Teresa
1826	"Any Change, Even A Change For The Better, Is Always Accompanied By Drawbacks And Discomforts." - Arnold Bennett
1827	"For Every Minute You Remain Angry, You Give Up Sixty Seconds Of Peace Of Mind." - Ralph Waldo Emerson
1828	"The Key Is Not To Prioritize What's On Your Schedule, But To Schedule Your Priorities." - Stephen Covey
1829	"There Is Nothing In A Caterpillar That Tells You It's Going To Be A Butterfly." - R. Buckminster Fuller
1830	"Science Is A Way Of Thinking Much More Than It Is A Body Of Knowledge." - Carl Sagan
1831	"The Best Thing Workers Can Bring To Their Jobs Is A Lifelong Thirst For Learning." - Jack Welch

1832	"A Child Of Five Would Understand This. Send Someone To Fetch A Child Of Five." - Groucho Marx
1833	"Government In The U.S. Today Is A Senior Partner In Every Business In The Country." - Norman Cousins
1834	"Whatever Poet, Orator Or Sage May Say Of It, Old Age Is Still Old Age." - Sinclair Lewis
1835	"We've Arranged A Civilization In Which Most Crucial Elements Profoundly Depend On Science And Technology." - Carl Sagan
1836	"Good Advertising Is A Happy Wedding Of Words And Pictures, Not A Contest Between Them." - Leo Burnett
1837	"California Is A Fine Place To Live - If You Happen To Be An Orange." - Fred Allen
1838	"The Toughest Thing About Success Is That You've Got To Keep On Being A Success." - Irving Berlin
1839	"The Difference In Golf And Government Is That In Golf You Can't Improve Your Lie." - George Deukmejian
1840	"Patriotism Is A Kind Of Religion; It Is The Egg From Which Wars Are Hatched." - Guy De Maupassant
1841	"I Am Always Doing Things I Can't Do, That's How I Get To Do Them." - Pablo Picasso
1842	"You Must Begin To Think Of Yourself As Becoming The Person You Want To Be." - David Viscott
1843	"Shoot A Few Scenes Out Of Focus. I Want To Win The Foreign Film Award." - Billy Wilder
1844	"If I Had Learned Education I Would Not Have Had Time To Learn Anything Else." - Cornelius Vanderbilt
1845	"The Act Of Taking The First Step Is What Separates The Winners From The Losers." - Brian Tracy
1846	"The Best Minds Are Not In Government. If Any Were, Business Would Steal Them Away." - Ronald Reagan
1847	"Love Is Only A Dirty Trick Played On Us To Achieve Continuation Of The Species." - W. Somerset Maugham
1848	"Age Is An Issue Of Mind Over Matter. If You Don't Mind, It Doesn't Matter." - Mark Twain
1849	"There's A Great Power In Words, If You Don't Hitch Too Many Of Them Together." - Josh Billings
1850	"One Important Key To Success Is Self-Confidence. An Important Key To Self- Confidence Is Preparation." - Arthur Ashe
1851	"Youth Is The Best Time To Be Rich, And The Best Time To Be Poor." - Euripides

1852	"Friendship Is A Word, The Very Sight Of Which In Print Makes The Heart Warm." - Augustine Birrell
1853	"In Three Words I Can Sum Up Everything I've Learned About Life: It Goes On." - Robert Frost
1854	"Too Many Of Us Are Not Living Our Dreams Because We Are Living Our Fears." - Les Brown
1855	"If Truth Is Beauty, How Come No One Has Their Hair Done In The Library?" - Lily Tomlin
1856	"Obstacles Are Those Frightful Things You See When You Take Your Eyes Off Your Goal." - Henry Ford
1857	"I Think There Is One Higher Office Than President And I Would Call That Patriot." - Gary Hart
1858	"The Wisdom Of The Wise And The Experience Of The Ages Are Perpetuated By Quotations." - Benjamin Disraeli
1859	"Be Like A Duck. Calm On The Surface, But Always Paddling Like The Dickens Underneath." - Michael Caine
1860	"Our Greatest Glory Is Not In Never Falling, But In Rising Every Time We Fall." - Confucius
1861	"A Person Is Always Startled When He Hears Himself Called Old For The First Time." - Oliver Wendell Holmes
1862	"A Husband Is What Is Left Of A Lover, After The Nerve Has Been Extracted." - Helen Rowland
1863	"Man Becomes Man Only By His Intelligence, But He Is Man Only By His Heart." - Henri Frederic Amiel
1864	"He's The Kind Of Man A Woman Would Have To Marry To Get Rid Of." - Mae West
1865	"The Bells And Stones Have Voices But, Unless They Are Struck, They Will Never Sound." - Chuang-Tzu
1866	"Only In Our Dreams Are We Free. The Rest Of The Time We Need Wages." - Terry Pratchett
1867	"All That Is Necessary For Evil To Triumph Is For Good Men To Do Nothing." - Edmund Burke
1868	"I Will Not Eat Oysters. I Want My Food Dead. Not Sick. Not Wounded. Dead." - Woody Allen
1869	"It Is Only When They Go Wrong That Machines Remind You How Powerful They Are." - Clive James
1870	"The Movies Are The Only Business Where You Can Go Out Front And Applaud Yourself." - Will Rogers
1871	"I Sang In The Choir For Years, Even Though My Family Belonged To Another Church." - Paul Lynde

1872	"Being Considerate Of Others Will Take Your Children Further In Life Than Any College Degree." - Marian Wright Edelman
1873	"My Reading Of History Convinces Me That Most Bad Government Results From Too Much Government." - Thomas Jefferson
1874	" It Is Wise To Keep In Mind That No Success Or Failure Is Necessarily Final." - Anonymous
1875	"Someone's Sitting In The Shade Today Because Someone Planted A Tree A Long Time Ago." - Les Brown
1876	"This Life Is Worth Living, We Can Say, Since It Is What We Make It." - William James
1877	"Dreams Are The Wanderings Of The Spirit Though All Nine Heavens And All Nine Earths." - Lu Yen
1878	"Time Is The Scarcest Resource And Unless It Is Managed Nothing Else Can Be Managed." - Peter Drucker
1879	"Our Scientific Power Has Outrun Our Spiritual Power. We Have Guided Missiles And Misguided Men." - Martin Luther King, Jr.
1880	"How Incessant And Great Are The Ills With Which A Prolonged Old Age Is Replete." - C. S. Lewis
1881	"I'm The Only Person Of Distinction Who Has Ever Had A Depression Named For Him." - Herbert Hoover
1882	"Nature Knows No Pause In Progress And Development, And Attaches Her Curse On All Inaction." - Johann Wolfgang Von Goethe
1883	"Only Those Who Risk Going Too Far Can Possibly Know How Far One Can Go." - T.S. Elliot
1884	" Most Great People Have Attained Their Greatest Success J ust One Step Beyond Their Greatest Failure." - Napoleon Hill
1885	"Continuous Effort - Not Strength Or Intelligence - Is The Key To Unlocking Our Potential" - Sir Winston Churchill
1886	"Poetry Is An Orphan Of Silence. The Words Never Quite Equal The Experience Behind Them." - Charles Simic
1887	"Those Who Bring Sunshine Into The Lives Of Others Can Not Keep It From Themselves." - J.M. Barrie
1888	"In Order To Make An Apple Pie From Scratch, You Must First Create The Universe." - Carl Sagan
1889	"Our Greatest Glory Consists Not In Never Falling... But In Rising Every Time We Fall." - Ralph Waldo Emerson
1890	"I Believe A Leaf Of Grass Is No Less Than The Journey - Work Of The Stars." - Walt Whitman
1891	"Russians Can Give You Arms But Only The United States Can Give You A Solution." - Anwar Sadat

1892	"If The Headline Doesn't Stop People, The Copy Might As Well Be Written In Greek." - John Caples
1893	"It Requires Wisdom To Understand Wisdom: The Music Is Nothing If The Audience Is Deaf." - Walter Lippmann
1894	"The Past Is Really Almost As Much A Work Of The Imagination As The Future." - Jessamyn West
1895	"It Is No Measure Of Health To Be Well Adjusted To A Profoundly Sick Society." - Jiddu Krishnamurti
1896	"Each Problem That I Solved Became A Rule, Which Served Afterwards To Solve Other Problems." - Rene Descartes
1897	"For Death Is No More Than A Turning Of Us Over From Time To Eternity." - William Penn
1898	"The Purpose Of Human Life Is To Show Compassion And The Will To Help Others." - Albert Schweitzer
1899	"Originality And The Feeling Of One's Own Dignity Are Achieved Only Through Work And Struggle." - Fyodor Dostoyevsky
1900	"More And More People Care About Religious Tolerance As Fewer And Fewer Care About Religion." - H. Jackson Brown, Jr.
1901	"History Is A Gallery Of Pictures In Which There Are Few Originals And Many Copies." - Alexis De Tocqueville
1902	"Suburbia Is Where The Developer Bulldozes Out The Trees, Then Names The Streets After Them." - Bill Vaughan
1903	"To Love Abundantly Is To Live Abundantly, And To Love Forever Is To Live Forever." - Henry Drummond
1904	"The Thing I Enjoyed Most Were Visits From Children. They Did Not Want Public Office." - Herbert Hoover
1905	"Let The Gentle Bush Dig Its Root Deep And Spread Upward To Split The Boulder." - Carl Sandburg
1906	"The Older I Grow The More I Distrust The Familiar Doctrine That Age Brings Wisdom." - H. L. Mencken
1907	"You Don't Have To Suffer To Be A Poet; Adolescence Is Enough Suffering For Anyone." - John Ciardi
1908	"I Found There Was Only One Way To Look Thin, Hang Out With Fat People." - Rodney Dangerfield
1909	"It Is Well That War Is So Terrible. We Should Grow Too Fond Of It." - Robert E. Lee
1910	"An Artist Is Never Ahead Of His Time But Most People Are Far Behind Theirs." - Edgard Varese
1911	"As We Look Ahead Into The Next Century, Leaders Will Be Those Who Empower Others." - Bill Gates

1912	"I Have A Simple Philosophy: Fill What's Empty. Empty What's Full. Scratch Where It Itches." - Alice Roosevelt Longworth
1913	"Art Is Not A Study Of Positive Reality, It Is The Seeking For Ideal Truth." - John Ruskin
1914	"Do You Know What My Favorite Part Of The Game Is? The Opportunity To Play." - Mike Singletary
1915	"I Play In The Low 80s. If It's Any Hotter Than That, I Won't Play." - Joe E. Lewis
1916	"Be Happy In The Moment, That's Enough. Each Moment Is All We Need, Not More." - Mother Teresa
1917	"One May Know How To Gain A Victory, And Know Not How To Use It." - Pedro Calderon De La Barca
1918	"It's A Round Ball And A Round Bat, And You Got To Hit It Square." - Pete Rose
1919	"Poetry Is A Phantom Script Telling How Rainbows Are Made And Why They Go Away." - Carl Sandburg
1920	"Flowers Are The Sweetest Things God Ever Made And Forgot To Put A Soul Into." - Henry Ward Beecher
1921	"I Have Never Killed A Man, But I Have Read Many Obituaries With Great Pleasure." - Clarence Darrow
1922	"I Am Not Afraid Of Storms, For I Am Learning How To Sail My Ship." - Louisa May Alcott
1923	"If My Films Make One More Person Miserable, I'll Feel I Have Done My Job." - Woody Allen
1924	"What's Unfortunate About Buying A Pitcher For $12 Million Is That He Carries No Warranty." - Bob Verdi
1925	"The Great Use Of Life Is To Spend It For Something That Will Outlast It." - William James
1926	"Bachelors Know More About Women Than Married Men; If They Didn't They'd Be Married Too." - H. L. Mencken
1927	"If You're Never Scared Or Embarrassed Or Hurt, It Means You Never Take Any Chances." - Julia Sorel
1928	"Patriots Always Talk Of Dying For Their Country And Never Of Killing For Their Country." - Bertrand Russell
1929	"Success Seems To Be Largely A Matter Of Hanging On After Others Have Let Go." - William Feather
1930	"You Can't Put A Limit On Anything. The More You Dream, The Farther You Get." - Michael Phelps
1931	"Pray That Success Will Not Come Any Faster Than You Are Able To Endure It." - Elbert Hubbard

1932	"For My Part I Believe In The Forgiveness Of Sin And The Redemption Of Ignorance." - Adlai E. Stevenson
1933	"Let Us Not Look Back In Anger, Nor Forward In Fear, But Around In Awareness." - James Thurber
1934	"When That Shutter Clicks, Anything Else That Can Be Done Afterward Is Not Worth Consideration." - Edward Steichen
1935	"We Perceive When Love Begins And When It Declines By Our Embarrassment When Alone Together." - Jean De La Bruyere
1936	"The Greatest Potential Of Control Tends To Exist At The Point Where Action Takes Place." - Louis A. Allen
1937	"Creative Thought Is The Only Reality, Everything Else Is Merely The By-Product Of That Thought." - Walter Russell
1938	"Our Individual Lives Cannot, Generally, Be Works Of Art Unless The Social Order Is Also." - Charles Horton Cooley
1939	"A Poet Is, Before Anything Else, A Person Who Is Passionately In Love With Language." - W. H. Auden
1940	"Thank God Men Cannot Fly, And Lay Waste The Sky As Well As The Earth." - Henry David Thoreau
1941	"The Most Pitiful Among Men Is He Who Turns His Dreams Into Silver And Gold." - Kahlil Gibran
1942	"Man Maintains His Balance, Poise, And Sense Of Security Only As He Is Moving Forward." - Maxwell Maltz
1943	"Things Alter For The Worse Spontaneously, If They Be Not Altered For The Better Designedly." - Francis Bacon
1944	"I Prayed For Twenty Years But Received No Answer Until I Prayed With My Legs." - Frederick Douglass
1945	"Not A Shred Of Evidence Exists In Favor Of The Idea That Life Is Serious." - Brendan Gill
1946	"Just Because Something Doesn't Do What You Planned It To Do Doesn't Mean It's Useless." - Thomas A. Edison
1947	"The Fewer Rules A Coach Has, The Fewer Rules There Are For Players To Break." - John Madden
1948	"I Can't Tell You If Genius Is Hereditary, Because Heaven Has Granted Me No Offspring." - James Whistler
1949	"Be As A Tower Firmly Set; Shakes Not Its Top For Any Blast That Blows." - Dante Alighieri
1950	"It Is An Unfortunate Fact That We Can Secure Peace Only By Preparing For War." - John F. Kennedy
1951	"All Men Are Created Equal, It Is Only Men Themselves Who Place Themselves Above Equality." - David Allan Coe

1952	"If You Take Responsibility For Yourself You Will Develop A Hunger To Accomplish Your Dreams." - Les Brown
1953	"There Is Nothing So Easy To Learn As Experience And Nothing So Hard To Apply." - Josh Billings
1954	"We Would Like To Live As We Once Lived, But History Will Not Permit It." - John F. Kennedy
1955	"My Greatest Strength As A Consultant Is To Be Ignorant And Ask A Few Questions." - Peter Drucker
1956	"The Wedding March Always Reminds Me Of The Music Played When Soldiers Go Into Battle." - Heinrich Heine
1957	"If We Don't Change, We Don't Grow. If We Don't Grow, We Aren't Really Living." - Gail Sheehy
1958	"The Practice Of Forgiveness Is Our Most Important Contribution To The Healing Of The World." - Marianne Williamson
1959	"Love, Work, And Knowledge Are The Wellsprings Of Our Lives, They Should Also Govern It." - Wilhelm Reich
1960	"Nolan Ryan Is Pitching Much Better Now That He Has His Curve Ball Straightened Out." - Joe Garagiola
1961	" It Is Hard To Fail, But It Is Worse Never To Have Tried To Succeed." - Theodore Roosevelt
1962	"When Your Desires Are Strong Enough You Will Appear To Possess Superhuman Powers To Achieve." - Napoleon Hill
1963	"Few People Even Scratch The Surface, Much Less Exhaust The Contemplation Of Their Own Experience." - Randolph Bourne
1964	"Statutes Authorizing Unreasonable Searches Were The Core Concern Of The Framers Of The 4th Amendment." - Sandra Day O'connor
1965	"Movies Are Not Scripts - Movies Are Films; They're Not Books, They're Not The Theatre." - Nicolas Roeg
1966	"Being Deeply Loved By Someone Gives You Strength, While Loving Someone Deeply Gives You Courage." - Lao Tzu
1967	"Poetry Is When An Emotion Has Found Its Thought And The Thought Has Found Words." - Robert Frost
1968	"I Did Not Have Three Thousand Pairs Of Shoes, I Had One Thousand And Sixty." - Imelda Marcos
1969	"Any Healthy Man Can Go Without Food For Two Days - But Not Without Poetry." - Charles Baudelaire
1970	"I Hear And I Forget. I See And I Remember. I Do And I Understand." - Chinese Proverb
1971	"All Through Nature, You Will Find The Same Law. First The Need, Then The Means." - Robert Collier

1972	"Bad Times Have A Scientific Value. These Are Occasions A Good Learner Would Not Miss." - Ralph Waldo Emerson
1973	"Wisdom Is The Quality That Keeps You From Getting Into Situations Where You Need It." - Doug Larson
1974	"Give Me Odorous At Sunrise A Garden Of Beautiful Flowers Where I Can Walk Undisturbed." - Walt Whitman
1975	"Patriotism Is Supporting Your Country All The Time, And Your Government When It Deserves It." - Mark Twain
1976	"Middle Age Is The Awkward Period When Father Time Starts Catching Up With Mother Nature." - Harold Coffin
1977	"The Object Of Education Is To Prepare The Young To Educate Themselves Throughout Their Lives." - Robert M. Hutchins
1978	"Those Who Hate You Don't Win Unless You Hate Them, And Then You Destroy Yourself." - Richard M. Nixon
1979	"Dream No Small Dreams For They Have No Power To Move The Hearts Of Men." - Johann Wolfgang Von Goethe
1980	"It's Good Sportsmanship To Not Pick Up Lost Golf Balls While They Are Still Rolling." - Mark Twain
1981	" It Is Literally True That You Can Succeed Best And Quickest By Helping Others To Succeed." - Napoleon Hill
1982	"Originality Is The Fine Art Of Remembering What You Hear But Forgetting Where You Heard It." - Laurence J. Peter
1983	"Wise Men Speak Because They Have Something To Say; Fools Because They Have To Say Something." - Plato
1984	"Education Is Simply The Soul Of A Society As It Passes From One Generation To Another." - Gilbert K. Chesterton
1985	"The Trouble With The Rat Race Is That Even If You Win, You're Still A Rat." - Lily Tomlin
1986	"Courage Is Doing What You're Afraid To Do. There Can Be No Courage Unless You're Scared." - Eddie Rickenbacker
1987	"If I Have Seen Further Than Others, It Is By Standing Upon The Shoulders Of Giants." - Isaac Newton
1988	"This Film Cost $31 Million. With That Kind Of Money I Could Have Invaded Some Country." - Clint Eastwood
1989	"Politics Has Become So Expensive That It Takes A Lot Of Money Even To Be Defeated." - Will Rogers
1990	"Regard It As Just As Desirable To Build A Chicken House As To Build A Cathedral." - Frank Lloyd Wright
1991	"If You Fall, Fall On Your Back. If You Can Look Up, You Can Get Up." - Les Brown

1992	"Follow Effective Action With Quiet Reflection. From The Quiet Reflection Will Come Even More Effective Action." - Peter Drucker
1993	"If Past History Was All There Was To The Game, The Richest People Would Be Librarians." - Warren Buffett
1994	"My Brother Bob Doesn't Want To Be In Government – He Promised Dad He'd Go Straight." - John F. Kennedy
1995	"You Can Be A King Or A Street Sweeper, But Everybody Dances With The Grim Reaper." - Robert Alton Harris
1996	"The World Needs Anger. The World Often Continues To Allow Evil Because It Isn't Angry Enough." - Bede Jarrett
1997	"The Day People Stop Bringing You Their Problems Is The Day You Have Stopped Leading Them." - Colin Powell
1998	"There Is Nobody So Irritating As Somebody With Less Intelligence And More Sense Than We Have." - Don Herold
1999	"I Think Your Whole Life Shows In Your Face And You Should Be Proud Of That." - Lauren Bacall
2000	"The Richest Man Is Not He Who Has The Most, But He Who Needs The Least." - Anonymous
2001	" They May Forget What You Said, But They Will Never Forget How You Make Them Feel." - Carol Buchner
2002	"The Digital Revolution Is Far More Significant Than The Invention Of Writing Or Even Of Printing." - Douglas Engelbart
2003	"The Only Thing Necessary For The Triumph Of Evil Is For Good Men To Do Nothing." - Edmund Burke
2004	"In The First Place, God Made Idiots. That Was For Practice. hen He Made School Boards." - Mark Twain
2005	"I Prefer The Company Of Peasants Because They Have Not Been Educated Sufficiently To Reason Incorrectly." - Michel De Montaigne
2006	"Giving Money And Power To Government Is Like Giving Whiskey And Car Keys To Teenage Boys." - P. J. O'Rourke
2007	"The Real Voyage Of Discovery Consists Not In Seeking New Lands But Seeing With New Eyes." - Marcel Proust
2008	"For In All Adversity Of Fortune The Worst Sort Of Misery Is To Have Been Happy." - Boethius
2009	"To Err Is Human - And To Blame It On A Computer Is Even More So." - Robert Orben
2010	"A Wedding Is Just Like A Funeral Except That You Get To Smell Your Own Flowers." - Grace Hansen
2011	"Human Beings Are The Only Creatures On Earth That Allow Their Children To Come Back Home." - Bill Cosby

2012	"The Emotional, Sexual, And Psychological Stereotyping Of Females Begins When The Doctor Says: It's A Girl." - Shirley Chisholm
2013	"Speak When You Are Angry And You Will Make The Best Speech You Will Ever Regret." - Ambrose Bierce
2014	"The Simplest Schoolboy Is Now Familiar With Truths For Which Archimedes Would Have Sacrificed His Life." - Ernest Renan
2015	"Women Are Like Teabags. We Don't Know Our True Strength Until We Are In Hot Water!" - Eleanor Roosevelt
2016	"We've Got To Have A Dream If We Are Going To Make A Dream Come True." - Denis Waitley
2017	"Common Sense And Education Are Highly Compatible; In Fact, Neither Is Worth Much Without The Other." - Donald G. Smith
2018	"Oh, The Tiger Will Love You. There Is No Sincerer Love Than The Love Of Food." - George Bernard Shaw
2019	"History Is Indeed Little More Than The Register Of The Crimes, Follies, And Misfortunes Of Mankind." - Edward Gibbon
2020	"In Order To Succeed, Your Desire For Success Should Be Greater Than Your Fear Of Failure." - Bill Cosby
2021	"There Are Many Who Dare Not Kill Themselves For Fear Of What The Neighbors Will Say." - Cyril Connolly
2022	"It Is Even Harder For The Average Ape To Believe That He Has Descended From Man." - H. L. Mencken
2023	"He Is Richest Who Is Content With The Least, For Content Is The Wealth Of Nature." - Socrates
2024	"If You Look Deep Enough You Will See Music; The Heart Of Nature Being Everywhere Music." - Thomas Carlyle
2025	"There Is Nothing Wrong With America That Cannot Be Cured With What Is Right In America." - William J. Clinton
2026	"Don't Ever Wrestle With A Pig. You'll Both Get Dirty, But The Pig Will Enjoy It." - Cale Yarborough
2027	"A Word To The Wise Ain't Necessary - It's The Stupid Ones That Need The Advice." - Bill Cosby
2028	"Face Reality As It Is, Not As It Was Or As You Wish It To Be." - Jack Welch
2029	"Remind People That Profit Is The Difference Between Revenue And Expense. This Makes You Look Smart." - Scott Adams
2030	"I Don't Understand Why People Are Frightened Of New Ideas. I'm Frightened Of The Old Ones." - John Cage
2031	"Mighty Proud I Am That I Am Able To Have A Spare Bed For My Friends." - Samuel Pepys

2032	"It's Not What You Are That Holds You Back, It's What You Think You Are Not." - Denis Waitley
2033	"Education - That Which Discloses The Wise And Disguises From The Foolish Their Lack Of Understanding." - Ambrose Bierce
2034	"Laughing At Our Mistakes Can Lengthen Our Own Life. Laughing At Someone Else's Can Shorten It." - Cullen Hightower
2035	"The Trouble With Our Times Is That The Future Is Not What It Used To Be." - Paul Valery
2036	"Imagination Will Often Carry Us To Worlds That Never Were. But Without It We Go Nowhere." - Carl Sagan
2037	"A World Without Nuclear Weapons Would Be Less Stable And More Dangerous For All Of Us." - Margaret Thatcher
2038	"All The Art Of Living Lies In A Fine Mingling Of Letting Go And Holding On." - Henry Ellis
2039	"How Many Cares One Loses When One Decides Not To Be Something But To Be Someone." - Coco Chanel
2040	"I Think The Next Best Thing To Solving A Problem Is Finding Some Humor In It." - Frank A. Clark
2041	"I Didn't Attend The Funeral, But I Sent A Nice Letter Saying I Approved Of It." - Mark Twain
2042	" Not Every Successful Man Is A Good Father. But Every Good Father Is A Successful Man." - R. Duvall
2043	"The Length Of A Film Should Be Directly Related To The Endurance Of The Human Bladder." - Alfred Hitchcock
2044	"A Government That Robs Peter To Pay Paul Can Always Depend On The Support Of Paul." - George Bernard Shaw
2045	"A Budget Tells Us What We Can't Afford, But It Doesn't Keep Us From Buying It." - William Feather
2046	"When You Have A Number Of Disagreeable Duties To Perform, Always Do The Most Disagreeable First." - Josiah Quincy
2047	"Thus To Be Independent Of Public Opinion Is The First Formal Condition Of Achieving Anything Great." - G. W. F. Hegel
2048	"Don't Forget Mother's Day. Or As They Call It In Beverly Hills, Dad's Third Wife Day." - Jay Leno
2049	"You Can't Say Civilization Don't Advance... In Every War They Kill You In A New Way." - Will Rogers
2050	"We Are All Born For Love. It Is The Principle Of Existence, And Its Only End." - Benjamin Disraeli
2051	"In Olden Times Sacrifices Were Made At The Altar – A Practice Which Is Still Continued." - Helen Rowland

2052	"No Amount Of Experimentation Can Ever Prove Me Right; A Single Experiment Can Prove Me Wrong." - Albert Einstein
2053	"The Only Limits To The Possibilities In Your Life Tomorrow Are The Buts You Use Today." - Les Brown
2054	"Confronted With The Choice, The American People Would Choose The Policeman's Truncheon Over The Anarchist's Bomb." - Spiro T. Agnew
2055	"I Always Wanted To Be Somebody, But Now I Realize I Should Have Been More Specific." - Lily Tomlin
2056	"Winners Are Those People Who Make A Habit Of Doing The Things Losers Are Uncomfortable Doing." - Ed Foreman
2057	"Bill Gates Is The Pope Of The Personal Computer Industry. He Decides Who's Going To Build." - Larry Ellison
2058	"Out Of Clutter, Find Simplicity. From Discord Find Harmony. In The Middle Of Difficulty Lies Opportunity." - Albert Einstein
2059	"One Cannot Subdue A Man By Holding Back His Hands. Lasting Peace Comes Not From Force." - David Borenstein
2060	"Thank You For Sending Me A Copy Of Your Book; I'll Waste No Time Reading It." - Moses Hadas
2061	"My Son Is Now An Entrepreneur. That's What You're Called When You Don't Have A Job." - Ted Turner
2062	"I'd Never Been In Play Long Enough For The Flowers To Die In The Dressing Room." - Mercedes Mccambridge
2063	"To An Engineer, Good Enough Means Perfect. With An Artist, There's No Such Thing As Perfect." - Alexander Calder
2064	"We've Put More Effort Into Helping Folks Reach Old Age Than Into Helping Them Enjoy It." - Frank A. Clark
2065	"Whenever A Man Has Cast A Longing Eye On Offices, A Rottenness Begins In His Conduct." - Thomas Jefferson
2066	"If We Do Not Learn To Live Together As Friends, We Will Die Apart As Fools." - Martin Luther King
2067	"In The Depth Of Winter I Finally Learned That There Was In Me An Invincible Summer." - Albert Camus
2068	"Any Girl Can Be Glamorous. All You Have To Do Is Stand Still And Look Stupid." - Hedy Lamarr
2069	"Even A Mistake May Turn Out To Be The One Thing Necessary To A Worthwhile Achievement." - Henry Ford
2070	"There Is Nothing So Useless As Doing Efficiently That Which Should Not Be Done At All." - Peter F. Ducker
2071	"The Leader Who Exercises Power With Honor Will Work From The Inside Out, Starting With Himself." - Blaine Lee

2072	"If You Think It's Hard To Meet New People, Try Picking Up The Wrong Golf Ball." - Jack Lemmon
2073	"People With Goals Succeed Because They Know Where They Are Going... It's As Simple As That." - Earl Nightingale
2074	" Six Essential Qualities That Are The Key To Success: Sincerity, Personal Integrity, Humility, Courtesy, Wisdom, Charity." - William Menninger
2075	"As Every Divided Kingdom Falls, So Every Mind Divided Between Many Studies Confounds And Saps Itself." - Leonardo Da Vinci
2076	"Art Is A Step From What Is Obvious And Well-Known Toward What Is Arcane And Concealed." - Kahlil Gibran
2077	"Develop Success From Failures. Discouragement And Failure Are Two Of The Surest Stepping Stones To Success." - Dale Carnegie
2078	"Art Is The Stored Honey Of The Human Soul, Gathered On Wings Of Misery And Travail." - Theodore Dreiser
2079	"Many A Man In Love With A Dimple Makes The Mistake Of Marrying The Whole Girl." - Stephen Leacock
2080	"A Diplomat Is A Man Who Always Remembers A Woman's Birthday But Never Remembers Her Age." - Robert Frost
2081	"It Is Necessary For Me To Establish A Winner Image. Therefore, I Have To Beat Somebody." - Richard M. Nixon
2082	"It's Just A Job. Grass Grows, Birds Fly, Waves Pound The Sand. I Beat People Up." - Muhammad Ali
2083	"Ask Five Economists And You'll Get Five Different Answers – Six If One Went To Harvard." - Edgar R. Fiedler
2084	"Have Enough Sense To Know, Ahead Of Time, When Your Skills Will Not Extend To Wallpapering." - Marilyn Vos Savant
2085	"Music Hath Charms To Soothe A Savage Breast, To Soften Rocks, Or Bend A Knotted Oak." - William Congreve
2086	"When You Jump For Joy, Beware That No One Moves The Ground From Beneath Your Feet." - Stanislaw Lec
2087	"The State Of Your Life Is Nothing More Than A Reflection Of Your State Of Mind." - Wayne Dyer
2088	"Great Things Are Not Done By Impulse, But By A Series Of Small Things Brought Together." - Vincent Van Gogh
2089	"Some People Are Born On Third Base And Go Through Life Thinking They Hit A Triple." - Barry Switzer
2090	"Science Is Organized Common Sense Where Many A Beautiful Theory Was Killed By An Ugly Fact." - Thomas Huxley
2091	"From My Rotting Body, Flowers Shall Grow And I Am In Them And That Is Eternity." - Edvard Munch

2092	"Even If You're On The Right Track, You'll Get Run Over If You Just Sit There." - Will Rogers
2093	"The Great Tragedy Of Science - The Slaying Of A Beautiful Hypothesis By An Ugly Fact." - Thomas Huxley
2094	"Absence Diminishes Mediocre Passions And Increases Great Ones, As The Wind Extinguishes Candles And Fans Fires. - Francois De La Rochefoucauld
2095	"Two Things Are Infinite: The Universe And Human Stupidity; And I'm Not Sure About The Universe." - Albert Einstein
2096	"The Philosophers Have Only Interpreted The World In Different Ways; The Point Is To Change It." - Karl Marx
2097	"The Real Voyage Of Discovery Consists Not In Making New Landscapes But In Having New Eyes." - Marcel Proust
2098	"The Secret Of Happiness Is To Count Your Blessings While Others Are Adding Up Their Troubles." - William Penn
2099	"I Am Not Afraid Of Death, I Just Don't Want To Be There When It Happens." - Woody Allen
2100	"Education Is The Ability To Listen To Almost Anything Without Losing Your Temper Or Your Self-Confidence." - Robert Frost
2101	"How Committed Are You? There Is A Remarkable Difference Between A Commitment Of 99% And 100%." - Vic Conant
2102	"I Stand For Freedom Of Expression, Doing What You Believe In, And Going After Your Dreams." - Madonna Ciccone
2103	"Never Get Married In The Morning - You Never Know Who You Might Meet That Night." - Paul Hornung
2104	"If You Want To Read About Love And Marriage, You've Got To Buy Two Separate Books." - Alan King
2105	"He Is Free Who Knows How To Keep In His Own Hand The Power To Decide." - Salvador De Madariaga
2106	"Employees Make The Best Dates. You Don't Have To Pick Them Up And They're Always Tax-Deductible." - Andy Warhol
2107	"When A Girl Marries, She Exchanges The Attentions Of Many Men For The Inattention Of One." - Helen Rowland
2108	"Abstract Art Is A Product Of The Untalented, Sold By The Unprincipled To The Utterly Bewildered." - Al Capp
2109	"You Do Live Longer With Bran, But You Spend The Last Fifteen Years On The Toilet." - Alan King
2110	"If It's Natural To Kill, How Come Men Have To Go Into Training To Learn How?" - Joan Baez
2111	"Your Chances Of Success In Any Undertaking Can Always Be Measured By Your Belief In Yourself." - Robert Collier

2112	"Advice Is What We Ask For When We Already Know The Answer But Wish We Didn't." - Erica Jong
2113	"The Trouble With The Rat Race Is That Even If You Win, You're Still A Rat." - Lily Tomlin
2114	"Secretly, I Wanted To Look Like Jimi Hendrix, But I Could Never Quite Pull It Off." - Bryan Ferry
2115	"To Be Successful, A Woman Has To Be Much Better At Her Job Than A Man." - Golda Meir
2116	"A Lot Of People Like Snow. I Find It To Be An Unnecessary Freezing Of Water." - Carl Reiner
2117	"For A Successful Technology, Reality Must Take Precedence Over Public Relations, For Nature Cannot Be Fooled." - Richard P. Feynman
2118	"Poetry Is A Deal Of Joy And Pain And Wonder, With A Dash Of The Dictionary." - Kahlil Gibran
2119	"Microsoft Is Engaging In Unlawful Predatory Practices That Go Well Beyond The Scope Of Fair Competition." - Orrin Hatch
2120	"Opportunity Is Missed By Most People Because It Is Dressed In Overalls And Looks Like Work." - Thomas A. Edison
2121	"Brought Up To Respect The Conventions, Love Had To End In Marriage. I'm Afraid It Did." - Bette Davis
2122	"It's Fine To Celebrate Success But It Is More Important To Heed The Lessons Of Failure." - Bill Gates
2123	"Tennis Is A Perfect Combination Of Violent Action Taking Place In An Atmosphere Of Total Tranquility." - Billie Jean King
2124	"People Always Ask Me, 'Were You Funny As A Child?' Well, No, I Was An Accountant." - Ellen Degeneres
2125	"We Didn't Actually Overspend Our Budget. The Health Commission Allocation Simply Fell Short Of Our Expenditure." - Frank A. Clark
2126	"Data Is Not Information, Information Is Not Knowledge, Knowledge Is Not Understanding, Understanding Is Not Wisdom." - Clifford Stoll
2127	"You Must Have Long Range Goals To Keep You From Being Frustrated By Short Range Failures." - Charles C. Noble
2128	"A Man May Be A Fool And Not Know It, But Not If He Is Married." - H. L. Mencken
2129	"There Are No Extraordinary Men... Just Extraordinary Circumstances That Ordinary Men Are Forced To Deal With." - William Halsey
2130	"I Can't Understand Why People Are Frightened Of New Ideas. I'm Frightened Of The Old Ones." - John Cage
2131	"Technology Is The Knack Of So Arranging The World That We Don't Have To Experience It." - Max Frisch

2132	"Life Has Meaning Only If One Barters It Day By Day For Something Other Than Itself." - Antoine De Saint-Exupery
2133	"The Hardest Thing To Learn In Life Is Which Bridge To Cross And Which To Burn." - David Russell
2134	"Without Wearing Any Mask We Are Conscious Of, We Have A Special Face For Each Friend." - Oliver Wendell Holmes
2135	"A Dog Is The Only Thing On Earth That Loves You More Than You Love Yourself." - Josh Billings
2136	"No Man Is Regular In His Attendance At The House Of Commons Until He Is Married." - Benjamin Disraeli
2137	"Before You Can Really Start Setting Financial Goals, You Need To Determine Where You Stand Financially." - David Bach
2138	"Anger, If Not Restrained, Is Frequently More Hurtful To Us Than The Injury That Provokes It." - Lucius Annaeus Seneca
2139	"Informed Decision-Making Comes From A Long Tradition Of Guessing And Then Blaming Others For Inadequate Results." - Scott Adams
2140	"A Bird Doesn't Sing Because It Has An Answer, It Sings Because It Has A Song." - Lou Holtz
2141	"Time Is The School In Which We Learn, Time Is The Fire In Which We Burn." - Delmore Schwartz
2142	"I Not Only Use All The Brains That I Have, But All That I Can Borrow." - Woodrow Wilson
2143	"You Better Take Advantage Of The Good Cigars. You Don't Get Much Else In That Job." - Thomas P. O'neill
2144	"Old Age Is The Most Unexpected Of All The Things That Can Happen To A Man." - James Thurber
2145	"Everywhere In The World, Music Enhances A Hall, With One Exception: Carnegie Hall Enhances The Music." - Isaac Stern
2146	"You'll Never Have A Quiet World Till You Knock The Patriotism Out Of The Human Race." - George Bernard Shaw
2147	"I Don't Think Meals Have Any Business Being Deductible. I'm For Separation Of Calories And Corporations." - Ralph Nader
2148	"What The World Needs Is More Geniuses With Humility, There Are So Few Of Us Left." - Oscar Levant
2149	"Music Is The Movement Of Sound To Reach The Soul For The Education Of Its Virtue." - Plato
2150	"The Past Is Malleable And Flexible, Changing As Our Recollection Interprets And Re-Explains What Has Happened." - Peter Berger
2151	"Never Forget The Three Powerful Resources You Always Have Available To You: Love, Prayer, And Forgiveness." - H. Jackson Brown, Jr.

2152	"More Marriages Might Survive If The Partners Realized That Sometimes The Better Comes After The Worse." - Doug Larson
2153	"Any Idiot Can Face A Crisis - It's Day To Day Living That Wears You Out." - Anton Chekhov
2154	"We Would All Like To Vote For The Best Man But He Is Never A Candidate." - Kin Hubbard
2155	"Healthy Children Will Not Fear Life If Their Elders Have Integrity Enough Not To Fear Death." - Erik H. Erikson
2156	"We All Have Big Changes In Our Lives That Are More Or Less A Second Chance." - Harrison Ford
2157	"Relax? How Can Anybody Relax And Play Golf? You Have To Grip The Club, Don't You?" - Ben Hogan
2158	"Music Expresses That Which Cannot Be Said And On Which It Is Impossible To Be Silent." - Victor Hugo
2159	"Though Bitter, Good Medicine Cures Illness. Though It May Hurt, Loyal Criticism Will Have Beneficial Effects." - Sima Qian
2160	"I Don't Know Whether War Is An Interlude During Peace, Or Peace An Interlude During War." - Georges Clemenceau
2161	"My Son Is Now An "Entrepreneur." That's What You're Called When You Don't Have A Job." - Ted Turner
2162	"Always Bear In Mind That Your Own Resolution To Succeed Is More Important Than Any Other." - Abraham Lincoln
2163	"A Kiss Is A Lovely Trick Designed By Nature To Stop Speech When Words Become Superfluous." - Ingrid Bergman
2164	"Since There Is Nothing So Well Worth Having As Friends, Never Lose A Chance To Make Them." - Francesco Guicciardini
2165	"Our Whole Constitutional Heritage Rebels At The Thought Of Giving Government The Power To Control Men's Minds." - Thurgood Marshall
2166	"'We Sure Shook That Bridge,' The Mouse Said To The Elephant After They Had Crossed The Bridge." - Anonymous
2167	"For In Reason, All Government Without The Consent Of The Governed Is The Very Definition Of Slavery." - Jonathan Swift
2168	"Wisdom Is The Reward You Get For A Lifetime Of Listening When You'd Have Preferred To Talk." - Doug Larson
2169	"Fishes Live In The Sea, As Men Do A-Land; The Great Ones Eat Up The Little Ones." - William Shakespeare
2170	"I Have Made This Letter Longer Than Usual Because I Lack The Time To Make It Shorter." - Blaise Pascal
2171	"Fine Art Is That In Which The Hand, The Head, And The Heart Of Man Go Together." - John Ruskin

2172	"Flowers... Are A Proud Assertion That A Ray Of Beauty Outvalues All The Utilities Of The World." - Ralph Waldo Emerson
2173	"It Is A Man's Own Mind, Not His Enemy Or Foe That Lures Him To Evil Ways." - The Buddha
2174	"Breathless, We Flung Us On A Windy Hill, Laughed In The Sun, And Kissed The Lovely Grass." - Rupert Brooke
2175	"He Has Never Been Known To Use A Word That Might Send A Reader To The Dictionary." - William Faulkner
2176	"When A Man Steals Your Wife, There Is No Better Revenge Than To Let Him Keep Her." - Sacha Guitry
2177	"Success In Life Comes Not From Holding A Good Hand, But In Playing A Poor Hand Well." - Kenneth Hildebrand
2178	"Swans Sing Before They Die - 'Twere No Bad Thing Should Certain Persons Die Before They Sing." - Samuel Taylor Coleridge
2179	"Effective Leadership Is Not About Making Speeches Or Being Liked; Leadership Is Defined By Results Not Attributes." - Peter Drucker
2180	"Man Has Lost The Capacity To Foresee And To Forestall. He Will End By Destroying The Earth." - Albert Schweitzer
2181	"Every Government Is A Parliament Of Whores. The Trouble Is, In A Democracy, The Whores Are Us." - P. J. O'Rourke
2182	"The Way To Get Things Done Is Not To Mind Who Gets The Credit For Doing Them." - Benjamin Jowett
2183	"Art Is A Collaboration Between God And The Artist, And The Less The Artist Does The Better." - Andre Gide
2184	"While I Thought That I Was Learning How To Live, I Have Been Learning How To Die." - Leonardo Da Vinci
2185	"To Send Light Into The Darkness Of Men's Hearts – Such Is The Duty Of The Artist." - Robert Schumann
2186	"In Wilderness I Sense The Miracle Of Life, And Behind It Our Scientific Accomplishments Fade To Trivia." - Charles Lindbergh
2187	"Success Or Failure In Business Is Caused More By The Mental Attitude Even Than By Mental Capacities." - Walter Scott
2188	"If You Think Your Teacher Is Tough, Wait Until You Get A Boss. He Doesn't Have Tenure." - Bill Gates
2189	"No Country Can Act Wisely Simultaneously In Every Part Of The Globe At Every Moment Of Time." - Henry A. Kissinger
2190	" You Make A Living By What You Get, But You Make A Life By What You Give." - Anonymous
2191	"If You Could Choose One Characteristic That Would Get You Through Life, Choose A Sense Of Humor." - Jennifer Jones

2192	"A Leader In The Democratic Party Is A Boss, In The Republican Party He Is A Leader." - Harry S. Truman
2193	"Wise Are Those Who Learn That The Bottom Line Doesn't Always Have To Be Their Top Priority." - William A. Ward
2194	"I Don't Wish To Be Everything To Everyone, But I Would Like To Be Something To Someone." - Javan
2195	"In All Science, Error Precedes The Truth, And It Is Better It Should Go First Than Last." - Hugh Walpole
2196	"Approach The Game With No Preset Agendas And You'll Probably Come Away Surprised At Your Overall Efforts." - Phil Jackson
2197	"I Took A Speed Reading Course And Read 'War And Peace' In Twenty Minutes. It Involves Russia." - Woody Allen
2198	"Human Beings Must Be Known To Be Loved; But Divine Beings Must Be Loved To Be Known." - Blaise Pascal
2199	"Most Of The Things Worth Doing In The World Had Been Declared Impossible Before They Were Done." - Louis D. Brandeis
2200	"I Always Voted At My Party's Call, And I Never Thought Of Thinking For Myself At All." - William Gilbert
2201	"Character Is Higher Than Intellect. A Great Soul Will Be Strong To Live As Well As Think." - Ralph Waldo Emerson
2202	"The Greatest Glory In Living Lies Not In Never Falling, But In Rising Every Time We Fall." - Nelson Mandela
2203	"A Man Of Genius Makes No Mistakes; His Errors Are Volitional And Are The Portals Of Discovery." - James Joyce
2204	"My List Of Ingredients For Success Is Divided Into Four Basic Groups: Inward, Outward, Upward And Onward." - David Thomas
2205	"One Merit Of Poetry Few Persons Will Deny: It Says More And In Fewer Words Than Prose." - Voltaire
2206	"Millions Long For Immortality Who Don't Know What To Do With Themselves On A Rainy Sunday Afternoon." - Susan Ertz
2207	"You Cannot Tailor-Make The Situations In Life But You Can Tailor-Make The Attitudes To Fit Those Situations." - Zig Ziglar
2208	"Honest Criticism Is Hard To Take, Particularly From A Relative, A Friend, An Acquaintance, Or A Stranger." - Franklin P. Jones
2209	"The Excitement Of Learning Separates Youth From Old Age. As Long As You're Learning You're Not Old." - Rosalyn S. Yalow
2210	"He Dares To Be A Fool, And That Is The First Step In The Direction Of Wisdom." - James Huneker
2211	"I've Been Married To One Marxist And One Fascist, And Neither One Would Take The Garbage Out." - Lee Grant

2212	"A Wise Man Among The Ignorant Is As A Beautiful Girl In The Company Of Blind Men." - Saadi
2213	"I've Failed Over And Over And Over Again In My Life And That Is Why I Succeed." - Michael Jordan
2214	"He That Will Not Apply New Remedies Must Expect New Evils; For Time Is The Greatest Innovator." - Francis Bacon
2215	"There Are No Great People In This World, Only Great Challenges Which Ordinary People Rise To Meet." - William Frederick Halsey, Jr.
2216	"All Our Knowledge Merely Helps Us To Die A More Painful Death Than Animals That Know Nothing." - Maurice Maeterlinck
2217	"All Water Has A Perfect Memory And Is Forever Trying To Get Back To Where It Was." - Toni Morrison
2218	"I Like Your Christ, I Do Not Like Your Christians. Your Christians Are So Unlike Your Christ." - Mohandas Gandhi
2219	"Things Turn Out Best For The People Who Make The Best Of The Way Things Turn Out." - John Wooden
2220	"Analyzing Humor Is Like Dissecting A Frog. Few People Are Interested And The Frog Dies Of It." - E. B. White
2221	"Golf Is Played By Twenty Million Mature American Men Whose Wives Think They Are Out Having Fun." - Jim Bishop
2222	"A Poem Begins As A Lump In The Throat, A Sense Of Wrong, A Homesickness, A Lovesickness." - Robert Frost
2223	"It Is Only In The Country That We Can Get To Know A Person Or A Book." - Cyril Connolly
2224	"Chains Of Habit Are Too Light To Be Felt Until They Are Too Heavy To Be Broken." - Warren Buffett
2225	"Success Without Honor Is An Unseasoned Dish; It Will Satisfy Your Hunger, But It Won't Taste Good." - Joe Paterno
2226	"Children And Lunatics Cut The Gordian Knot Which The Poet Spends His Life Patiently Trying To Untie." - Jean Cocteau
2227	"Most People Do Not Consider Dawn To Be An Attractive Experience - Unless They Are Still Up." - Ellen Goodman
2228	"The Writer, When He Is Also An Artist, Is Someone Who Admits What Others Don't Dare Reveal." - Elia Kazan
2229	"You Can Find Your Way Across This Country Using Burger Joints The Way A Navigator Uses Stars." - Charles Kuralt
2230	"The Aim Of Art Is To Represent Not The Outward Appearance Of Things, But Their Inward Significance." - Aristotle
2231	"Every Artist Dips His Brush In His Own Soul, And Paints His Own Nature Into His Pictures." - Henry Ward Beecher

2232	"If You Don't Like Something, Change It. If You Can't Change It, Change Your Attitude. Don't Complain." - Maya Angelou
2233	" It Is High Time That The Ideal Of Success Should Be Replaced By The Ideal Of Service." - Albert Einstein
2234	"An Organization's Ability To Learn, And Translate That Learning Into Action Rapidly, Is The Ultimate Competitive Advantage." - Jack Welch
2235	"Thank You, God, For This Good Life And Forgive Us If We Do Not Love It Enough." - Garrison Keillor
2236	"Movies Are Something People See All Over The World Because There Is A Certain Need For It." - Wim Wenders
2237	"A Computer Once Beat Me At Chess, But It Was No Match For Me At Kick Boxing." - Emo Philips
2238	"Music, In Performance, Is A Type Of Sculpture. The Air In The Performance Is Sculpted Into Something." - Frank Zappa
2239	" Try Not To Become A Man Of Success But Rather Try To Become A Man Of Value." - Albert Einstein
2240	"What Most Persons Consider As Virtue, After The Age Of 40 Is Simply A Loss Of Energy." - Voltaire
2241	"A Man Who Dares To Waste One Hour Of Time Has Not Discovered The Value Of Life." - Charles Darwin
2242	"There Ought To Be One Day - Just One - When There Is Open Season On Senators." - Will Rogers
2243	"The Best Time To Plant A Tree Was 20 Years Ago. The Second Best Time Is Now." - Chinese Proverb
2244	"Every Adversity, Every Failure, Every Heartache Carries With It The Seed On An Equal Or Greater Benefit." - Napoleon Hill
2245	"Any Intelligent Woman Who Reads The Marriage Contract, And Then Goes Into It, Deserves All The Consequences." - Isadora Duncan
2246	"There Is A Single Light Of Science, And To Brighten It Anywhere Is To Brighten It Everywhere." - Isaac Asimov
2247	"Without Tradition, Art Is A Flock Of Sheep Without A Shepherd. Without Innovation, It Is A Corpse." - Winston Churchill
2248	"As Soon Go Kindle Fire With Snow, As Seek To Quench The Fire Of Love With Words." - William Shakespeare
2249	"If We Become Increasingly Humble About How Little We Know, We May Be More Eager To Search." - Sir John Templeton
2250	"Inside Of A Ring Or Out, Ain't Nothing Wrong With Going Down. It's Staying Down That's Wrong." - Muhammad Ali
2251	"There Are Only Two Lasting Bequests We Can Give Our Children... One Is Roots, The Other Wings." - Stephen Covey

2252	"If We Have No Peace, It Is Because We Have Forgotten That We Belong To Each Other." - Mother Teresa
2253	"Before I Met My Husband, I'd Never Fallen In Love. I'd Stepped In It A Few Times." - Rita Rudner
2254	"You Can't Expect To Hit The Jackpot If You Don't Put A Few Nickels In The Machine." - Flip Wilson
2255	"A Fool Thinks Himself To Be Wise, But A Wise Man Knows Himself To Be A Fool." - William Shakespeare
2256	"The Work Of The Individual Still Remains The Spark That Moves Mankind Ahead Even More Than Teamwork." - Igor Sikorsky
2257	"Contempt Is The Weapon Of The Weak And A Defense Against One's Own Despised And Unwanted Feelings." - Alice Duer Miller
2258	"I Don't Know The Key To Success, But The Key To Failure Is Trying To Please Everybody." - Bill Cosby
2259	"History Is A Pack Of Lies About Events That Never Happened Told By People Who Weren't There." - George Santayana
2260	"No Good Opera Plot Can Be Sensible, For People Do Not Sing When They Are Feeling Sensible." - W. H. Auden
2261	"Careers, Like Rockets, Don't Always Take Off On Schedule. The Key Is To Keep Working The Engines." - Gary Sinise
2262	" Success Is A State Of Mind. If You Want Success, Start Thinking Of Yourself As A Success." - Dr. Joyce Brothers
2263	"Every Child Is An Artist. The Problem Is How To Remain An Artist Once We Grow Up." - Pablo Picasso
2264	"The Best Portion Of A Good Man's Life: His Little, Nameless, Unre-membered Acts Of Kindness And Love." - William Wordsworth
2265	"The Only Time A Woman Really Succeeds In Changing A Man Is When He Is A Baby." - Natalie Wood
2266	"The United States Is Not Stingy. We Are The Greatest Contributor To International Efforts In The World." - Colin Powell
2267	"The Flower Is The Poetry Of Reproduction. It Is An Example Of The Eternal Seductiveness Of Life." - Jean Giraudoux
2268	"The Highest Art Is Always The Most Religious, And The Greatest Artist Is Always A Devout Person." - Abraham Lincoln
2269	"Life Is Like Playing A Violin Solo In Public And Learning The Instrument As One Goes On." - Samuel Butler
2270	"The Love Of One's Country Is A Splendid Thing. But Why Should Love Stop At The Border?" - Pablo Casals
2271	"Real Education Must Ultimately Be Limited To Men Who Insist On Knowing, The Rest Is Mere Sheep-Herding." - Ezra Pound

2272	"I Was Showing Early Symptoms Of Becoming A Professional Baseball Man. I Was Lying To The Press." - Roger Kahn
2273	"After Much Prayerful Consideration, I Feel That I Must Say I Have Climbed My Last Political Mountain." - George C. Wallace
2274	"The Sovereign Invigorator Of The Body Is Exercise, And Of All The Exercises Walking Is The Best." - Thomas Jefferson
2275	"I Don't Feel Old. I Don't Feel Anything Till Noon. That's When It's Time For My Nap." - Bob Hope
2276	" Know Where To Find The Information And How To Use It – That's The Secret Of Success." - Albert Einstein
2277	"Maybe Nature Is Fundamentally Ugly, Chaotic And Complicated. But If It's Like That, Then I Want Out." - Steven Weinberg
2278	"Love Does Not Consist In Gazing At Each Other But In Looking Together In The Same Direction." - Antoine De Saint-Exupéry
2279	"I Must Study Politics And War That My Sons May Have Liberty To Study Mathematics And Philosophy." - John Adams
2280	"They Are Ill Discoverers That Think There Is No Land, When They Can See Nothing But Sea." - Francis Bacon
2281	"Love Takes Off Masks That We Fear We Cannot Live Without And Know We Cannot Live Within." - James A. Baldwin
2282	"A Story Should Have A Beginning, A Middle, And An End... But Not Necessarily In That Order." - Jean-Luc Godard
2283	"Civilization Advances By Extending The Number Of Important Operations Which We Can Perform Without Thinking Of Them." - Alfred North Whitehead
2284	"The Saddest Aspect Of Life Right Now Is That Science Gathers Knowledge Faster Than Society Gathers Wisdom." - Isaac Asimov
2285	"The Invisible Hand Of The Market Always Moves Faster And Better Than The Heavy Hand Of Government." - Mitt Romney
2286	"The Wisdom Of Man Never Yet Contrived A System Of Taxation That Would Operate With Perfect Equality." - Andrew Jackson
2287	"Let Us Follow Our Destiny, Ebb And Flow. Whatever May Happen, We Master Fortune By Accepting It." - Virgil
2288	"An Idea Not Coupled With Action Will Never Get Any Bigger Than The Brain Cell It Occupied." - Arnold H. Glasow
2289	"I Don't Want To Achieve Immortality Through My Work. I Want To Achieve It Through Not Dying." - Woody Allen
2290	"I'm Afraid That If You Look At A Thing Long Enough, It Loses All Of Its Meaning." - Andy Warhol
2291	"There Is No Defense Against Adverse Fortune Which Is So Effectual As An Habitual Sense Of Humor." - Thomas W. Higginson

2292	"I Go To Nature To Be Soothed And Healed, And To Have My Senses Put In Order." - John Burroughs
2293	"True Friendship Is Like Sound Health; The Value Of It Is Seldom Known Until It Is Lost." - Charles Caleb Colton
2294	"There's No Limit To What A Man Can Achieve, If He Doesn't Care Who Gets The Credit." - Laing Burns, Jr.
2295	"Give Me Beauty In The Inward Soul; May The Outward And The Inward Man Be At One." - Socrates
2296	"Some Painters Transform The Sun Into A Yellow Spot, Others Transform A Yellow Spot Into The Sun." - Pablo Picasso
2297	"Don't Bother Just To Be Better Than Your Contemporaries Or Predecessors. Try To Be Better Than Yourself." - William Faulkner
2298	"Simple Kindness To One's Self And All That Lives Is The Most Powerful Transformational Force Of All." - David R. Hawkins
2299	"Take Your Life In Your Own Hands, And What Happens? A Terrible Thing: No One To Blame." - Erica Jong
2300	"A True Poet Does Not Bother To Be Poetical. Nor Does A Nursery Gardener Scent His Roses." - Jean Cocteau
2301	"Do Not Seek To Follow In The Footsteps Of The Men Of Old; Seek What They Sought." - Basho
2302	"An Excuse Is Worse And More Terrible Than A Lie, For An Excuse Is A Lie Guarded." - Pope John Paul II
2303	"A Journey Is Like Marriage. The Certain Way To Be Wrong Is To Think You Control It." - John Steinbeck
2304	"Your Own Mind Is A Sacred Enclosure Into Which Nothing Harmful Can Enter Except By Your Permission." - Ralph Waldo Emerson
2305	"It Is Sad Not To Love, But It Is Much Sadder Not To Be Able To Love." - Miguel De Unamuno
2306	"Marriage Is Like A Bank Account. You Put It In, You Take It Out, You Lose Interest." - Irwin Corey
2307	"If The United Nations Is A Country Unto Itself, Then The Commodity It Exports Most Is Words." - Esther B. Fein
2308	"The Only Person Who Is Educated Is The One Who Has Learned How To Learn And Change." - Carl Rogers
2309	"Most People Never Run Far Enough On Their First Wind To Find Out They've Got A Second." - William James
2310	"It Is Not So Much Our Friends' Help That Helps Us, As The Confidence Of Their Help." - Epicurus
2311	"I Have Been All Things Unholy. If God Can Work Through Me, He Can Work Through Anyone." - Saint Francis Of Assisi

2312	"If We Could Sell Our Experiences For What They Cost Us ... We Would All Be Millionaires." - Abigail Van Buren
2313	"Shall I Not Have Intelligence With The Earth? Am I Not Partly Leaves And Vegetable Mould Myself." - Henry David Thoreau
2314	"The Only Reason I Would Take Up Jogging Is So That I Could Hear Heavy Breathing Again." - Erma Bombeck
2315	"In The Last Analysis, What We Are Communicates Far More Eloquently Than Anything We Say Or Do." - Stephen Covey
2316	"Aim At Heaven And You Will Get Earth Thrown In. Aim At Earth And You Get Neither." - C. S. Lewis
2317	"People Think Computers Will Keep Them From Making Mistakes. They're Wrong. With Computers You Make Mistakes Faster." - Adam Osborne
2318	"This I Conceive To Be The Chemical Function Of Humor: To Change The Character Of Our Thought." - Lin Yutang
2319	"Education... Has Produced A Vast Population Able To Read But Unable To Distinguish What Is Worth Reading." - Malcolm Forbes
2320	"Experiences Are Savings Which A Miser Puts Aside. Wisdom Is An Inheritance Which A Wastrel Cannot Exhaust." - Karl Kraus
2321	"Dreams Will Get You Nowhere, A Good Kick In The Pants Will Take You A Long Way." - Baltasar Gracian
2322	"Heaven Has No Rage Like Love To Hatred Turned, Nor Hell A Fury Like A Woman Scorned." - William Congreve
2323	"If Galileo Had Said In Verse That The World Moved, The Inquisition Might Have Let Him Alone." - Thomas Hardy
2324	"The Christian Resolution To Find The World Ugly And Bad Has Made The World Ugly And Bad." - Friedrich Nietzsche
2325	"Sleep Is The Most Moronic Fraternity In The World, With The Heaviest Dues And The Crudest Rituals." - Vladimir Nabokov
2326	"Always Bear In Mind, That Your Own Resolution To Succeed Is More Important Than Any Other Thing." - Abraham Lincoln
2327	"Suppose You Were An Idiot, And Suppose You Were A Member Of Congress; But I Repeat Myself." - Mark Twain
2328	"Old Age Is Like Everything Else. To Make A Success Of It, You've Got To Start Young." - Theodore Roosevelt
2329	"To The Man Who Only Has A Hammer, Everything He Encounters Begins To Look Like A Nail." - Abraham Maslow
2330	"Work Like You Don't Need The Money. Love Like You've Never Been Hurt. Dance Like Nobody's Watching." - Satchel Paige
2331	"We Make A Living By What We Get, But We Make A Life By What We Give." - Winston Churchill

2332	"Good, Better, Best. Never Let It Rest. Until Your Good Is Better And Your Better Is Best." - Tim Duncan
2333	"Every Man Has His Follies - And Often They Are The Most Interesting Thing He Has Got." - Josh Billings
2334	"You May Get Skinned Knees And Elbows, But It's Worth It If You Score A Spectacular Goal." - Mia Hamm
2335	"Whenever You Find Yourself On The Side Of The Majority, It Is Time To Pause And Reflect." - Mark Twain
2336	"A Woman Knows The Face Of The Man She Loves As A Sailor Knows The Open Sea." - Honore De Balzac
2337	"I Got The Bill For My Surgery. Now I Know What Those Doctors Were Wearing Masks For." - James H. Boren
2338	"Try Not To Become A Man Of Success, But Rather Try To Become A Man Of Value." - Albert Einstein
2339	"Number One, Cash Is King ... Number Two, Communicate ... Number Three, Buy Or Bury The Competition." - Jack Welch
2340	"Determination Gives You The Resolve To Keep Going In Spite Of The Roadblocks That Lay Before You." - Denis Waitley
2341	"If You Want To Make Beautiful Music, You Must Play The Black And The White Notes Together." - Richard M. Nixon
2342	"To Fear Love Is To Fear Life, And Those Who Fear Life Are Already Three Parts Dead." - Bertrand Russell
2343	"Only Two Things Are Infinite, The Universe And Human Stupidity, And I'm Not Sure About The Former." - Albert Einstein
2344	"Patriotism Is Not Short, Frenzied Outbursts Of Emotion, But The Tranquil And Steady Dedication Of A Lifetime." - Adlai E. Stevenson
2345	"He Who Reigns Within Himself And Rules His Passions, Desires, And Fears Is More Than A King." - John Milton
2346	"The Darkest Places In Hell Are Reserved For Those Who Maintain Their Neutrality In Times Of Moral Crisis." - Dante Alighieri
2347	"Poetry Is Just The Evidence Of Life. If Your Life Is Burning Well, Poetry Is Just The Ash." - Leonard Cohen
2348	"Many Men Go Fishing All Of Their Lives Without Knowing That It Is Not Fish They Are After." - Henry David Thoreau
2349	"It Is Difficult To Discern A Serious Threat To Religious Liberty From A Room Of Silent, Thoughtful Schoolchildren." - Sandra Day O'connor
2350	"To Enlarge Or Illustrate This Power And Effect Of Love Is To Set A Candle In The Sun." - Robert Burton
2351	"People Are Pretty Much Alike. It's Only That Our Differences Are More Susceptible To Definition Than Our Similarities." - Linda Ellerbee

2352	"Science Investigates Religion Interprets. Science Gives Man Knowledge Which Is Power Religion Gives Man Wisdom Which Is Control." - Martin Luther King, Jr.
2353	"Work Like You Don't Need Money, Love Like You've Never Been Hurt, And Dance Like No One's Watching." - Anonymous
2354	"In Order To Succeed You Must Fail, So That You Know What Not To Do The Next Time." - Anthony J. D'angelo
2355	"Gold Medals Aren't Really Made Of Gold. They're Made Of Sweat, Determination, And A Hard-To-Find Alloy Called Guts." - Dan Gable
2356	"In The Affairs Of This World, Men Are Saved Not By Faith, But By The Want Of It." - Benjamin Franklin
2357	"Growing Old Is No More Than A Bad Habit Which A Busy Person Has No Time To Form." - Andre Maurois
2358	"You Know You're Getting Old When All The Names In Your Black Book Have M. D. After Them." - Harrison Ford
2359	"We Must View Young People Not As Empty Bottles To Be Filled But As Candles To Be Lit." - Robert Shaffer
2360	"Our Very Business In Life Is Not To Get Ahead Of Others... But To Get Ahead Of Ourselves." - Thomas L. Monson
2361	"Does Wisdom Perhaps Appear On The Earth As A Raven Which Is Inspired By The Smell Of Carrion?" - Friedrich Nietzsche
2362	"Looking Back, I Have This To Regret, That Too Often When I Loved, I Did Not Say So." - David Grayson
2363	"An Artist Is Always Alone - If He Is An Artist. No, What The Artist Needs Is Loneliness." - Henry Miller
2364	"The Artist Alone Sees Spirits. But After He Has Told Of Their Appearing To Him, Everybody Sees Them." - Johann Wolfgang Von Goethe
2365	"The Easiest Way To Get Rich Is To Find Someone Who Is Rich And Do What They Do." - J. Paul Getty
2366	"You, Too, Can Determine What You Want. You Can Decide On Your Major Objectives, Targets, Aims, And Destination." - W. Clement Stone
2367	"The Art Of Art, The Glory Of Expression And The Sunshine Of The Light Of Letters, Is Simplicity." - Walt Whitman
2368	"An Economist Is An Expert Who Will Know Tomorrow Why The Things He Predicted Yesterday Didn't Happen Today." - Laurence J. Peter
2369	"Concentration, In Its Truest, Unadulterated Form, Means Being Able To Focus The Mind On One Single Solitary Thing." - Komar
2370	"Size Matters Not. Look At Me. Judge Me By My Size, Do You? That Is Why You Fail." - Yoda

2371	"There Are No Great Limits To Growth Because There Are No Limits Of Human Intelligence, Imagination, And Wonder." - Ronald Reagan
2372	"It Is The Mark Of An Educated Mind To Be Able To Entertain A Thought Without Accepting It." - Aristotle
2373	"Peace Is A Journey Of A Thousand Miles And It Must Be Taken One Step At A Time." - Lyndon B. Johnson
2374	"When A Person Can No Longer Laugh At Himself, It Is Time For Others To Laugh At Him." - Thomas Szasz
2375	"No Matter What We Want Of Life We Have To Give Up Something In Order To Get It." - Raymond Holliwell
2376	"Nothing In The Universe Can Travel At The Speed Of Light, They Say, Forgetful Of The Shadow's Speed." - Howard Nemerov
2377	"Patriotism Is Your Conviction That This Country Is Superior To All Others Because You Were Born In It." - George Bernard Shaw
2378	"A Business Absolutely Devoted To Service Will Have Only One Worry About Profits. They Will Be Embarrassingly Large." - Henry Ford
2379	"Liberalism Is Trust Of The People Tempered By Prudence. Conservatism Is Distrust Of The People Tempered By Fear." - William E. Gladstone
2380	"There Is Only One Thing More Painful Than Learning From Experience And That Is Not Learning From Experience." - Archibald Mcleish
2381	"I Never Expected To See The Day When Girls Would Get Sunburned In The Places They Now Do." - Will Rogers
2382	"'Tis Not Where We Lie, But Whence We Fell; The Loss Of Heaven's The Greatest Pain In Hell." - Pedro Calderon De La Barca
2383	" The Thing Always Happens That You Really Believe In; And The Belief In A Thing Makes It Happen." - Frank Lloyd Wright
2384	"Everything One Invents Is True, You May Be Perfectly Sure Of That. Poetry Is As Precise As Geometry." - Gustave Flaubert
2385	"I Have Tried To Know Absolutely Nothing About A Great Many Things, And I Have Succeeded Fairly Well." - Robert Benchley
2386	"You Don't Suffer, Kill Yourself And Take The Risks I Take Just For Money. I Love Bike Racing." - Greg Lemond
2387	"If We Cannot Now End Our Differences, At Least We Can Help Make The World Safe For Diversity." - John F. Kennedy
2388	"I Read Shakespeare And The Bible, And I Can Shoot Dice. That's What I Call A Liberal Education." - Tallulah Bankhead
2389	"Creationists Make It Sound As Though A 'Theory' Is Something You Dreamt Up After Being Drunk All Night." - Isaac Asimov
2390	"Nearly All Men Can Stand Adversity, But If You Want To Test A Man's Character, Give Him Power." - Abraham Lincoln

2391	"Those Who Do Not Know How To Weep With Their Whole Heart Don't Know How To Laugh Either." - Golda Meir
2392	"No Person Was Ever Honored For What He Received. Honor Has Been The Reward For What He Gave." - Calvin Coolidge
2393	"If You Wait To Do Everything Until You're Sure It's Right, You'll Probably Never Do Much Of Anything." - Win Borden
2394	"Study As If You Were Going To Live Forever; Live As If You Were Going To Die Tomorrow." - Maria Mitchell
2395	"In Seeking Wisdom Thou Art Wise; In Imagining That Thou Hast Attained It - Thou Art A Fool." - Lord Chesterfield
2396	"Inventor - A Person Who Makes An Ingenious Arrangement Of Wheels, Levers And Springs, And Believes It Civilization." - Ambrose Bierce
2397	"When Lip Service To Some Mysterious Deity Permits Bestiality On Wednesday And Absolution On Sunday, Cash Me Out." - Frank Sinatra
2398	"Most Of What We Call Management Consists Of Making It Difficult For People To Get Their Work Done." - Peter Drucker
2399	"Plan For The Future, Because That Is Where You Are Going To Spend The Rest Of Your Life." - Mark Twain
2400	"You Can't Make Up Anything Anymore. The World Itself Is A Satire. All You're Doing Is Recording It." - Art Buchwald
2401	"Unless A Tree Has Borne Blossoms In Spring, You Will Vainly Look For Fruit On It In Autumn." - Walter Scott
2402	"When Buying And Selling Are Controlled By Legislation, The First Things To Be Bought And Sold Are Legislators." - P. J. O'Rourke
2403	"Those Who Have Compared Our Life To A Dream Were Right... We Were Sleeping Wake, And Waking Sleep." - Michel De Montaigne
2404	"We Have Just Enough Religion To Make Us Hate, But Not Enough To Make Us Love One Another." - Jonathan Swift
2405	"If The Only Tool You Have Is A Hammer, You Tend To See Every Problem As A Nail." - Abraham Maslow
2406	"Birds Sing After A Storm; Why Shouldn't People Feel As Free To Delight In Whatever Remains To Them?" - Rose Kennedy
2407	"The Poor, The Unsuccessful, The Unhappy, The Unhealthy Are The Ones Who Use The Word Tomorrow The Most" - Robert Kiyosaki
2408	"Tragedy Is When I Cut My Finger. Comedy Is When You Fall Into An Open Sewer And Die." - Mel Brooks
2409	"Because You're Not What I Would Have You Be, I Blind Myself To Who, In Truth, You Are." - Madeline L'Engle
2410	"A Sense Of Humor Is The Ability To Understand A Joke And That The Joke Is Oneself." - Clifton Paul Fadiman

2411	"Poetry Should... Strike The Reader As A Wording Of His Own Highest Thoughts, And Appear Almost A Remembrance." - John Keats
2412	"Society Has Always Seemed To Demand A Little More From Human Beings Than It Will Get In Practice." - George Orwell
2413	"I Believe In General In A Dualism Between Facts And The Ideas Of Those Facts In Human Heads." - George Santayana
2414	"When You Forgive, You In No Way Change The Past - But You Sure Do Change The Future." - Bernard Meltzer
2415	"Men Who Have A Pierced Ear Are Better Prepared For Marriage - They've Experienced Pain And Bought Jewelry." - Rita Rudner
2416	"I Would Rather Entertain And Hope That People Learned Something Than Educate People And Hope They Were Entertained." - Walt Disney
2417	"An Edwardian Lady In Full Dress Was A Wonder To Behold, And Her Preparations For Viewing Were Awesome." - William Manchester
2418	"Old Age Has Deformities Enough Of Its Own. It Should Never Add To Them The Deformity Of Vice." - Eleanor Roosevelt
2419	"Man Will Never Be Free Until The Last King Is Strangled With The Entrails Of The Last Priest." - Denis Diderot
2420	"Some Books Are To Be Tasted, Others To Be Swallowed, And Some Few To Be Chewed And Digested." - Francis Bacon
2421	" You Have Reached The Pinnacle Of Success As Soon As You Become Uninterested In Money, Compliments, Or Publicity." - Thomas Wolfe
2422	"Only Choose In Marriage A Man Whom You Would Choose As A Friend If He Were A Woman." - Joseph Joubert
2423	"A Truly American Sentiment Recognizes The Dignity Of Labor And The Fact That Honor Lies In Honest Toil." - Grover Cleveland
2424	"Government, Even In Its Best State, Is But A Necessary Evil; In Its Worst State, An Intolerable One." - Thomas Paine
2425	"It Is One Of The Most Beautiful Compensations In Life... We Can Never Help Another Without Helping Ourselves." - Ralph Waldo Emerson
2426	"How Things Look On The Outside Of Us Depends On How Things Are On The Inside Of Us." - Parks Cousins
2427	"Why Should We Take Advice On Sex From The Pope? If He Knows Anything About It, He Shouldn't!" - George Bernard Shaw
2428	"Old Age Is Like A Plane Flying Through A Storm. Once You're Aboard, There's Nothing You Can Do." - Golda Meir
2429	"There Was No Before The Beginning Of Our Universe, Because Once Upon A Time There Was No Time." - John D. Barrow
2430	"Trust That Little Voice In Your Head That Says Wouldn't It Be Interesting If...; And Then Do It." - Duane Michals

2431	"The Danger Is Not That A Particular Class Is Unfit To Govern. Every Class Is Unfit To Govern." - Lord Acton
2432	"Age Does Not Diminish The Extreme Disappointment Of Having A Scoop Of Ice Cream Fall From The Cone." - Jim Fiebig
2433	"We All Live With The Objective Of Being Happy; Our Lives Are All Different And Yet The Same." - Anne Frank
2434	"I'm Not A Driven Businessman, But A Driven Artist. I Never Think About Money. Beautiful Things Make Money." - Lord Acton
2435	"What Is The Use Of A House If You Haven't Got A Tolerable Planet To Put It On?" - Henry David Thoreau
2436	"Then, The Cool Kindliness Of Sheets, That Soon Smooth Away Trouble; And The Rough Male Kiss Of Blankets...." - Rupert Brooke
2437	"You Can Map Your Life Through Your Favorite Movies, And No Two People's Maps Will Be The Same." - Mary Schmich
2438	"I'm Fed Up To The Ears With Old Men Dreaming Up Wars For Young Men To Die In." - George Mcgovern
2439	"Equality May Perhaps Be A Right, But No Power On Earth Can Ever Turn It Into A Fact." - Honore De Balzac
2440	"One Of The Tests Of Leadership Is The Ability To Recognize A Problem Before It Becomes An Emergency." - Arnold H. Glasow
2441	"When I Was A Boy I Was Told That Anybody Could Become President; I'm Beginning To Believe It." - Clarence Darrow
2442	"Every Young Man Would Do Well To Remember That All Successful Business Stands On The Foundation Of Morality." - Henry Ward Beecher
2443	"We Are Made Wise Not By The Recollection Of Our Past, But By The Responsibility For Our Future." - George Bernard Shaw
2444	"Flaming Enthusiasm, Backed Up By Horse Sense And Persistence, Is The Quality That Most Frequently Makes For Success." - Dale Carnegie
2445	"The Most Important Single Ingredient In The Formula Of Success Is Knowing How To Get Along With People." - Theodore Roosevelt
2446	"Like Everyone Else Who Makes The Mistake Of Getting Older, I Begin Each Day With Coffee And Obituaries." - Bill Cosby
2447	"In Politics, If You Want Anything Said, Ask A Man; If You Want Anything Done, Ask A Woman." - Margaret Thatcher
2448	"Break Open A Cherry Tree And There Are No Flowers, But The Spring Breeze Brings Forth Myriad Blossoms." - Ikkyu Sojun
2449	"There Are No Secrets To Success. It Is The Result Of Preparation, Hard Work, And Learning From Failure." - Colin Powell

2450	"A Man Begins Cutting His Wisdom Teeth The First Time He Bites Off More Than He Can Chew." - Herb Caen
2451	"The Only Way To Discover The Limits Of The Possible Is To Go Beyond Them Into The Impossible." - Arthur C. Clarke
2452	"A Good Painting To Me Has Always Been Like A Friend. It Keeps Me Company, Comforts And Inspires." - Hedy Lamarr
2453	"Visualize This Thing You Want. See It, Feel It, Believe In It. Make Your Mental Blueprint And Begin." - Robert Collier
2454	"I Learned More From The One Restaurant That Didn't Work Than From All The Ones That Were Successes." - Wolfgang Puck
2455	"Those Who Dream By Day Are Cognizant Of Many Things That Escape Those Who Dream Only At Night." - Edgar Allan Poe
2456	"There Are Many Men Of Principle In Both Parties In America, But There Is No Party Of Principle." - Alexis De Tocqueville
2457	"People Often Say That Motivation Doesn't Last. Well, Neither Does Bathing - That's Why We Recommend It Daily." - Zig Ziglar
2458	"All Men Are Frauds. The Only Difference Between Them Is That Some Admit It. I Myself Deny It." - H. L. Mencken
2459	"A Visitor From Mars Could Easily Pick Out The Civilized Nations. They Have The Best Implements Of War." - Herbert V. Prochnow
2460	"Like Music And Art, Love Of Nature Is A Common Language That Can Transcend Political Or Social Boundaries." - Jimmy Carter
2461	"When Grace Is Joined With Wrinkles, It Is Adorable. There Is An Unspeakable Dawn In Happy Old Age." - Victor Hugo
2462	"The Reason There Are Two Senators For Each State Is So That One Can Be The Designated Driver." - Jay Leno
2463	"Your Work Is To Discover Your Work And Then With All Your Heart To Give Yourself To It." - The Buddha
2464	"Trying To Sneak A Fastball Past Hank Aaron Is Like Trying To Sneak The Sunrise Past A Rooster." - Joe Adcock
2465	"Don't Fight With The Pillow, But Lay Down Your Head And Kick Every Worriment Out Of The Bed." - Edmund Vance Cooke
2466	"One's Dignity May Be Assaulted, Vandalized And Cruelly Mocked, But Cannot Be Taken Away Unless It Is Surrendered." - Michael J. Fox
2467	"Our Habitual Monetary Path Reflects Whether We Continue To Create Or Sabotage Our Own Personal & Financial Freedoms." - Richard Marvin Voigt
2468	"Close Scrutiny Will Show That Most Crisis Situations Are Opportunities To Either Advance, Or Stay Where You Are." - Maxwell Maltz

2469	"The Three Great Essentials To Achieve Anything Worth While Are, First, Hard Work; Second, Stick-To-Itiveness; Third, Common Sense." - Thomas Edison
2470	"To Sit In The Shade On A Fine Day And Look Upon Verdure Is The Most Perfect Refreshment." - Jane Austen
2471	"Some People Like My Advice So Much That They Frame It Upon The Wall Instead Of Using It." - Gordon R. Dickson
2472	"The Tree Of Liberty Must Be Refreshed From Time To Time With The Blood Of Patriots And Tyrants." - Thomas Jefferson
2473	"If A Tie Is Like Kissing Your Sister, Losing Is Like Kissing You Grandmother With Her Teeth Out." - George Brett
2474	"All Books Are Divisible Into Two Classes, The Books Of The Hour, And The Books Of All Time." - John Ruskin
2475	"I Believe In The Imagination. What I Cannot See Is Infinitely More Important Than What I Can See." - Duane Michals
2476	"It Was One Of Those Perfect English Autumnal Days Which Occur More Frequently In Memory Than In Life." - P. D. James
2477	"It Is Astonishing With How Little Wisdom Mankind Can Be Governed, When That Little Wisdom Is Its Own." - William Ralph Inge
2478	"Some Of The World's Greatest Feats Were Accomplished By People Not Smart Enough To Know They Were Impossible." - Doug Larson
2479	"It Has Been Well Said That A Hungry Man Is More Interested In Four Sandwiches Than Four Freedoms." - Henry Cabot Lodge, Jr.
2480	"It Is Almost Impossible To Remember How Tragic A Place The World Is When One Is Playing Golf." - Robert Wilson Lynd
2481	"Is What Happens When Painters Stop Looking At Girls And Persuade Themselves That They Have A Better Idea." - John Ciardi
2482	"Instead Of Giving A Politician The Keys To The City, It Might Be Better To Change The Locks." - Doug Larson
2483	"Always Bear In Mind That Your Own Resolution To Success Is More Important Than Any Other One Thing." - Abraham Lincoln
2484	"Here Is The Test To Find Whether Your Mission On Earth Is Finished: If You're Alive, It Isn't." - Richard Bach
2485	"A Film Is Never Really Good Unless The Camera Is An Eye In The Head Of A Poet." - Orson Welles
2486	"If You Want To Conquer Fear, Don't Sit Home And Think About It. Go Out And Get Busy." - Dale Carnegie
2487	"The Best Scientist Is Open To Experience And Begins With Romance - The Idea That Anything Is Possible." - Ray Bradbury
2488	"The Key To Most Difficulties Does Not Lie In The Dilemmas Themselves, But In Our Relationship To Them." - David Seabury

2489	"Christians Are Supposed Not Merely To Endure Change, Nor Even To Profit By It, But To Cause It." - Harry Emerson Fosdick
2490	"All Love Shifts And Changes. I Don't Know If You Can Be Wholeheartedly In Love All The Time." - Julie Andrews
2491	"A Man Who Carries A Cat By The Tail Learns Something He Can Learn In No Other Way." - Mark Twain
2492	"It Is One Of The Blessings Of Old Friends That You Can Afford To Be Stupid With Them." - Ralph Waldo Emerson
2493	"Supercomputers Will Achieve One Human Brain Capacity By 2010, And Personal Computers Will Do So By About 2020." - Douglas Engelbart
2494	"Literature Is Mostly About Having Sex And Not Much About Having Children. Life Is The Other Way Round." - David Lodge
2495	"Fall Is My Favorite Season In Los Angeles, Watching The Birds Change Color And Fall From The Trees." - David Letterman
2496	"I Did Not Become A Vegetarian For My Health, I Did It For The Health Of The Chickens." - Isaac Bashevis Singer
2497	"As I Grow Older, I Pay Less Attention To What Men Say. I Just Watch What They Do." - Andrew Carnegie
2498	"Those Who Try To Do Something And Fail Are Infinitely Better Than Those Who Try Nothing And Succeed." - Lloyd Jones (Adapted)
2499	"If A Small Thing Has The Power To Make You Angry, Does That Not Indicate Something About Your Size?" - Sydney J. Harris
2500	"A Successful Man Is One Who Can Lay A Firm Foundation With The Bricks Others Have Thrown At Him." - David Brinkley
2501	"I Always Knew I Was Going To Be Rich. I Don't Think I Ever Doubted It For A Minute." - Warren Buffett
2502	"It Is Hard To Feel Individually Responsible With Respect To The Invisible Processes Of A Huge And Distant Government." - John W. Gardner
2503	"It Is Lamentable, That To Be A Good Patriot One Must Become The Enemy Of The Rest Of Mankind." - Voltaire
2504	"Innovation Is The Specific Instrument Of Entrepreneurship. The Act That Endows Resources With A New Capacity To Create Wealth." - Peter Drucker
2505	"One Of The True Tests Of Leadership Is The Ability To Recognize A Problem Before It Becomes An Emergency." - Arnold H. Glasow
2506	"If We Continue To Develop Our Technology Without Wisdom Or Prudence, Our Servant May Prove To Be Our Executioner." - Omar N. Bradley

2507	"One Should Not Lose One's Temper Unless One Is Certain Of Getting More And More Angry To The End." - William Butler Yeats
2508	"Success Is Focusing The Full Power Of All You Are On What You Have A Burning Desire To Achieve." - Wilfred A. Peterson
2509	"Soon I Will Rest, Yes, Forever Sleep. Earned It I Have. Twilight Is Upon Me, Sonn Night Must Fall." - Yoda
2510	"When I Was A Boy I Was Told That Anybody Could Become President. Now I'm Beginning To Believe It." - Clarence Darrow
2511	"Avoid Having Your Ego So Close To Your Position That When Your Position Falls, Your Ego Goes With It." - Colin Powell
2512	"Better To Write For Yourself And Have No Public, Than To Write For The Public And Have No Self." - Cyril Connolly
2513	"Music Was My Refuge. I Could Crawl Into The Space Between The Notes And Curl My Back To Loneliness." - Maya Angelou
2514	"In These Times You Have To Be An Optimist To Open Your Eyes When You Awake In The Morning." - Carl Sandburg
2515	"Don't Go Around Saying The World Owes You A Living. The World Owes You Nothing. It Was Here First." - Mark Twain
2516	"When A Man Opens A Car Door For His Wife, It's Either A New Car Or A New Wife." - Prince Philip
2517	"Perseverance Is The Hard Work You Do After You Get Tired Of Doing The Hard Work You Already Did." - Newt Gingrich
2518	"I Can't Let Important Policy Decisions Hinge On The Fact That An Election Is Coming Up Every 90 Days." - Gerhard Schroeder
2519	"Yes, We Love Peace, But We Are Not Willing To Take Wounds For It, As We Are For War." - John Andrew Holmes
2520	"I Don't Need You To Remind Me Of My Age. I Have A Bladder To Do That For Me." - Stephen Fry
2521	"More Than Anything Else, I Believe It's Our Decisions, Not The Conditions Of Our Lives, That Determine Our Destiny." - Anthony Robbins
2522	"When I Make Art, I Think About Its Ability To Connect With Others, To Bring Them Into The Process." - Jim Hodges
2523	"If I Had To Choose A Religion, The Sun As The Universal Giver Of Life Would Be My God." - Napoleon Bonaparte
2524	"Patriotism Is Easy To Understand In America. It Means Looking Out For Yourself By Looking Out For Your Country." - Calvin Coolidge
2525	"There Are Many Truths Of Which The Full Meaning Cannot Be Realized Until Personal Experience Had Brought It Home." - John Stuart Mill

2526	"I Find It Rather Easy To Portray A Businessman. Being Bland, Rather Cruel And Incompetent Comes Naturally To Me." - John Cleese
2527	"For Behind All Imperialism Is Ultimately The Imperialistic Individual, Just As Behind All Peace Is Ultimately The Peaceful Individual." - Irving Babbitt
2528	"I Am Not The Only Person Who Uses His Computer Mainly For The Purpose Of Diddling With His Computer." - Dave Barry
2529	"In Politics It Is Necessary Either To Betray One's Country Or The Electorate. I Prefer To Betray The Electorate." - Charles De Gaulle
2530	"It Takes Time To Succeed Because Success Is Merely The Natural Reward Of Taking Time To Do Anything Well." - Joseph Ross
2531	"There Was A Time When A Fool And His Money Were Soon Parted, But Now It Happens To Everybody." - Adlai E. Stevenson
2532	"When I've Heard All I Need To Make A Decision, I Don't Take A Vote. I Make A Decision." - Ronald Reagan
2533	"Without Freedom, No Art; Art Lives Only On The Restraints It Imposes On Itself, And Dies Of All Others." - Albert Camus
2534	"Marriage - A Book Of Which The First Chapter Is Written In Poetry And The Remaining Chapters In Prose." - Beverley Nichols
2535	"The Revenues Of Cuban State-Run Companies Are Used Exclusively For The Benefit Of The People, To Whom They Belong." - Fidel Castro
2536	"Executives Owe It To The Organization And To Their Fellow Workers Not To Tolerate Nonperforming Individuals In Important Jobs." - Peter Drucker
2537	"The Indispensable First Step To Getting The Things You Want Out Of Life Is This: Decide What You Want." - Ben Stein
2538	"If There Is A God, Whence Proceed So Many Evils? If There Is No God, Whence Cometh Any Good?" - Boethius
2539	"Every Other Artist Begins With A Blank Canvas, A Piece Of Paper The Photographer Begins With The Finished Product." - Edward Steichen
2540	"If The Romans Had Been Obliged To Learn Latin, They Would Never Have Found Time To Conquer The World." - Heinrich Heine
2541	"Between Two Groups Of People Who Want To Make Inconsistent Kinds Of Worlds, I See No Remedy But Force." - Oliver Wendell Holmes
2542	"Courage Is Not The Absence Of Fear, But Rather The Judgment That Something Else Is More Important Than Fear." - Ambrose Redmoon
2543	"If You Listen To Your Fears, You Will Die Never Knowing What A Great Person You Might Have Been." - Robert H. Schuller

2544	"I Decided That If I Could Paint That Flower In A Huge Scale, You Could Not Ignore Its Beauty." - Georgia O'keeffe
2545	"Bitterness Is Like Cancer. It Eats Upon The Host. But Anger Is Like Fire. It Burns It All Clean." - Maya Angelou
2546	"We Come To Love Not By Finding A Perfect Person But By Learning To See An Imperfect Person Perfectly." - Sam Keen
2547	"I Will Never Be An Old Man. To Me, Old Age Is Always 15 Years Older Than I Am." - Francis Bacon
2548	"Anyone Who Attempts To Generate Random Numbers By Deterministic Means Is, Of Course, Living In A State Of Sin." - John Von Neumann
2549	"It Appears That Every Man's Insomnia Is As Different From His Neighbour's As Are Their Daytime Hopes And Aspirations." - F. Scott Fitzgerald
2550	" Success Is A Matter Of Adjusting One's Efforts To Obstacles And One's Abilities To A Service Needed By Others." - Henry Ford
2551	"Education Is A Social Process. Education Is Growth. Education Is, Not A Preparation For Life; Education Is Life Itself." - John Dewey
2552	"If You Cannot Work With Love But Only With Distaste, It Is Better That You Should Leave Your Work." - Kahlil Gibran
2553	"Life Is Hard If You Live It The Easy Way And Easy If You Live It The Hard Way." - Joe Polish
2554	"He That Is Of The Opinion Money Will Do Everything May Well Be Suspected Of Doing Everything For Money." - Ben Franklin
2555	"A Market Is Never Saturated With A Good Product, But It Is Very Quickly Saturated With A Bad One." - Henry Ford
2556	"You Can Do What You Think You Can Do And You Cannot Do What You Think You Cannot Do." - Ben Stein
2557	"Insomnia Is A Gross Feeder. It Will Nourish Itself On Any Kind Of Thinking, Including Thinking About Not Thinking." - Clifton Fadiman
2558	"What Other People May Find In Poetry Or Art Museums, I Find In The Flight Of A Good Drive." - Arnold Palmer
2559	"The Universe Is One Great Kindergarten For Man. Everything That Exists Has Brought With It Its Own Peculiar Lesson." - Orison Swett Marden
2560	"Never Accept The Proposition That Just Because A Solution Satisfies A Problem, That It Must Be The Only Solution." - Raymond E. Feist
2561	"Take The First Step In Faith. You Don't Have To See The Whole Staircase, Just Take The First Step." - Martin Luther King, Jr.
2562	"A Nation Is A Society United By A Delusion About Its Ancestry And By Common Hatred Of Its Neighbors." - William Ralph Inge

2563	"Sometimes In Movies, I Still Have To Be The Hero, But It's Not All That Important To Me Anymore." - Dennis Quaid
2564	"To Cherish What Remains Of The Earth And To Foster Its Renewal Is Our Only Legitimate Hope Of Survival." - Wendell Berry
2565	"Everyone Is A Genius At Least Once A Year. The Real Geniuses Simply Have Their Bright Ideas Closer Together." - Georg C. Lichtenberg
2566	"The Most Rewarding Things You Do In Life Are Often The Ones That Look Like They Cannot Be Done." - Arnold Palmer
2567	"The Difficulty With Marriage Is That We Fall In Love With A Personality, But Must Live With A Character." - Peter De Vries
2568	"No Enterprise Is More Likely To Succeed Than One Concealed From The Enemy Until It Is Ripe For Execution." - Niccolo Machiavelli
2569	"He Who Rejects Change Is The Architect Of Decay. The Only Human Institution Which Rejects Progress Is The Cemetery." - Harold Wilson
2570	"The Machine Does Not Isolate Man From The Great Problems Of Nature But Plunges Him More Deeply Into Them." - Antoine De Saint-Exupery
2571	"Drawing Is The Honesty Of The Art. There Is No Possibility Of Cheating. It Is Either Good Or Bad." - Salvador Dali
2572	"If There Is Such A Thing As A Good Marriage, It Is Because It Resembles Friendship Rather Than Love." - Michel De Montaigne
2573	"Politics: A Strife Of Interests Masquerading As A Contest Of Principles. The Conduct Of Public Affairs For Private Advantage." - Ambrose Bierce
2574	"People Who Lean On Logic And Philosophy And Rational Exposition End By Starving The Best Part Of The Mind." - William Butler Yeats
2575	"One Secret Of Success In Life Is For A Man To Be Ready For His Opportunity When It Comes." - Benjamin Disraeli
2576	"Never Feel Remorse For What You Have Thought About Your Wife; She Has Thought Much Worse Things About You." - Jean Rostand
2577	"Do Not Dwell In The Past, Do Not Dream Of The Future, Concentrate The Mind On The Present Moment." - The Buddha
2578	"It Was A Greek Tragedy. Nixon Was Fulfilling His Own Nature. Once It Started It Could Not End Otherwise." - Henry A. Kissinger
2579	"Do Not Dwell In The Past; Do Not Dream Of The Future, Concentrate The Mind On The Present Moment." - The Buddha
2580	"A Conservative Is A Man With Two Perfectly Good Legs Who, However, Has Never Learned How To Walk Forward." - Franklin D. Roosevelt
2581	"He That Would Live In Peace And At Ease Must Not Speak All He Knows Or All He Sees." - Benjamin Franklin

2582	"Relying On The Government To Protect Your Privacy Is Like Asking A Peeping Tom To Install Your Window Blinds." - John Perry Barlow
2583	"Money Won't Buy Happiness, But It Will Pay The Salaries Of A Large Research Staff To Study The Problem." - Bill Vaughan
2584	"No Real Social Change Has Ever Been Brought About Without A Revolution... Revolution Is But Thought Carried Into Action." - Emma Goldman
2585	"Doing Linear Scans Over An Associative Array Is Like Trying To Club Someone To Death With A Loaded Uzi." - Larry Wall
2586	"Give Me Six Hours To Chop Down A Tree And I Will Spend The First Four Sharpening The Axe." - Abraham Lincoln
2587	"I'm Not Interested In Age. People Who Tell Me Their Age Are Silly. You're As Old As You Feel." - Henri Frederic Amiel
2588	"I Like Trees Because They Seem More Resigned To The Way They Have To Live Than Other Things Do." - Willa Cather
2589	"Be Not Afraid Of Life. Believe That Life Is Worth Living, And Your Belief Will Help Create The Fact." - Henry James
2590	"If You Were My Husband I'd Give You Poison. He Said, If You Were My Wife, I'd Drink It." - Exchange Between Churchill & Lady Astor
2591	"Ability Is What You're Capable Of Doing. Motivation Determines What You Do. Attitude Determines How Well You Do It." - Lou Holtz
2592	"There Ain't No Answer. There Ain't Gonna Be Any Answer. There Never Has Been An Answer. That's The Answer." - Gertrude Stein
2593	"A Lot Of People Do Not Muster The Courage To Live Their Dreams Because They Are Afraid To Die." - Les Brown
2594	"Look At Market Fluctuations As Your Friend Rather Than Your Enemy; Profit From Folly Rather Than Participate In It." - Warren Buffett
2595	"It Is A Thousand Times Better To Have Common Sense Without Education Than To Have Education Without Common Sense." - Robert Green Ingersoll
2596	" Success Is Always Temporary. When All Is Said And Done, The Only Thing You'll Have Left Is Your Character." - Vince Gill
2597	"What We've Gone Through In The Last Several Years Has Caused Some People To Question 'Can We Trust Microsoft?'" - Steve Ballmer
2598	"I Think I've Discovered The Secret Of Life - You Just Hang Around Until You Get Used To It." - Charles M. Schulz
2599	"Fortunately Analysis Is Not The Only Way To Resolve Inner Conflicts. Life Itself Still Remains A Very Effective Therapist." - Karen Horney
2600	"The Mistakes Made By Congress Wouldn't Be So Bad If The Next Congress Didn't Keep Trying To Correct Them." - Cullen Hightower

2601	"Do Not Go Where The Path May Lead, Go Instead Where There Is No Path And Leave A Trail." - Ralph Waldo Emerson
2602	"Faith Has To Do With Things That Are Not Seen And Hope With Things That Are Not At Hand." - Saint Thomas Aquinas
2603	"Silences Make The Real Conversations Between Friends. Not The Saying But The Never Needing To Say Is What Counts." - Margaret Lee Runbeck
2604	"One Needs To Be Slow To Form Conviction, But Once Formed, They Must Be Defended Against The Heaviest Odds." - Mohandas Gandhi
2605	"What We Actually Learn, From Any Given Set Of Circumstances, Determines Whether We Become Increasingly Powerless Or More Powerful." - Blaine Lee
2606	"A Constant Struggle, A Ceaseless Battle To Bring Success From Inhospitable Surroundings, Is The Price Of All Great Achievements." - Orison Swett Marden
2607	"Nothing In Education Is So Astonishing As The Amount Of Ignorance It Accumulates In The Form Of Inert Facts." - Henry B. Adams
2608	"The Scientific Theory I Like Best Is That The Rings Of Saturn Are Composed Entirely Of Lost Airline Luggage." - Mark Russell
2609	"To Me, Photography Is The Simultaneous Recognition, In A Fraction Of A Second, Of The Significance Of An Event." - Robert Schumann
2610	"Everyone Is A Genius At Least Once A Year. The Real Geniuses Simply Have Their Bright Ideas Closer Together." - Georg Christoph Lichtenberg
2611	"A Good Film Is When The Price Of The Dinner, The Theatre Admission And The Babysitter Were Worth It." - Alfred Hitchcock
2612	"Company Cultures Are Like Country Cultures. Never Try To Change One. Try, Instead, To Work With What You've Got." - Peter Drucker
2613	"I Busted A Mirror And Got Seven Years Bad Luck, But My Lawyer Thinks He Can Get Me Five." - Steven Wright
2614	"The Person Who Reads Too Much And Uses His Brain Too Little Will Fall Into Lazy Habits Of Thinking." - Albert Einstein
2615	"Ocean: A Body Of Water Occupying About Two-Thirds Of A World Made For Man - Who Has No Gills." - Ambrose Bierce
2616	"Religion Is Essentially The Art And The Theory Of The Remaking Of Man. Man Is Not A Finished Creation." - Edmund Burke
2617	"War Will Never Cease Until Babies Begin To Come Into The World With Larger Cerebrums And Smaller Adrenal Glands." - H. L. Mencken
2618	"I Don't Want To Play Golf. When I Hit A Ball, I Want Someone Else To Go Chase It." - Rogers Hornsby

2619	"Life May Not Be The Party We Hoped For, But While We Are Here, We May As Well Dance." - Herm Albright
2620	"We Learn Something Every Day, And Lots Of Times It's That What We Learned The Day Before Was Wrong." - Bill Vaughan
2621	"You Can't Live A Perfect Day Without Doing Something For Someone Who Will Never Be Able To Repay You." - John Wooden
2622	"Have You Ever Seen A Headstone With These Words - If Only I Had Spent More Time At Work" - Anonymous
2623	"It Is Questionable If All The Mechanical Inventions Yet Made Have Lightened The Day's Toil Of Any Human Being." - John Stuart Mill
2624	"I Tell Ya When I Was A Kid, All I Knew Was Rejection. My Yo-Yo, It Never Came Back!" - Rodney Dangerfield
2625	"I Am Accustomed To Sleep And In My Dreams To Imagine The Same Things That Lunatics Imagine When Awake." - Rene Descartes
2626	"The More Sand That Has Escaped From The Hourglass Of Our Life, The Clearer We Should See Through It." - Jean Paul
2627	"It Will Free Man From The Remaining Chains, The Chains Of Gravity Which Still Tie Him To This Planet." - Wernher Von Braun
2628	"Sleep Lingers All Our Lifetime About Our Eyes, As Night Hovers All Day In The Boughs Of The Fir-Tree." - Ralph Waldo Emerson
2629	"Any American Who Is Prepared To Run For President Should Automatically, By Definition, Be Disqualified From Ever Doing So." - Gore Vidal
2630	"When You Take Stuff From One Writer It's Plagiarism; But When You Take It From Many Writers, It's Research." - Wilson Mizner
2631	"You Fall Out Of Your Mother's Womb, You Crawl Across Open Country Under Fire, And Drop Into Your Grave." - Quentin Crisp
2632	"You Can Free Yourself From Aging By Reinterpreting Your Body And By Grasping The Link Between Belief And Biology." - Deepak Chopra
2633	"Do Not Be Bullied Out Of Your Common Sense By The Specialist; Two To One, He Is A Pedant." - Oliver Wendell Holmes
2634	"Always End The Name Of Your Child With A Vowel, So That When You Yell The Name Will Carry." - Bill Cosby
2635	"Even If I Set Out To Make A Film About A Fillet Of Sole, It Would Be About Me." - Federico Fellini
2636	"The Linux Philosophy Is 'Laugh In The Face Of Danger'. Oops. Wrong One. 'Do It Yourself'. Yes, That's It." - Linus Torvalds
2637	"We Must Walk Consciously Only Part Way Toward Our Goal And Then Leap In The Dark To Our Success." - Henry David Thoreau
2638	"If The Lessons Of History Teach Us Anything It Is That Nobody Learns The Lessons That History Teaches Us." - Anonymous

2639	"Asking A Working Writer What He Thinks About Critics Is Like Asking A Lamppost How It Feels About Dogs." - Christopher Hampton
2640	"If You Want To Sacrifice The Admiration Of Many Men For The Criticism Of One, Go Ahead, Get Married." - Katharine Hepburn
2641	"Experience Is Not What Happens To A Man; It Is What A Man Does With What Happens To Him." - Aldous Huxley
2642	"True Terror Is To Wake Up One Morning And Discover That Your High School Class Is Running The Country." - Kurt Vonnegut
2643	"Anthropology Was The Science That Gave Her The Platform From Which She Surveyed, Scolded And Beamed At The World." - Jane Howard
2644	"I'm Not A Real Movie Star. I've Still Got The Same Wife I Started Out With Twenty-Eight Years Ago." - Will Rogers
2645	"The World Can Only Be Grasped By Action, Not By Contemplation...The Hand Is The Cutting Edge Of The Mind." - Jacob Bronowski
2646	"If We Don't Believe In Freedom Of Expression For People We Despise, We Don't Believe In It At All." - Noam Chomsky
2647	"For Everything You Have Missed, You Have Gained Something Else; And For Everything You Gain, You Lose Something Else." - Ralph Waldo Emerson
2648	"How Absurd And Delicious It Is To Be In Love With Somebody Younger Than Yourself. Everybody Should Try It." - Barbara Pym
2649	"Remember That No One Is Ever Rewarded Or Promoted Because Of A Bad Disposition And A Negative Mental Attitude." - Napoleon Hill
2650	"If You Don't Set Goals For Yourself, You Are Doomed To Work To Achieve The Goals Of Someone Else." - Brian Tracy
2651	"Golf Is A Game In Which One Endeavors To Control A Ball With Implements Ill Adapted For The Purpose." - Woodrow Wilson
2652	"A Government That Is Big Enough To Give You All You Want Is Big Enough To Take It All Away." - Barry Goldwater
2653	"The Only Difference Between The Democrats And The Republicans Is That The Democrats Allow The Poor To Be Corrupt, Too." - Oscar Levant
2654	"Inflation Is As Violent As A Mugger, As Frightening As An Armed Robber And As Deadly As A Hit Man." - Ronald Reagan
2655	"Democracy Is The Recurrent Suspicion That More Than Half Of The People Are Right More Than Half Of The Time." - E. B. White
2656	"Academe - An Ancient School Where Morality And Philosophy Were Taught. Academy - A Modern School Where Football Is Taught." - Ambrose Bierce

2657	"A Poem Is True If It Hangs Together. Information Points To Something Else. A Poem Points To Nothing But Itself." - E. M. Forster
2658	"When They See Me Holding Fish, They Can See That I Am Comfortable With Kings As Well As With Paupers." - Imelda Marcos
2659	"It Is Difficult To Know At What Moment Love Begins; It Is Less Difficult To Know That It Has Begun." - Henry Wadsworth Longfellow
2660	"I Don't Mind If My Skull Ends Up On A Shelf As Long As It's Got My Name On It." - Debbie Harry
2661	"The Greater The Artist, The Greater The Doubt. Perfect Confidence Is Granted To The Less Talented As A Consolation Prize." - Robert Hughes
2662	"A Small Body Of Determined Spirits Fired By An Unquenchable Faith In Their Mission Can Alter The Course Of History." - Mohandas Gandhi
2663	"Giving Connects Two People, The Giver And The Receiver, And This Connection Gives Birth To A New Sense Of Belonging." - Deepak Chopra
2664	"The Most Exciting Phrase To Hear In Science, The One That Heralds New Discoveries, Is Not 'Eureka!' But 'That's Funny...'" - Isaac Asimov
2665	"I Am Enclosing Two Tickets To The First Night Of My New Play; Bring A Friend.... If You Have One." - George Bernard Shaw
2666	"For Sleep, One Needs Endless Depths Of Blackness To Sink Into; Day-light Is Too Shallow, It Will Not Cover One." - Anne Morrow Lindbergh
2667	"If You're In A Bad Situation, Don't Worry It'll Change. If You're In A Good Situation, Don't Worry It'll Change." - John A. Simone, Sr.
2668	"We Should Take Care Not To Make The Intellect Our God; It Has, Of Course, Powerful Muscles, But No Personality." - Albert Einstein
2669	"Baseball Is A Public Trust. Players Turn Over, Owners Turn Over And Certain Commissioners Turn Over. But Baseball Goes On." - Peter Ueberroth
2670	"The Very Essence Of The Creative Is Its Novelty, And Hence We Have No Standard By Which To Judge It." - Carl Rogers
2671	"I Think Cinema, Movies, And Magic Have Always Been Closely Associated. The Very Earliest People Who Made Film Were Magicians." - Francis Ford Coppola
2672	"Go As Far As You Can See And When You Get There, You Will Always Be Able To See Farther." - Zig Ziglar
2673	"To Me A Lush Carpet Of Pine Needles Or Spongy Grass Is More Welcome Than The Most Luxurious Persian Rug." - Helen Keller
2674	"Never Be Afraid To Laugh At Yourself, After All, You Could Be Missing Out On The Joke Of The Century." - Dame Edna Everage

2675	"There Is That In The Glance Of A Flower Which May At Times Control The Greatest Of Creation's Braggart Lords." - John Muir
2676	"Cyberspace. A Consensual Hallucination Experienced Daily By Billions Of Legitimate Operators, In Every Nation, By Children Being Taught Mathematical Concepts." - William Gibson
2677	"Everything Has Been Said Before, But Since Nobody Listens We Have To Keep Going Back And Beginning All Over Again." - Andre Gide
2678	"Comedy Has To Be Based On Truth. You Take The Truth And You Put A Little Curlicue At The End." - Sid Caesar
2679	"I Always Turn To The Sports Pages First, Which Records People's Accomplishments. The Front Page Has Nothing But Man's Failures." - Earl Warren
2680	"If You Are Going To Sin, Sin Against God, Not The Bureaucracy. God Will Forgive You But The Bureaucracy Won't." - Hyman Rickover
2681	"It Is A Scientific Fact That Your Body Will Not Absorb Cholesterol If You Take It From Another Person's Plate." - Dave Barry
2682	"There Is Nothing So Stupid As The Educated Man If You Get Him Off The Thing He Was Educated In." - Will Rogers
2683	"By Working Faithfully Eight Hours A Day You May Eventually Get To Be Boss And Work Twelve Hours A Day." - Robert Frost
2684	"We Can Chart Our Future Clearly And Wisely Only When We Know The Path Which Has Led To The Present." - Adlai Stevenson
2685	"I Have A Fantasy Where Ted Turner Is Elected President But Refuses Because He Doesn't Want To Give Up Power." - Arthur C. Clarke
2686	"Science Is Wonderfully Equipped To Answer The Question How? But It Gets Terribly Confused When You Ask The Question Why?" - Erwin Chargaff
2687	"A Peace Is Of The Nature Of A Conquest; For Then Both Parties Nobly Are Subdued, And Neither Party Loser." - William Shakespeare
2688	"Before I Got Married I Had Six Theories About Bringing Up Children; Now I Have Six Children And No Theories." - John Wilmot
2689	"Peace, Plenty, And Contentment Reign Throughout Our Borders, And Our Beloved Country Presents A Sublime Moral Spectacle To The World." - James Polk
2690	"There Are Risks And Costs To Action. But They Are Far Less Than The Long Range Risks Of Comfortable Inaction." - John Fitzgerald Kennedy
2691	"Show Me A Person Who Has Never Made A Mistake And I'll Show You Somebody Who Has Never Achieved Much." - Joan Collins
2692	"Accept Everything About Yourself-I Mean Everything. You Are You And That Is The Beginning And The End-No Apologies, No Regrets." - Clark Moustakas

2693	"I Think Complexity Is Mostly Sort Of Crummy Stuff That Is There Because It's Too Expensive To Change The Interface." - Jaron Lanier
2694	"I Have No Country To Fight For; My Country Is The Earth, And I Am A Citizen Of The World." - Eugene V. Debs
2695	"I Always Felt That The Great High Privilege, Relief And Comfort Of Friendship Was That One Had To Explain Nothing." - Katherine Mansfield
2696	"Don't Marry The Person You Think You Can Live With; Marry Only The Individual You Think You Can't Live Without." - James C. Dobson
2697	"Cherish Your Visions And Your Dreams As They Are The Children Of Your Soul, The Blueprints Of Your Ultimate Achievements." - Napoleon Hill
2698	"Technology Is So Much Fun But We Can Drown In Our Technology. The Fog Of Information Can Drive Out Knowledge." - Daniel J. Boorstin
2699	"The Negative Is Comparable To The Composer's Score And The Print To Its Performance. Each Performance Differs In Subtle Ways." - Ansel Adams
2700	"The Internet Is So Big, So Powerful And Pointless That For Some People It Is A Complete Substitute For Life." - Andrew Brown
2701	"Life Is Not Measured By The Number Of Breaths We Take, But By The Moments That Take Our Breath Away." - Maya Angelou
2702	"The Best Measure Of A Man's Honesty Isn't His Income Tax Return. It's The Zero Adjust On His Bathroom Scale." - Arthur C. Clarke
2703	"The Greatest Discovery Of My Generation Is That Human Beings Can Alter Their Lives By Altering Their Attitudes Of Mind." - William James
2704	"Art Is The Right Hand Of Nature. The Latter Has Only Given Us Being, The Former Has Made Us Men." - Friedrich Schiller
2705	"Washington Is A Place Where Politicians Don't Know Which Way Is Up And Taxes Don't Know Which Way Is Down." - Robert Orben
2706	"One Of The Penalties For Refusing To Participate In Politics Is That You End Up Being Governed By Your Inferiors." - Plato
2707	"If The Career You Have Chosen Has Some Unexpected Inconvenience, Console Yourself By Reflecting That No Career Is Without Them." - Jane Fonda
2708	"Never Tell People How To Do Things. Tell Them What To Do And They Will Surprise You With Their Ingenuity." - General George S. Patton
2709	"Achievement Seems To Be Connected With Action. Successful Men And Women Keep Moving. They Make Mistakes, But They Don't Quit." - Woodrow Wilson

2710	"Forget Not That The Earth Delights To Feel Your Bare Feet And The Winds Long To Play With Your Hair." - Kahlil Gibran
2711	"Be As Smart As You Can, But Remember That It Is Always Better To Be Wise Than To Be Smart." - Alan Alda
2712	"Management Is Efficiency In Climbing The Ladder Of Success; Leadership Determines Whether The Ladder Is Leaning Against The Right Wall." - Stephen Covey
2713	"If You Watch A Game, It's Fun. If You Play It, It's Recreation. If You Work At It, It's Golf." - Bob Hope
2714	"Youth Is When You're Allowed To Stay Up Late On New Year's Eve. Middle Age Is When You're Forced To." - Bill Vaughan
2715	"Music Doesn't Lie. If There Is Something To Be Changed In This World, Then It Can Only Happen Through Music." - Jimi Hendrix
2716	"There Is No Disguise Which Can Hide Love For Long Where It Exists, Or Simulate It Where It Does Not." - Francois De La Rochefoucauld
2717	"Every Man Is A Damn Fool For At Least Five Minutes Every Day; Wisdom Consists In Not Exceeding The Limit." - Elbert Hubbard
2718	"Treat Your Password Like Your Toothbrush. Don't Let Anybody Else Use It, And Get A New One Every Six Months." - Clifford Stoll
2719	"The System Of Nature, Of Which Man Is A Part, Tends To Be Self-Balancing, Self-Adjusting, Self-Cleansing. Not So With Technology." - E. F. Schumacher
2720	"Peace And Friendship With All Mankind Is Our Wisest Policy, And I Wish We May Be Permitted To Pursue It." - Thomas Jefferson
2721	"The Ineffable Joy Of Forgiving And Being Forgiven Forms An Ecstasy That Might Well Arouse The Envy Of The Gods." - Elbert Hubbard
2722	"Concentrate All Your Thoughts Upon The Work At Hand. The Sun's Rays Do Not Burn Until Brought To A Focus." - Alexander Graham Bell
2723	"We Change The World Not By What We Say Or Do, But As A Consequence Of What We Have Become." - David R. Hawkins
2724	"Singleness Of Purpose Is One Of The Chief Essentials For Success In Life, No Matter What May Be One's Aim." - John D. Rockefeller
2725	"Give Me A Lever Long Enough And A Fulcrum On Which To Place It, And I Shall Move The World." - Archimedes
2726	"The Supreme Court's Only Armor Is The Cloak Of Public Trust; Its Sole Ammunition, The Collective Hopes Of Our Society." - Irving R. Kaufman
2727	"Perfection Is Achieved, Not When There Is Nothing More To Add, But When There Is Nothing Left To Take Away." - Antoine De Saint-Exupéry

2728	"The Movies We Love And Admire Are To Some Extent A Function Of Who We Are When We See Them." - Mary Schmich
2729	"Liberalism Is, I Think, Resurgent. One Reason Is That More And More People Are So Painfully Aware Of The Alternative." - John Kenneth Galbraith
2730	"Science Is Simply Common Sense At Its Best, That Is, Rigidly Accurate In Observation, And Merciless To Fallacy In Logic." - Thomas Huxley
2731	"When You Do The Common Things In Life In An Uncommon Way, You Will Command The Attention Of The World." - George Washington Carver
2732	"Once You Have A Clear Picture Of Your Priorities- That Is Values, Goals, And High Leverage Activities- Organize Around Them." - Stephen Covey
2733	"Apparently, A Democracy Is A Place Where Numerous Elections Are Held At Great Cost Without Issues And With Interchangeable Candidates." - Gore Vidal
2734	"If A Man Speaks Or Acts With A Pure Thought, Happiness Follows Him, Like A Shadow That Never Leaves Him." - The Buddha
2735	"Nothing Can Add More Power To Your Life Than Concentrating All Of Your Energies On A Limited Set Of Targets." - Nido Qubein
2736	"While One Finds Company In Himself And His Pursuits, He Cannot Feel Old, No Matter What His Years May Be." - Amos Bronson Alcott
2737	"I've Never Been Poor, Only Broke. Being Poor Is A Frame Of Mind. Being Broke Is Only A Temporary Situation." - Mike Todd
2738	"Give Me Golf Clubs, Fresh Air And A Beautiful Partner, And You Can Keep The Clubs And The Fresh Air." - Jack Benny
2739	"Any Time Detroit Scores More Than 100 Points And Holds The Other Team Below 100 Points They Almost Always Win." - Doug Collins
2740	"If You Wish To Know The Road Up The Mountain, Ask The Man Who Goes Back And Forth On It." - Zenrin
2741	"The Internet Is The Most Important Single Development In The History Of Human Communication Since The Invention Of Call Waiting." - Dave Barry
2742	"Immature Love Says: 'I Love You Because I Need You.' Mature Love Says 'I Need You Because I Love You.'" - Erich Fromm
2743	"We Cannot Banish Dangers, But We Can Banish Fears. We Must Not Demean Life By Standing In Awe Of Death." - David Sarnoff
2744	"Publishing A Volume Of Verse Is Like Dropping A Rose Petal Down The Grand Canyon And Waiting For The Echo." - Don Marquis

2745	"Can Miles Truly Separate You From Friends... If You Want To Be With Someone You Love, Aren't You Already There?" - Richard Bach
2746	"The World Has Achieved Brilliance Without Wisdom, Power Without Conscience. Our Is A World Of Nuclear Giants And Ethical Infants." - Omar N. Bradley
2747	"When Written In Chinese, The Word Crisis Is Composed Of Two Characters. One Represents Danger And The Other Represents Opportunity." - John F. Kennedy
2748	"Don't Knock The Weather; Nine-Tenths Of The People Couldn't Start A Conversation If It Didn't Change Once In A While." - Kin Hubbard
2749	"Think Of Yourself As On The Threshold Of Unparalleled Success. A Whole Clear, Glorious Life Lies Before You. Achieve! Achieve! " - Andrew Carnegie
2750	"Everything's In The Mind. That's Where It All Starts. Knowing What You Want Is The First Step Toward Getting It." - Mae West
2751	"In Faith There Is Enough Light For Those Who Want To Believe And Enough Shadows To Blind Those Who Don't." - Blaise Pascal
2752	"Attach Yourself To Your Passion, But Not To Your Pain. Adversity Is Your Best Friend On The Path To Success." - Anonymous
2753	"One Of The Definitions Of Sanity Is The Ability To Tell Real From Unreal. Soon We'll Need A New Definition." - Alvin Toffler
2754	"But No One Ever Is Allowed In Sleepytown, Unless He Goes To Bed In Time To Take The Sleepytown Express! " - James Jackson Montague
2755	"Let Us Be Grateful To People Who Make Us Happy, They Are The Charming Gardeners Who Make Our Souls Blossom." - Marcel Proust
2756	"One Machine Can Do The Work Of Fifty Ordinary Men. No Machine Can Do The Work Of One Extraordinary Man." - Elbert Hubbard
2757	"If You Owe The Bank $100 That's Your Problem. If You Owe The Bank $100 Million, That's The Bank's Problem." - J. Paul Getty
2758	"I Have Friends In Overalls Whose Friendship I Would Not Swap For The Favor Of The Kings Of The World." - Thomas A. Edison
2759	"A Wedding Anniversary Is The Celebration Of Love, Trust, Partnership, Tolerance And Tenacity. The Order Varies For Any Given Year." - Paul Sweeney
2760	" Getting Divorced Just Because You Don't Love A Man Is Almost As Silly As Getting Married Just Because You Do." - Zsa Zsa Gabor
2761	"Most Of The Change We Think We See In Life Is Due To Truths Being In And Out Of Favor." - Robert Frost
2762	"If There Is Anything That A Man Can Do Well, I Say Let Him Do It. Give Him A Chance." - Abraham Lincoln

2763	" Many Of Life's Failures Are People Who Did Not Realize How Close They Were To Success When They Gave Up." - Thomas Edison
2764	"It Is A Fine Thing To Have Ability, But The Ability To Discover Ability In Others Is The True Test." - Lou Holtz
2765	"Age Is Not A Particularly Interesting Subject. Anyone Can Get Old. All You Have To Do Is Live Long Enough." - Don Marquis
2766	"Do Not Overrate What You Have Received, Nor Envy Others. He Who Envies Others Does Not Obtain Peace Of Mind." - The Buddha
2767	"A Woman Is Like A Tea Bag. You Never Know How Strong She Is Until She Gets In Hot Water." - Nancy Reagan
2768	"I Knew I Was An Unwanted Baby When I Saw That My Bath Toys Were A Toaster And A Radio." - Joan Rivers
2769	"There Are More Love Songs Than Anything Else. If Songs Could Make You Do Something We'd All Love One Another." - Frank Zappa
2770	"Never Tell People How To Do Things. Tell Them What To Do And They Will Surprise You With Their Ingenuity." - George S. Patton
2771	"Half Of The Modern Drugs Could Well Be Thrown Out Of The Window, Except That The Birds Might Eat Them." - Martin Henry Fischer
2772	"Faith Is To Believe What You Do Not See; The Reward Of This Faith Is To See What You Believe." - Saint Augustine
2773	"I Don't Mind What Congress Does, As Long As They Don't Do It In The Streets And Frighten The Horses." - Victor Hugo
2774	"We Have War When At Least One Of The Parties To A Conflict Wants Something More Than It Wants Peace." - Jeane Kirkpatrick
2775	"I Am Certainly Not One Of Those Who Need To Be Prodded. In Fact, If Anything, I Am The Prod." - Winston Churchill
2776	"You Know It's Going To Hell When The Best Rapper Out There Is White And The Best Golfer Is Black." - Charles Barkley
2777	"Try, Try, Try, And Keep On Trying Is The Rule That Must Be Followed To Become An Expert In Anything." - W. Clement Stone
2778	"I'm Tired Of Hearing It Said That Democracy Doesn't Work. Of Course It Doesn't Work. We Are Supposed To Work It." - Alexander Woollcott
2779	"Thanksgiving Dinners Take Eighteen Hours To Prepare. They Are Consumed In Twelve Minutes. Half-Times Take Twelve Minutes. This Is Not Coincidence." - Erma Bombeck
2780	"Courage Means To Keep Working A Relationship, To Continue Seeking Solutions To Difficult Problems, And To Stay Focused During Stressful Periods." - Denis Waitley
2781	" Success Has Nothing To Do With What You Gain In Life Or Accomplish For Yourself. It's What You Do For Others." - Danny Thomas

2782	"Don't Worry About People Stealing Your Ideas. If Your Ideas Are Any Good, You'll Have To Ram Them Down People's Throats." - Howard Aiken
2783	"A Leader, Once Convinced That A Particular Course Of Action Is The Right One, Must...Be Undaunted When The Going Gets Tough." - Ronald Reagan
2784	"If You Decide To Go For It, Do It With Spirit: Sometimes Success Is Due Less To Ability Than To Zeal." - Charles Buxton
2785	"If You Got The Game, You Got The Game. That's Why Tiger Woods Is Out There Playing Golf With Greg Norman." - Shaquille O'Neal
2786	"People Think Of The Inventor As A Screwball, But No One Ever Asks The Inventor What He Thinks Of Other People." - Charles F. Kettering
2787	"Most Women Set Out To Try To Change A Man, And When They Have Changed Him They Do Not Like Him." - Marlene Dietrich
2788	"In Its Early Stages, Insomnia Is Almost An Oasis In Which Those Who Have To Think Or Suffer Darkly Take Refuge." - Colette
2789	"I Have Found The Paradox, That If You Love Until It Hurts, There Can Be No More Hurt, Only More Love." - Mother Teresa
2790	"The Satirist Shoots To Kill While The Humorist Brings His Prey Back Alive And Eventually Releases Him Again For Another Chance." - Peter De Vries
2791	"A Sculptor Is A Person Who Is Interested In The Shape Of Things, A Poet In Words, A Musician By Sounds." - Henry Moore
2792	"The Judicial System Is The Most Expensive Machine Ever Invented For Finding Out What Happened And What To Do About It." - Irving R. Kaufman
2793	"The Way You Think, The Way You Behave, The Way You Eat, Can Influence Your Life By 30 To 50 Years." - Deepak Chopra
2794	"Be Courteous To All, But Intimate With Few, And Let Those Few Be Well Tried Before You Give Them Your Confidence." - George Washington
2795	"If A Lot Of People Gripped A Knife And Fork The Way They Do A Golf Club, They'd Starve To Death." - Sam Snead
2796	"When We Get Piled Upon One Another In Large Cities, As In Europe, We Shall Become As Corrupt As Europe ." - Thomas Jefferson
2797	"Just As We Could Have Rode Into The Sunset, Along Came The Internet, And It Tripled The Significance Of The Pc." - Andy Grove
2798	"What A Distressing Contrast There Is Between The Radiant Intelligence Of The Child And The Feeble Mentality Of The Average Adult." - Sigmund Freud

2799	"A Person Without A Sense Of Humor Is Like A Wagon Without Springs. It's Jolted By Every Pebble On The Road." - Henry Ward Beecher
2800	"The Future Is Something Which Everyone Reaches At The Rate Of 60 Minutes An Hour, Whatever He Does, Whoever He Is." - C. S. Lewis
2801	" To Establish True Self-Esteem We Must Concentrate On Our Successes And Forget About The Failures And The Negatives In Our Lives." - Denis Waitley
2802	"A Successful Person Is One Who Can Lay A Firm Foundation With The Bricks That Others Throw At Him Or Her." - David Brinkley
2803	"Death Is A Very Dull, Dreary Affair, And My Advice To You Is To Have Nothing Whatsoever To Do With It." - W. Somerset Maugham
2804	"No Man Ever Believes That The Bible Means What It Says: He's Always Convinced That It Says What He Means." - George Bernard Shaw
2805	"The Instant Formal Government Is Abolished, Society Begins To Act. A General Association Takes Place, And Common Interest Produces Common Security." - Thomas Paine
2806	"Pay No Attention To What The Critics Say; There Has Never Been Set Up A Statue In Honor Of A Critic." - Jean Sibelius
2807	"When A Noble Life Has Prepared Old Age, It Is Not Decline That It Reveals, But The First Days Of Immortality." - Muriel Spark
2808	"In Youth The Days Are Short And The Years Are Long. In Old Age The Years Are Short And Day's Long." - Pope Paul VI
2809	"If At First You Don't Succeed, Try, Try Again. Then Quit. There's No Point In Being A Damn Fool About It." - W. C. Fields
2810	"Whenever Men Take The Law Into Their Own Hands, The Loser Is The Law. And When The Law Loses, Freedom Languishes." - Robert Kennedy
2811	"I'm Tired Of Hearing About Money, Money, Money, Money, Money. I Just Want To Play The Game, Drink Pepsi, Wear Reebok." - Shaquille O'neal
2812	"You Can't Stay The Same. If You're A Musician And A Singer, You Have To Change, That's The Way It Works." - Van Morrison
2813	"Profit In Business Comes From Repeat Customers, Customers That Boast About Your Project Or Service, And That Bring Friends With Them." - W. Edwards Deming
2814	"Peace Is Not An Absence Of War, It Is A Virtue, A State Of Mind, A Disposition For Benevolence, Confidence, Justice." - Baruch Spinoza
2815	"To Be Interested In The Changing Seasons Is A Happier State Of Mind Than To Be Hopelessly In Love With Spring." - George Santayana

2816	"The Human Brain Starts Working The Moment You Are Born And Never Stops Until You Stand Up To Speak In Public." - George Jessel
2817	"They Were Afraid, Never Having Learned What I Taught Myself: Defeat The Fear Of Death And Welcome The Death Of Fear." - G. Gordon Liddy
2818	"The Danger Of The Past Was That Men Became Slaves. The Danger Of The Future Is That Man May Become Robots." - Erich Fromm
2819	"It's A Funny Thing That When A Man Hasn't Anything On Earth To Worry About, He Goes Off And Gets Married." - Robert Frost
2820	"Life Does Not Cease To Be Funny When People Die Any More Than It Ceases To Be Serious When People Laugh." - George Bernard Shaw
2821	"The Great Leaders Are Like The Best Conductors - They Reach Beyond The Notes To Reach The Magic In The Players." - Blaine Lee
2822	"It Took Me 17 Years To Get 3,000 Hits In Baseball. I Did It In One Afternoon On The Golf Course." - Hank Aaron
2823	"Discipline Is The Soul Of An Army. It Makes Small Numbers Formidable, Procures Success To The Weak And Esteem To All." - George Washington
2824	"Nothing So Conclusively Proves A Man's Ability To Lead Others As What He Does From Day To Day To Lead Himself." - Thomas J. Watson
2825	"As You Walk Down The Fairway Of Life You Must Smell The Roses, For You Only Get To Play One Round." - Ben Hogan
2826	"I Can See Clearly Now... That I Was Wrong In Not Acting More Decisively And More Forthrightly In Dealing With Watergate." - Richard M. Nixon
2827	"I Don't Think You Can Ever Do Your Best. Doing Your Best Is A Process Of Trying To Do Your Best." - Townes Van Zandt
2828	"The Game Of Golf Would Lose A Great Deal If Croquet Mallets And Billiard Cues Were Allowed On The Putting Green." - Ernest Hemingway
2829	" The Greatest Compliment That Was Ever Paid Me Was When One Asked Me What I Thought, And Attended To My Answer." - Henry David Thoreau
2830	"I Think It Pisses God Off If You Walk By The Color Purple In A Field Somewhere And Don't Notice It." - Alice Walker
2831	"The Big Difference Between Sex For Money And Sex For Free Is That Sex For Money Usually Costs A Lot Less." - Brendan Behan
2832	"Reduce Your Plan To Writing... The Moment You Complete This, You Will Have Definitely Given Concrete Form To The Intangible Desire." - Napoleon Hill

2833	"Nobody's A Natural. You Work Hard To Get Good And Then Work To Get Better. It's Hard To Stay On Top." - Paul Coffey
2834	"The Man Who Has Done His Level Best... Is A Success, Even Though The World May Write Him Down A Failure." - B. C. Forbes
2835	"No Matter Who You Are It's The Simple Things In Life That Lead You To Believe That You Can Achieve Anything." - Aristotle
2836	" If You Want To Succeed, You Should Strike Out On New Paths Rather Than Travel The Worn Paths Of Accepted Success." - John D. Rockefeller
2837	"I Believe That If You Show People The Problems And You Show Them The Solutions They Will Be Moved To Act." - Bill Gates
2838	" To Be Successful, You Must Decide Exactly What You Want To Accomplish; Then Resolve To Pay The Price To Get It." - Bunker Hunt
2839	"There Is One Thing Stronger Than All The Armies In The World, And That Is An Idea Whose Time Has Come." - Victor Hugo
2840	"So Long As We Have Enough People In This Country Willing To Fight For Their Rights, We'll Be Called A Democracy." - Roger Nash Baldwin
2841	"The Sweltering Summer Of The Negro's Legitimate Discontent Will Not Pass Until There Is An Invigorating Autumn Of Freedom And Equality." - Martin Luther King, Jr.
2842	"You Can Turn Painful Situations Around Through Laughter. If You Can Find Humor In Anything, Even Poverty, You Can Survive It." - Bill Cosby
2843	"There Is No Time For Cut-And-Dried Monotony. There Is Time For Work. And Time For Love. That Leaves No Other Time!" - Coco Chanel
2844	"Every Tomorrow Has Two Handles. We Can Take Hold Of It With The Handle Of Anxiety Or The Handle Of Faith." - Henry Ward Beecher
2845	"A Well-Developed Sense Of Humor Is The Pole That Adds Balance To Your Steps As You Walk The Tightrope Of Life." - William A. Ward
2846	"Confidence Is A Habit That Can Be Developed By Acting As If You Already Had The Confidence You Desire To Have." - Brian Tracy
2847	"Bill Gates Is A Very Rich Man Today... And Do You Want To Know Why? The Answer Is One Word: Versions." - Dave Barry
2848	"To Wear Your Heart On Your Sleeve Isn't A Very Good Plan; You Should Wear It Inside, Where It Functions Best." - Margaret Thatcher
2849	"Never Get Married In College; It's Hard To Get A Start If A Prospective Employer Finds You've Already Made One Mistake." - Elbert Hubbard
2850	"No Greater Nor More Affectionate Honor Can Be Conferred On An American Than To Have A Public School Named After Him." - Herbert Hoover

2851	"Everything Human Is Pathetic. The Secret Source Of Humor Itself Is Not Joy But Sorrow. There Is No Humor In Heaven." - Mark Twain
2852	"Life Does Not Require Us To Make Good; It Asks Only That We Give Our Best At Each Level Of Experience." - Harold Ruopp
2853	"They Say Women Talk Too Much. If You Have Worked In Congress You Know That The Filibuster Was Invented By Men." - Clare Boothe Luce
2854	"The Most Terrible Job In Warfare Is To Be A Second Lieutenant Leading A Platoon When You Are On The Battlefield." - Dwight D. Eisenhower
2855	"One Who Comes To The Court Must Come To Adore, Not To Protest. That's The New Gloss On The 1st Amendment." - William O. Douglas
2856	"It Is The Eye Of Ignorance That Assigns A Fixed And Unchangeable Color To Every Object; Beware Of This Stumbling Block." - Paul Gauguin
2857	"There's Always A Period Of Curious Fear Between The First Sweet-Smelling Breeze And The Time When The Rain Comes Cracking Down." - Don Delillo
2858	"The Men Who Try To Do Something And Fail Are Infinitely Better Than Those Who Try To Do Nothing And Succeed." - Lloyd Jones
2859	"Being President Is Like Being A Jackass In A Hailstorm. There's Nothing To Do But To Stand There And Take It." - Lyndon B. Johnson
2860	"In My Dreams I Hear Again The Crash Of Guns, The Rattle Of Musketry, The Strange, Mournful Mutter Of The Battlefield." - Douglas Macarthur
2861	"The Best Job Goes To The Person Who Can Get It Done Without Passing The Buck Or Coming Back With Excuses." - Napoleon Hill
2862	"Never Measure The Height Of A Mountain Until You Have Reached The Top. Then You Will See How Low It Was." - Dag Hammarskjold
2863	"I Must Have A Prodigious Quantity Of Mind; It Takes Me As Much As A Week Sometimes To Make It Up." - Mark Twain
2864	"Always Acknowledge A Fault. This Will Throw Those In Authority Off Their Guard And Give You An Opportunity To Commit More." - Mark Twain
2865	"All This Talk About Equality. The Only Thing People Really Have In Common Is That They Are All Going To Die." - Bob Dylan
2866	"The Proper Means Of Increasing The Love We Bear Our Native Country Is To Reside Some Time In A Foreign One." - William Shenstone
2867	"Telephone - An Invention Of The Devil Which Abrogates Some Of The Advantages Of Making A Disagreeable Person Keep His Distance." - Ambrose Bierce

2868	"One Of The Greatest Casualties Of The War In Vietnam Is The Great Society... Shot Down On The Battlefield Of Vietnam." - Martin Luther King, Jr.
2869	"The Advantage Of A Classical Education Is That It Enables You To Despise The Wealth That It Prevents You From Achieving." - Russell Green
2870	"Marrying For Love May Be A Bit Risky, But It Is So Honest That God Can't Help But Smile On It." - Josh Billings
2871	"A Positive Attitude May Not Solve All Your Problems, But It Will Annoy Enough People To Make It Worth The Effort." - Herm Albright
2872	"The Feeling Of Sleepiness When You Are Not In Bed, And Can't Get There, Is The Meanest Feeling In The World." - Edgar Watson Howe
2873	"Time Is Our Most Valuable Asset, Yet We Tend To Waste It, Kill It, And Spend It Rather Than Invest It." - Jim Rohn
2874	"No Man Succeeds Without A Good Woman Behind Him. Wife Or Mother, If It Is Both, He Is Twice Blessed Indeed." - Harold Macmillan
2875	"Art Is An Invention Of Aesthetics, Which In Turn Is An Invention Of Philosophers... What We Call Art Is A Game." - Octavio Paz
2876	"All That I Desire To Point Out Is The General Principle That Life Imitates Art Far More Than Art Imitates Life." - Oscar Wilde
2877	"Until You Value Yourself, You Won't Value Your Time. Until You Value Your Time, You Will Not Do Anything With It." - M. Scott Peck
2878	"It's Impossible To Move, To Live, To Operate At Any Level Without Leaving Traces, Bits, Seemingly Meaningless Fragments Of Personal Information." - William Gibson
2879	"Even The Rich Are Hungry For Love, For Being Cared For, For Being Wanted, For Having Someone To Call Their Own." - Mother Teresa
2880	"Edison Failed 10, 000 Times Before He Made The Electric Light. Do Not Be Discouraged If You Fail A Few Times." - Napoleon Hill
2881	"Both Now And For Always, I Intend To Hold Fast To My Belief In The Hidden Strength Of The Human Spirit." - Andrei Sakharov
2882	"If We Could Have Just Screwed Another Head On His Shoulders, He Would Have Been The Greatest Golfer Who Ever Lived." - Ben Hogan
2883	"Part Of The Inhumanity Of The Computer Is That, Once It Is Competently Programmed And Working Smoothly, It Is Completely Honest." - Isaac Asimov
2884	"An Archaeologist Is The Best Husband A Woman Can Have. The Older She Gets The More Interested He Is In Her." - Agatha Christie
2885	"A Good Hockey Player Plays Where The Puck Is. A Great Hockey Player Plays Where The Puck Is Going To Be." - Wayne Gretzky

2886	"Forgiveness Is The Economy Of The Heart... Forgiveness Saves The Expense Of Anger, The Cost Of Hatred, The Waste Of Spirits." - Hannah More
2887	"Don't Aim For Success If You Want It; Just Do What You Love And Believe In, And It Will Come Naturally." - David Frost
2888	"I've Got A Theory That If You Give 100% All Of The Time, Somehow Things Will Work Out In The End." - Larry Bird
2889	"If A Man Had As Many Ideas During The Day As He Does When He Has Insomnia, He'd Make A Fortune." - Griff Niblack
2890	"Home Computers Are Being Called Upon To Perform Many New Functions, Including The Consumption Of Homework Formerly Eaten By The Dog." - Doug Larson
2891	"People Discuss My Art And Pretend To Understand As If It Were Necessary To Understand, When It's Simply Necessary To Love." - Claude Monet
2892	"The Reason There Are So Few Female Politicians Is That It Is Too Much Trouble To Put Makeup On Two Faces." - Maureen Murphy
2893	"Science Is A First-Rate Piece Of Furniture For A Man's Upper Chamber, If He Has Common Sense On The Ground Floor." - Oliver Wendell Holmes
2894	"There Is Only One Difference Between A Long Life And A Good Dinner: That, In The Dinner, The Sweets Come Last." - Robert Louis Stevenson
2895	"Those Who Admire The Massive, Rigid Bone Structures Of Dinosaurs Should Remember That Jellyfish Still Enjoy Their Very Secure Ecological Niche." - Beau Sheil
2896	"The Poet May Be Used As A Barometer, But Let Us Not Forget That He Is Also Part Of The Weather." - Lionel Trilling
2897	"A Quotation In A Speech, Article Or Book Is Like A Rifle In The Hands Of An Infantryman. It Speaks With Authority." - Brendan Francis
2898	"Justice, Sir, Is The Great Interest Of Man On Earth. It Is The Ligament Which Holds Civilized Beings And Civilized Nations Together." - Daniel Webster
2899	"Life Is A Dream For The Wise, A Game For The Fool, A Comedy For The Rich, A Tragedy For The Poor." - Sholom Aleichem
2900	"If We Wish To Make A New World We Have The Material Ready. The First One, Too, Was Made Out Of Chaos." - Robert Quillen
2901	"And So, My Fellow Americans, Ask Not What Your Country Can Do For You; Ask What You Can Do For Your Country." - John F. Kennedy

2902	"When Bad Men Combine, The Good Must Associate; Else They Will Fall One By One, An Unpitied Sacrifice In A Contemptible Struggle." - Edmund Burke
2903	"I Don't Need A Friend Who Changes When I Change And Who Nods When I Nod; My Shadow Does That Much Better." - Plutarch
2904	"To Compel A Man To Subsidize With His Taxes The Propagation Of Ideas Which He Disbelieves And Abhors Is Sinful And Tyrannical." - Thomas Jefferson
2905	"Fishing Is Much More Than Fish. It Is The Great Occasion When We May Return To The Fine Simplicity Of Our Forefathers." - Herbert Hoover
2906	"Our Character Is Basically A Composite Of Our Habits. Because They Are Consistent, Often Unconscious Patterns, They Constantly, Daily, Express Our Character." - Stephen Covey
2907	"Always Vote For Principle, Though You May Vote Alone, And You May Cherish The Sweetest Reflection That Your Vote Is Never Lost." - John Quincy Adams
2908	"Think Left And Think Right And Think Low And Think High. Oh, The Thinks You Can Think Up If Only You Try!" - Theodor Geisel
2909	"Do You Ever Get The Feeling That The Only Reason We Have Elections Is To Find Out If The Polls Were Right?" - Robert Orben
2910	"What Is Human Warfare But Just This; An Effort To Make The Laws Of God And Nature Take Sides With One Party." - Henry David Thoreau
2911	"You Will Know That Forgiveness Has Begun When You Recall Those Who Hurt You And Feel The Power To Wish Them Well." - Lewis B. Smedes
2912	" Your Vision Will Become Clear Only When You Can Look Into Your Own Heart. Who Looks Outside, Dreams; Who Looks Inside, Awakens." - Carl Jung
2913	"Much May Be Done In Those Little Shreds And Patches Of Time Which Every Day Produces, And Which Most Men Throw Away." - Charles Caleb Colton
2914	"My Advice To You Is Get Married: If You Find A Good Wife You'll Be Happy; If Not, You'll Become A Philosopher." - Socrates
2915	"Like All Sciences And All Valuations, The Psychology Of Women Has Hitherto Been Considered Only From The Point Of View Of Men." - Karen Horney
2916	"There Is More Refreshment And Stimulation In A Nap, Even Of The Briefest, Than In All The Alcohol Ever Distilled." - Edward Lucas
2917	"Old Age Is An Excellent Time For Outrage. My Goal Is To Say Or Do At Least One Outrageous Thing Every Week." - Louis Kronenberger

2918	"You Can Take My Factories, Burn Up My Buildings, But Give Me My People And I'll Build The Business Right Back Again." - Henry Ford
2919	"It Is Forbidden To Kill; Therefore All Murderers Are Punished Unless They Kill In Large Numbers And To The Sound Of Trumpets." - Voltaire
2920	"Individual Commitment To A Group Effort That Is What Makes A Team Work, A Company Work, A Society Work, A Civilization Work." - Vince Lombardi
2921	"Accept Responsibility For Your Life. Know That It Is You Who Will Get You Where You Want To Go, No One Else." - Les Brown
2922	"Men Have A Much Better Time Of It Than Women. For One Thing, They Marry Later; For Another Thing, They Die Earlier." - H. L. Mencken
2923	"The True Soldier Fights Not Because He Hates What Is In Front Of Him, But Because He Loves What Is Behind Him." - G. K. Chesteron
2924	"If You Make A Living, If You Earn Your Own Money, You're Free - However Free One Can Be On This Planet." - Theodore White
2925	"The Aim Of Marketing Is To Know And Understand The Customer So Well The Product Or Service Fits Him And Sells Itself." - Peter Drucker
2926	"Why Should Society Feel Responsible Only For The Education Of Children, And Not For The Education Of All Adults Of Every Age?" - Erich Fromm
2927	"I Get To Play Golf For A Living. What More Can You Ask For – Getting Paid For Doing What You Love." - Tiger Woods
2928	"No Married Man Is Genuinely Happy If He Has To Drink Worse Whisky Than He Used To Drink When He Was Single." - H. L. Mencken
2929	"Never Doubt That A Small Group Of Thoughtful, Committed Citizens Can Change The World; Indeed, It's The Only Thing That Ever Has." - Margaret Mead
2930	"Man, Alone, Has The Power To Transform His Thoughts Into Physical Reality; Man, Alone, Can Dream And Make His Dreams Come True." - Napoleon Hill
2931	"An Election Is Coming. Universal Peace Is Declared And The Foxes Have A Sincere Interest In Prolonging The Lives Of The Poultry." - T. S. Eliot
2932	"The Work An Unknown Good Man Has Done Is Like A Vein Of Water Flowing Hidden Underground, Secretly Making The Ground Green." - Thomas Carlyle
2933	"It's Wonderful To Climb The Liquid Mountains Of The Sky. Behind Me And Before Me Is God And I Have No Fears." - Helen Keller

2934	"Yes'm, Old Friends Is Always Best, 'Less You Can Catch A New One That's Fit To Make An Old One Out Of." - Sarah Orne Jewett
2935	"Desire Is The Starting Point Of All Achievement, Not A Hope, Not A Wish, But A Keen Pulsating Desire Which Transcends Everything." - Napoleon Hill
2936	"Art Begins With Resistance - At The Point Where Resistance Is Overcome. No Human Masterpiece Has Ever Been Created Without Great Labor." - Andre Gide
2937	"Hubert Humphrey Talks So Fast That Listening To Him Is Like Trying To Read Playboy Magazine With Your Wife Turning The Pages." - Barry Goldwater
2938	"The Activist Is Not The Man Who Says The River Is Dirty. The Activist Is The Man Who Cleans Up The River." - Ross Perot
2939	"Sometimes When You Innovate, You Make Mistakes. It Is Best To Admit Them Quickly, And Get On With Improving Your Other Innovations." - Steve Jobs
2940	"The Fastest Way To Succeed Is To Look As If You're Playing By Somebody Else's Rules, While Quietly Playing By Your Own." - Michael Korda
2941	"Except During The Nine Months Before He Draws His First Breath, No Man Manages His Affairs As Well As A Tree Does." - George Bernard Shaw
2942	"Capital Isn't That Important In Business. Experience Isn't That Important. You Can Get Both Of These Things. What Is Important Is Ideas." - Harvey S. Firestone
2943	"If You Want To Achieve Things In Life, You've Just Got To Do Them, And If You're Talented And Smart, You'll Succeed." - Juliana Hatfield
2944	"He That Cannot Forgive Others Breaks The Bridge Over Which He Must Pass Himself; For Every Man Has Need To Be Forgiven." - Thomas Fuller
2945	"It Is Impossible To Predict The Time And Progress Of Revolution. It Is Governed By Its Own More Or Less Mysterious Laws." - Vladimir Lenin
2946	"The Real Danger Is Not That Computers Will Begin To Think Like Men, But That Men Will Begin To Think Like Computers." - Sydney J. Harris
2947	"Beauty For Some Provides Escape, Who Gain A Happiness In Eyeing The Gorgeous Buttocks Of The Ape Or Autumn Sunsets Exquisitely Dying." - Langston Hughes
2948	"The Typewriting Machine, When Played With Expression, Is No More Annoying Than The Piano When Played By A Sister Or Near Relation." - Oscar Wilde

2949	"Nothing Interferes With My Concentration. You Could Put On An Orgy In My Office And I Wouldn't Look Up. Well, Maybe Once." - Isaac Asimov
2950	"Why Does A Woman Work Ten Years To Change A Man's Habits And Then Complain That He's Not The Man She Married?" - Barbra Streisand
2951	"Never Be Bullied Into Silence. Never Allow Yourself To Be Made A Victim. Accept No One's Definition Of Your Life; Define Yourself." - Harvey Fierstein
2952	"Confidence Doesn't Come Out Of Nowhere. It's A Result Of Something...Hours And Days And Weeks And Years Of Constant Work And Dedication." - Roger Staubach
2953	"Web Users Ultimately Want To Get At Data Quickly And Easily. They Don't Care As Much About Attractive Sites And Pretty Design." - Tim Bemers-Lee
2954	"A Man Is Not Idle Because He Is Absorbed In Thought. There Is A Visible Labor And There Is An Invisible Labor." - Victor Hugo
2955	"Whenever You Decide To Marry For Good, Make Sure Your Final And Only Selection Turns Out To Be To Your Best Friend. - Richard Marvin Voigt
2956	"Remember, A Real Decision Is Measured By The Fact That You've Taken New Action. If There's No Action, You Haven't Truly Decided." - Anthony Robbins
2957	"Pollution Is Nothing But The Resources We Are Not Harvesting. We Allow Them To Disperse Because We've Been Ignorant Of Their Value." - R. Buckminster Fuller
2958	"If A Composer Could Say What He Had To Say In Words He Would Not Bother Trying To Say It In Music." - Gustav Mahler
2959	"Friendship... Is Not Something You Learn In School. But If You Haven't Learned The Meaning Of Friendship, You Really Haven't Learned Anything." - Muhammad Ali
2960	"This Country Has Come To Feel The Same When Congress Is In Session As When The Baby Gets Hold Of A Hammer." - Will Rogers
2961	"I Still Get Wildly Enthusiastic About Little Things... I Play With Leaves. I Skip Down The Street And Run Against The Wind." - Leo Buscaglia
2962	"We've Collected The Most Common Service Complaints.... And Every One Of Them Is Rooted In A Lack Of Respect For The Customer." - Leonard Berry
2963	"One Cannot Get Through Life Without Pain... What We Can Do Is Choose How To Use The Pain Life Presents To Us." - Bernie Siegel

2964	"A Real Decision Is Measured By The Fact That You've Taken A New Action. If There's No Action, You Haven't Truly Decided." - Tony Robbins
2965	"Aerodynamically, The Bumble Bee Shouldn't Be Able To Fly, But The Bumble Bee Doesn't Know It So It Goes On Flying Anyway." - Mary Kay Ash
2966	"Faith And Doubt Both Are Needed - Not As Antagonists, But Working Side By Side To Take Us Around The Unknown Curve." - Lillian Smith
2967	"In A Controversy The Instant We Feel Anger We Have Already Ceased Striving For The Truth, And Have Begun Striving For Ourselves." - The Buddha
2968	"Conservative - A Statesman Who Is Enamored Of Existing Evils, As Distinguished From The Liberal Who Wishes To Replace Them With Others." - Ambrose Bierce
2969	"Half Of The American People Have Never Read A Newspaper. Half Never Voted For President. One Hopes It Is The Same Half." - Gore Vidal
2970	"In Most Places In The Country, Voting Is Looked Upon As A Right And A Duty, But In Chicago It's A Sport." - Dick Gregory
2971	"I Had A Mother Who Taught Me There Is No Such Thing As Failure. It Is Just A Temporary Postponement Of Success." - Buddy Ebsen
2972	"He Who Devotes Sixteen Hours A Day To Hard Study May Become At Sixty As Wise As He Thought Himself At Twenty." - Mary Wilson Little
2973	"You Can Always Tell A Real Friend: When You've Made A Fool Of Yourself He Doesn't Feel You've Done A Permanent Job." - Laurence J. Peter
2974	"It Is Impossible To Win The Race Unless You Venture To Run, Impossible To Win The Victory Unless You Dare To Battle." - Richard M. Devos
2975	"Inflation Is When You Pay Fifteen Dollars For The Ten-Dollar Haircut You Used To Get For Five Dollars When You Had Hair." - Sam Ewing
2976	"Eighteen Holes Of Match Play Will Teach You More About Your Foe Than 18 Years Of Dealing With Him Across A Desk." - Grantland Rice
2977	"Success Is Blocked By Concentrating On It And Planning For It... Success Is Shy - It Won't Come Out While You're Watching." - Tennessee Williams
2978	"If You Hear A Voice Within You Say You Cannot Paint, Then By All Means Paint, And That Voice Will Be Silenced." - Vincent Van Gogh
2979	"I Tell People I'm Too Stupid To Know What's Impossible. I Have Ridiculously Large Dreams, And Half The Time They Come True." - Debi Thomas

143

2980	"I Couldn't Wait For The Sun To Come Up The Next Morning So That I Could Get Out On The Course Again." - Ben Hogan
2981	"The Vice-Presidency Is Sort Of Like The Last Cookie On The Plate. Everybody Insists He Won't Take It, But Somebody Always Does." - Bill Vaughan
2982	"Government Is Not Reason; It Is Not Eloquent; It Is Force. Like Fire, It Is A Dangerous Servant And A Fearful Master." - George Washington
2983	"Life Is Better Than Death, I Believe, If Only Because It Is Less Boring, And Because It Has Fresh Peaches In It." - Alice Walker
2984	"I Don't Have To Write About The Future. For Most People, The Present Is Enough Like The Future To Be Pretty Scary." - William Gibson
2985	"History Is An Account, Mostly False, Of Events, Mostly Unimportant, Which Are Brought About By Rulers, Mostly Knaves, And Soldiers, Mostly Fools." - Ambrose Bierce
2986	"In The Business World, Everyone Is Paid In Two Coins: Cash And Experience. Take The Experience First; The Cash Will Come Later." - Harold S. Geneen
2987	"I've Been To War, And It's Not Easy To Kill. It's Bloody And Messy And Totally Horrifying, And The Consequences Are Serious." - Oliver Stone
2988	"The Research Rat Of The Future Allows Experimentation Without Manipulation Of The Real World. This Is The Cutting Edge Of Modeling Technology." - John Spencer
2989	"Baseball Happens To Be A Game Of Cumulative Tension But Football, Basketball And Hockey Are Played With Hand Grenades And Machine Guns." - John Leonard
2990	"Marriage - The State Or Condition Of A Community Consisting Of A Master, A Mistress, And Two Slaves, Making In All, Two." - Ambrose Bierce
2991	"Democracy Is The Only System That Persists In Asking The Powers That Be Whether They Are The Powers That Ought To Be." - Sydney J. Harris
2992	"We Are To Admit No More Causes Of Natural Things Than Such As Are Both True And Sufficient To Explain Their Appearances" - Isaac Newton
2993	"One's Mind Has A Way Of Making Itself Up In The Background, And It Suddenly Becomes Clear What One Means To Do." - A. C. Benson
2994	"The Fear Of Death Follows From The Fear Of Life. A Man Who Lives Fully Is Prepared To Die At Any Time." - Mark Twain
2995	"There Is A Boundary To Men's Passions When They Act From Feelings; But None When They Are Under The Influence Of Imagination." - Edmund Burke

2996	"People With Small Minds Talk About Other People. People With Average Minds Talk About Events. People With Great Minds Talk About Ideas " - Anonymous
2997	"The Most Tragic Paradox Of Our Time Is To Be Found In The Failure Of Nation-States To Recognize The Imperatives Of Internationalism." - Earl Warren
2998	"Ancient Rome Declined Because It Had A Senate, Now What's Going To Happen To Us With Both A House And A Senate?" - Will Rogers
2999	"When One May Pay Out Over Two Million Dollars To Presidential And Congressional Campaigns, The U.S. Government Is Virtually Up For Sale." - John W. Gardner
3000	"Keeping Books On Social Aid Is Capitalistic Nonsense. I Just Use The Money For The Poor. I Can't Stop To Count It." - Evita Peron
3001	"Information Technology And Business Are Becoming Inextricably Interwoven. I Don't Think Anybody Can Talk Meaningfully About One Without The Talking About The Other." - Bill Gates
3002	"The Final Test Of A Leader Is That He Leaves Behind Him In Other Men The Conviction And The Will To Carry On." - Walter Lippmann
3003	"Yosemite Valley, To Me, Is Always A Sunrise, A Glitter Of Green And Golden Wonder In A Vast Edifice Of Stone And Space." - Ansel Adams
3004	"It Takes Someone With A Vision Of The Possibilities To Attain New Levels Of Experience. Someone With The Courage To Live His Dreams." - Les Brown
3005	"Smartness Runs In My Family. When I Went To School I Was So Smart My Teacher Was In My Class For Five Years." - Gracie Allen
3006	"I Don't Think You Should Feel About A Film. You Should Feel About A Woman, Not A Movie. You Can't Kiss A Movie." - Jean-Luc Godard
3007	"It Is A Good Morning Exercise For A Research Scientist To Discard A Pet Hypothesis Every Day Before Breakfast. It Keeps Him Young." - Konrad Lorenz
3008	"God Writes A Lot Of Comedy... The Trouble Is, He's Stuck With So Many Bad Actors Who Don't Know How To Play Funny." - Garrison Keillor
3009	"If We All Worked On The Assumption That What Is Accepted As True Is Really True, There Would Be Little Hope For Advance." - Orville Wright
3010	"The March Of Science And Technology Does Not Imply Growing Intellectual Complexity In The Lives Of Most People. It Often Means The Opposite." - Thomas Sowell
3011	"Inanimate Objects Can Be Classified Scientifically Into Three Major Categories; Those That Don't Work, Those That Break Down And Those That Get Lost." - Russell Baker

145

3012	"Never Doubt That A Small Group Of Thoughtful Committed People Can Change The World; Indeed It Is The Only Thing That Ever Has." - Margaret Mead
3013	"No Man Who Worships Education Has Got The Best Out Of Education... Without A Gentle Contempt For Education No Man's Education Is Complete." - Gilbert K. Chesterton
3014	"How Can A Society That Exists On Instant Mashed Potatoes, Packaged Cake Mixes, Frozen Dinners, And Instant Cameras Teach Patience To Its Young?" - Paul Sweeney
3015	"You Can't Be Suspicious Of A Tree, Or Accuse A Bird Or A Squirrel Of Subversion Or Challenge The Ideology Of A Violet." - Hal Borland
3016	"There Is No Need For Temples, No Need For Complicated Philosophies. My Brain And My Heart Are My Temples; My Philosophy Is Kindness." - Dalai Lama
3017	"Dreams Pass Into The Reality Of Action. From The Actions Stems The Dream Again; And This Interdependence Produces The Highest Form Of Living." - Anais Nin
3018	"It Takes 20 Years To Build A Reputation And Five Minutes To Ruin It. If You Think About That, You'll Do Things Differently." - Warren Buffett
3019	" What We Have Done For Ourselves Alone Dies With Us; What We Have Done For Others And The World Remains And Are Immortal." - Albert Pike
3020	"Technology... Is A Queer Thing. It Brings You Great Gifts With One Hand, And It Stabs You In The Back With The Other." - Carrie P. Snow
3021	"Woe To The Man Whose Heart Has Not Learned While Young To Hope, To Love - And To Put Its Trust In Life." - Joseph Conrad
3022	"Usually, Terrible Things That Are Done With The Excuse That Progress Requires Them Are Not Really Progress At All, But Just Terrible Things." - Russell Baker
3023	"People From A Planet Without Flowers Would Think We Must Be Mad With Joy The Whole Time To Have Such Things About Us." - Iris Murdoch
3024	"You Know What Your Problem Is, It's That You Haven't Seen Enough Movies - All Of Life's Riddles Are Answered In The Movies." - Steve Martin
3025	"Many A Man Curses The Rain That Falls Upon His Head, And Knows Not That It Brings Abundance To Drive Away The Hunger." - Saint Basil
3026	"I'm Not Offended By All The Dumb Blonde Jokes Because I Know I'm Not Dumb... And I Also Know That I'm Not Blonde." - Dolly Parton
3027	"And The Day Came When The Risk To Remain Tight In A Bud Was More Painful Than The Risk It Took To Blossom." - Anais Nin

3028	"Poetry Is The Revelation Of A Feeling That The Poet Believes To Be Interior And Personal Which The Reader Recognizes As His Own." - Salvatore Quasimodo
3029	"One Thing You Learned As A Cubs Fan: When You Bought You Ticket, You Could Bank On Seeing The Bottom Of The Ninth." - Joe Garagiola
3030	"The Ultimate Secret To Living A Full Life Is In Man's Innate Ability To REFOCUS His Vision Rather Than To RETIRE His Dreams." - Richard Marvin Voigt
3031	"Death Most Resembles A Prophet Who Is Without Honor In His Own Land Or A Poet Who Is A Stranger Among His People." - Kahlil Gibran
3032	"Sometimes I Wonder If Men And Women Really Suit Each Other. Perhaps They Should Live Next Door And Just Visit Now And Then." - Katharine Hepburn
3033	"Success Is Like Death. The More Successful You Become, The Higher The Houses In The Hills Get And The Higher The Fences Get." - Kevin Spacey
3034	"All The King's Horses And All The King's Men Can't Put The Past Together Again. So Let's Remember: Don't Try To Saw Sawdust." - Dale Carnegie
3035	"I Have Great Hopes That We Shall Love Each Other All Our Lives As Much As If We Had Never Married At All." - Lord Byron
3036	"Let The Rain Kiss You. Let The Rain Beat Upon Your Head With Silver Liquid Drops. Let The Rain Sing You A Lullaby." - Langston Hughes
3037	"As Human Beings, Our Greatness Lies Not So Much In Being Able To Remake The World... As In Being Able To Remake Ourselves." - Mahatma Gandhi
3038	"Politics, It Seems To Me, For Years, Or All Too Long, Has Been Concerned With Right Or Left Instead Of Right Or Wrong." - Richard Armour
3039	"Baseball Is The Only Field Of Endeavor Where A Man Can Succeed Three Times Out Of Ten And Be Considered A Good Performer." - Ted Williams
3040	"It Is Important To Our Friends To Believe That We Are Unreservedly Frank With Them, And Important To Friendship That We Are Not." - Mignon Mclaughlin
3041	"Time Rushes Towards Us With Its Hospital Tray Of Infinitely Varied Narcotics, Even While It Is Preparing Us For Its Inevitably Fatal Operation." - Tennessee Williams
3042	"It's Said In Hollywood That You Should Always Forgive Your Enemies - Because You Never Know When You'll Have To Work With Them." - Lana Turner

3043	"One Of The Most Adventurous Things Left Us Is To Go To Bed. For No One Can Lay A Hand On Our Dreams." - E. V. Lucas
3044	"A Man May Fulfill The Object Of His Existence By Asking A Question He Cannot Answer, And Attempting A Task He Cannot Achieve." - Oliver Wendell Holmes
3045	"The Arts Are An Even Better Barometer Of What Is Happening In Our World Than The Stock Market Or The Debates In Congress." - Hendrik Willem Van Loon
3046	"When Hungry, Eat Your Rice; When Tired, Close Your Eyes. Fools May Laugh At Me, But Wise Men Will Know What I Mean." - Lin Chi
3047	"Definition Of A Statistician: A Man Who Believes Figures Don't Lie, But Admits Than Under Analysis Some Of Them Won't Stand Up Either." - Evan Esar
3048	"My Family Got All Over Me Because They Said Bush Is Only For The Rich People. Then I Reminded Them, 'Hey, I'm Rich'." - Charles Barkley
3049	"Reporters Thrive On The World's Misfortune. For This Reason They Often Take An Indecent Pleasure In Events That Dismay The Rest Of Humanity." - Russell Baker
3050	"To Himself Everyone Is Immortal; He May Know That He Is Going To Die, But He Can Never Know That He Is Dead." - Samuel Butler
3051	"Self-Managing Is Job One. Have A Vision And A Mission. Surround Yourself With Talented People. Rely On Effective Coaching, Not Managing Of Employees." - Tom Gegax
3052	"All My Life I Have Tried To Pluck A Thistle And Plant A Flower Wherever The Flower Would Grow In Thought And Mind." - Abraham Lincoln
3053	"Love Is That Splendid Triggering Of Human Vitality The Supreme Activity Which Nature Affords Anyone For Going Out Of Himself Toward Someone Else." - Jose Ortega Y Gasset
3054	"The Oppressed Are Allowed Once Every Few Years To Decide Which Particular Representatives Of The Oppressing Class Are To Represent And Repress Them." - Karl Marx
3055	"People Of Mediocre Ability Sometimes Achieve Outstanding Success Because They Don't Know When To Quit. Most People Succeed Because They Are Determined To." - George E. Allen
3056	"Basketball Is Like War In That Offensive Weapons Are Developed First, And It Always Takes A While For The Defense To Catch Up." - Red Auerbach
3057	"It Was Character That Got Us Out Of Bed, Commitment That Moved Us Into Action, And Discipline That Enabled Us To Follow Through." - Zig Ziglar

3058	"Confidence....Thrives Only On Honesty, On Honor, On The Sacredness Of Obligations, On Faithful Protection And On Unselfish Performance. Without Them, It Cannot Live." - Franklin D. Roosevelt
3059	"Love Is Always Bestowed As A Gift - Freely, Willingly And Without Expectation. We Don't Love To Be Loved; We Love To Love." - Leo Buscaglia
3060	"Business Is Never So Healthy As When, Like A Chicken, It Must Do A Certain Amount Of Scratching Around For What It Gets." - Henry Ford
3061	"I Think That There Is Nothing, Not Even Crime, More Opposed To Poetry, To Philosophy, Ay, To Life Itself Than This Incessant Business." - Henry David Thoreau
3062	"Art Is The Desire Of A Man To Express Himself, To Record The Reactions Of His Personality To The World He Lives In." - Amy Lowell
3063	"Poetry Is The Opening And Closing Of A Door, Leaving Those Who Look Through To Guess About What Is Seen During The Moment." - Carl Sandburg
3064	"If Jesus Had Been Killed Twenty Years Ago, Catholic School Children Would Be Wearing Little Electric Chairs Around Their Necks Instead Of Crosses." - Lenny Bruce
3065	"I Honestly Think It Is Better To Be A Failure At Something You Love Than To Be A Success At Something You Hate." - George Burns
3066	"A Most Important Key To Successful Leadership Is Your Ability To Direct And Challenge The Very Best That Is In Those Whom You Lead." - Anonymous
3067	"If You Are Carrying Strong Feelings About Something That Happened In Your Past, They May Hinder Your Ability To Live In The Present." - Les Brown
3068	"Beware Of Endeavoring To Become A Great Man In A Hurry. One Such Attempt In Ten Thousand May Succeed. These Are Fearful Odds." - Benjamin Disraeli
3069	" The Real Contest Is Always Between What You've Done And What You're Capable Of Doing. You Measure Yourself Against Yourself And Nobody Else." - Geoffrey Gaberino
3070	"Wisdom Stands At The Turn In The Road And Calls Upon Us Publicly, But We Consider It False And Despise Its Adherents - " - Kahlil Gibran
3071	"If One Morning I Walked On Top Of The Water Across The Potomac River, The Headline That Afternoon Would Read: President Can't Swim." - Lyndon B. Johnson
3072	"My Mother Taught Me Very Early To Believe I Could Achieve Any Accomplishment I Wanted To. The First Was To Walk Without Braces." - Wilma Rudolph

3073	"For It Was Not Into My Ear You Whispered, But Into My Heart. It Was Not My Lips You Kissed, But My Soul." - Judy Garland
3074	"Baseball Players Are Smarter Than Football Players. How Often Do You See A Baseball Team Penalized For Too Many Men On The Field?" - Jim Bouton
3075	"Boredom Is A Vital Problem For The Moralist, Since At Least Half The Sins Of Mankind Are Caused By The Fear Of It." - Bertrand Arthur William Russell
3076	"The Greatest Obstacle To Discovering The Shape Of The Earth, The Continents, And The Oceans Was Not Ignorance But The Illusion Of Knowledge." - Daniel Boorstin
3077	"We Peruse One Ideal, That Of Bringing People Together In Peace, Irrespective Of Race, Religion And Political Convictions, For The Benefit Of Mankind." - Juan Antonio Samaranch
3078	"Men Kick Friendship Around Like A Football, But It Doesn't Seem To Crack. Women Treat It Like Glass And It Goes To Pieces." - Anne Morrow Lindbergh
3079	"I Think The Most Important Factor In Getting Out Of The Recession Actually Is Just The Regenerative Capacity Of American Capitalism." - Warren Buffett
3080	"Let Go Of The Past And Go For The Future. Go Confidently In The Direction Of Your Dreams. Live The Life You've Imagined." - Henry David Thoreau
3081	"Where It Is A Duty To Worship The Sun It Is Pretty Sure To Be A Crime To Examine The Laws Of Heat." - John Morley
3082	"Democratic Nations Must Try To Find Ways To Starve The Terrorist And The Hijacker Of The Oxygen Of Publicity On Which They Depend." - Margaret Thatcher
3083	"It Isn't Tying Himself To One Woman That A Man Dreads When He Thinks Of Marrying; It's Separating Himself From All The Others." - Helen Rowland
3084	"For Disappearing Acts, It's Hard To Beat What Happens To The Eight Hours Supposedly Left After Eight Of Sleep And Eight Of Work." - Doug Larson
3085	"If You Want To Reach A Goal, You Must See The Reaching In Your Own Mind Before You Actually Arrive At Your Goal." - Zig Ziglar
3086	"A Lot Of People Don't Want To Make Their Own Decisions. They're Too Scared. It's Much Easier To Be Told What To Do." - Marilyn Manson
3087	"I Love Being Married. It's So Great To Find That One Special Person You Want To Annoy For The Rest Of Your Life." - Rita Rudner

3088	"What We Have Done For Ourselves Alone Dies With Us; What We Have Done For Others And The World Remains And Is Immortal." - Albert Pike
3089	"Business, More Than Any Other Occupation, Is A Continual Dealing With The Future; It Is A Continual Calculation, An Instinctive Exercise In Foresight." - Henry R. Luce
3090	"I Never Did Very Well In Math - I Could Never Seem To Persuade The Teacher That I Hadn't Meant My Answers Literally." - Calvin Trillin
3091	" Though No One Can Go Back And Make A Brand New Start, Anyone Can Start From Now And Make A Brand New Ending." - Anonymous
3092	"When I Have A Terrible Need Of - Shall I Say The Word - Religion. Then I Go Out And Paint The Stars." - Vincent Van Gogh
3093	"There Is No Such Thing As A Person That Nothing Has Happened To, And Each Person's Story Is As Different As His Fingertips." - Elsa Lanchester
3094	"Heroism On Command, Senseless Violence, And All The Loathsome Nonsense That Goes By The Name Of Patriotism - How Passionately I Hate Them!" - Albert Einstein
3095	"My Grandmother Started Walking Five Miles A Day When She Was Sixty. She's Ninety-Seven Now, And We Don't Know Where The Hell She Is." - Ellen Degeneres
3096	"Everything Is Blooming Most Recklessly; If It Were Voices Instead Of Colors, There Would Be An Unbelievable Shrieking Into The Heart Of The Night." - Rainer Maria Rilke
3097	"Abundance Has Made It Possible To Extend The Quest For Self-Realization From A Minute Fraction Of The Population To Almost The Whole Of It." - Robert William Fogel
3098	"When You Get Right Down To The Root Of The Meaning Of The Word 'Succeed,' You Find That It Simply Means To Follow Through." - F. W. Nichol
3099	"The Sun, The Moon And The Stars Would Have Disappeared Long Ago... Had They Happened To Be Within The Reach Of Predatory Human Hands." - Henry Ellis
3100	" In A World Where There Is So Much To Be Done, I Felt Strongly Impressed That There Must Be Something For Me To Do." - Dorothea Dix
3101	"Those Little Nimble Musicians Of The Air, That Warble Forth Their Curious Ditties, With Which Nature Hath Furnished Them To The Shame Of Art." - Izaak Walton
3102	"Education Is An Admirable Thing, But It Is Well To Remember From Time To Time That Nothing That Is Worth Knowing Can Be Taught." - Oscar Wilde

3103	"Middle Age Is The Time When A Man Is Always Thinking That In A Week Or Two He Will Feel As Good As Ever." - Don Marquis
3104	"Create A Definite Plan For Carrying Out Your Desire And Begin At Once, Whether You Ready Or Not, To Put This Plan Into Action." - Napoleon Hill
3105	"The Direct Use Of Force Is Such A Poor Solution To Any Problem, It Is Generally Employed Only By Small Children And Large Nations." - David Friedman
3106	"Overall The Fundamentals Seem To Be There And He's Obviously Got A Very Mature Head On His Shoulders. He's Got A Kind Of Presence." - Nick Price
3107	"I'm So Fast That Last Night I Turned Off The Light Switch In My Bed-room And Was In Bed Before The Room Was Dark." - Muhammad Ali
3108	"Knowledge Will Forever Govern Ignorance; And A People Who Mean To Be Their Own Governors Must Arm Themselves With The Power Which Knowledge Gives." - James Madison
3109	"I Do Not Bring Forgiveness With Me, Nor Forgetfulness. The Only Ones Who Can Forgive Are Dead; The Living Have No Right To Forget." - Chaim Herzog
3110	"We Succeed In Enterprises Which Demand The Positive Qualities We Possess, But We Excel In Those Which Can Also Make Use Of Our Defects." - Alexis De Tocqueville
3111	"Imagination Was Given To Man To Compensate Him For What He Is Not; A Sense Of Humor To Console Him For What He Is." - Francis Bacon
3112	"Computers Are Magnificent Tools For The Realization Of Our Dreams, But No Machine Can Replace The Human Spark Of Spirit, Compassion, Love, And Understanding." - Louis Gerstner
3113	"When A Machine Begins To Run Without Human Aid, It Is Time To Scrap It - Whether It Be A Factory Or A Government." - Alexander Chase
3114	"I Always Try To Balance The Light With The Heavy - A Few Tears Of Human Spirit In With The Sequins And The Fringes." - Bette Midler
3115	"A Man Marries To Have A Home, But Also Because He Doesn't Want To Be Bothered With Sex And All That Sort Of Thing." - W. Somerset Maugham
3116	"Common Sense And A Sense Of Humor Are The Same Thing, Moving At Different Speeds. A Sense Of Humor Is Just Common Sense, Dancing." - William James
3117	"It Is Possible To Provide Security Against Other Ills, But As Far As Death Is Concerned, We Men Live In A City Without Walls." - Epicurus

3118	"I Never Looked At The Consequences Of Missing A Big Shot... When You Think About The Consequences You Always Think Of A Negative Result." - Michael Jordan
3119	"We Are Not Animals. We Are Not A Product Of What Has Happened To Us In Our Past. We Have The Power Of Choice." - Stephen Covey
3120	"Nothing Has Such Power To Broaden The Mind As The Ability To Investigate Systematically And Truly All That Comes Under Thy Observation In Life." - Marcus Aurelius
3121	"From Now On We Live In A World Where Man Has Walked On The Moon. It's Not A Miracle; We Just Decided To Go." - Tom Hanks
3122	"We Are Not Held Back By The Love We Didn't Receive In The Past, But By The Love We're Not Extending In The Present." - Marianne Williamson
3123	"Love Is Much Nicer To Be In Than An Automobile Accident, A Tight Girdle, A Higher Tax Bracket Or A Holding Pattern Over Philadelphia." - Judith Viorst
3124	"I Know Many Writers Who First Dictate Passages, Then Polish What They Have Dictated. I Speak, Then I Polish – Occasionally I Do Windows." - Edward Koch
3125	"When We Do The Best That We Can, We Never Know What Miracle Is Wrought In Our Life, Or In The Life Of Another." - Helen Keller
3126	"For A Lot Of People, The Weekly Paycheck Is Take-Home Pay Because Home Is The Only Place They Can Afford To Go With It." - Charles A. Jaffe
3127	"A Rock Pile Ceases To Be A Rock Pile The Moment A Single Man Contemplates It, Bearing Within Him The Image Of A Cathedral." - Antoine De Saint-Exupery
3128	"What's Sort Of Interesting About The Whole Public Relations Disaster That Is The Net, In Some Ways, Is That The Fundamentals Are Really Good." - Meg Whitman
3129	"If You've Had Wonderful Family Relationships, You Will Be Able To Call Yourself A True Success In Life No Matter What Else You've Achieved." - Vic Conant
3130	"For Every Failure, There's An Alternative Course Of Action. You Just Have To Find It. When You Come To A Roadblock, Take A Detour." - Mary Kay Ash
3131	"Teach This Triple Truth To All: A Generous Heart, Kind Speech, And A Life Of Service And Compassion Are The Things, Which Renew Humanity." - The Buddha
3132	"I've Said That Playing The Blues Is Like Having To Be Black Twice. Stevie Ray Vaughan Missed On Both Counts, But I Never Noticed." - B. B. King

153

3133	"What Law, What Reason Can Deny That Gift So Sweet, So Natural That God Has Given A Stream, A Fish, A Beast, A Bird?" - Pedro Calderon De La Barca
3134	"The Internet Is Not Just One Thing, It's A Collection Of Things – Of Numerous Communications Networks That All Speak The Same Digital Language." - Jim Clark
3135	"The Deliberate And Deadly Attacks Which Were Carried Out Yesterday Against Our Country Were More Than Acts Of Terror. They Were Acts Of War." - George W. Bush
3136	"Creative Ideas Reside In People's Minds But Are Trapped By Fear Or Rejection. Create A Judgment-Free Environment And You'll Unleash A Torrent Of Creativity." - Alex Osborn
3137	"The First Responsibility Of A Leader Is To Define Reality. The Last Is To Say Thank You. In Between, The Leader Is A Servant." - Max De Pree
3138	"Recounting Of A Life Story, A Mind Thinking Aloud Leads One Inevitably To The Consideration Of Problems Which Are No Longer Psychological But Spiritual." - Paul Tournier
3139	"If You Put Yourself In A Position Where You Have To Stretch Outside Your Comfort Zone, Then You Are Forced To Expand Your Consciousness." - Les Brown
3140	"For A Lot Of People, The Weekly Paycheck Is "Take-Home Pay" Because Home Is The Only Place They Can Afford To Go With It." - Charles A. Jaffe
3141	"In Old Age We Are Like A Batch Of Letters That Someone Has Sent. We Are No Longer In The Past, We Have Arrived." - Knut Hamsun
3142	"Don't Let Your Ego Get Too Close To Your Position, So That If Your Position Gets Shot Down, Your Ego Doesn't Go With It." - Colin Powell
3143	"So Many Of Our Dreams At First Seem Impossible, Then They Seem Improbable, And Then, When We Summon The Will, They Soon Become Inevitable." - Christopher Reeve
3144	"I Found I Could Say Things With Color And Shapes That I Couldn't Say Any Other Way - Things I Had No Words For." - Georgia O'keeffe
3145	"Regret For The Things We Did Can Be Tempered By Time; It Is Regret For The Things We Did Not Do That Is Inconsolable." - Sydney J. Harris
3146	"Movies Can And Do Have Tremendous Influence In Shaping Young Lives In The Realm Of Entertainment Towards The Ideals And Objectives Of Normal Adulthood." - Walt Disney
3147	"The Beef Industry Has Contributed To More American Deaths Than All The Wars Of This Century, All Natural Disasters, And All Automobile Accidents Combined." - Neal Barnard

3148	"The Democracy Will Cease To Exist When You Take Away From Those Who Are Willing To Work And Give To Those Who Would Not." - Thomas Jefferson
3149	"You Will Never Change Your Life Until You Change Something You Do Daily. The Secret Of Your Success Is Found In Your Daily Routine." - John C. Maxwell
3150	"Citizen Kane Is Perhaps The One American Talking Picture That Seems As Fresh Now As The Day It Opened. It May Seem Even Fresher." - Pauline Kael
3151	"Old Age Adds To The Respect Due To Virtue, But It Takes Nothing From The Contempt Inspired By Vice; It Whitens Only The Hair." - Ira Gershwin
3152	"When You Get Right Down To The Root Of The Meaning Of The Word Succeed, You Find That It Simply Means To Follow Through." - F. W. Nichol
3153	"I Was The Kind Nobody Thought Could Make It. I Had A Funny Boston Accent. I Couldn't Pronounce My R's. I Wasn't A Beauty." - Barbara Walters
3154	"He Who Draws Noble Delights From Sentiments Of Poetry Is A True Poet, Though He Has Never Written A Line In All His Life." - George Sand
3155	"Isn't It Enough To See That A Garden Is Beautiful Without Having To Believe That There Are Fairies At The Bottom Of It Too?" - Douglas Adams
3156	" Success Is Not The Key To Happiness. Happiness Is The Key To Success. If You Love What You Are Doing, You Will Be Successful." - Albert Schweitzer
3157	"If You Press Me To Say Why I Loved Him, I Can Say No More Than Because He Was He, And I Was I." - Michel De Montaigne
3158	" I Am More Afraid Of An Army Of 100 Sheep Led By A Lion Than An Army Of 100 Lions Led By A Sheep." - Charles Maurice de Talleyrand
3159	"Nobody Climbs Mountains For Scientific Reasons. Science Is Used To Raise Money For The Expeditions, But You Really Climb For The Hell Of It." - Edmund Hillary
3160	"Courage Does Not Always Roar. Sometimes It Is A Quiet Voice At The End Of The Day That Says, "I Will Try Again Tomorrow."" - Anonymous
3161	"We All Have Dreams. But In Order To Make Dreams Come Into Reality, It Takes An Awful Lot Of Determination, Dedication, Self-Discipline, And Effort." - Jesse Owens
3162	"In Films Murders Are Always Very Clean. I Show How Difficult It Is And What A Messy Thing It Is To Kill A Man." - Alfred Hitchcock

3163	"The Happiness Of Your Life Depends Upon The Quality Of Your Thoughts....Take Care That You Entertain No Notions Unsuitable To Virtue And Reasonable Nature." - Marcus Aurelius
3164	"I Doubt That The Imagination Can Be Suppressed. If You Truly Eradicated It In A Child, He Would Grow Up To Be An Eggplant." - Ursula K. Le Guin
3165	"If You Make Learning Fun And Interesting You Will Most Likely Retain That Knowledge And Benefit Greatly In Both Your Professional And Personal Life." - Blaine Athorn
3166	"Holding Anger Is Like Grasping A Hot Coal With The Intent Of Throwing It At Someone Else; You Are The One Who Gets Burned." - The Buddha
3167	"Friendship Is Unnecessary, Like Philosophy, Like Art... It Has No Survival Value; Rather It Is One Of Those Things That Give Value To Survival." - C. S. Lewis
3168	"It Is Better To Be Violent, If There Is Violence In Our Hearts, Than To Put On The Cloak Of Nonviolence To Cover Impotence." - Mohandas Gandhi
3169	"And This, Our Life, Exempt From Public Haunt, Finds Tongues In Trees, Books In The Running Brooks, Sermons In Stones, And Good In Everything." - William Shakespeare
3170	"Take Young Researchers, Put Them Together In Virtual Seclusion, Give Them An Unprecedented Degree Of Freedom And Turn Up The Pressure By Fostering Competitiveness." - James D. Watson
3171	" To Achieve The Impossible, One Must Think The Absurd; To Look Where Everyone Else Has Looked, But To See What No Else Has Seen."" - Anonymous
3172	"The Protean Nature Of The Computer Is Such That It Can Act Like A Machine Or Like A Language To Be Shaped And Exploited." - Alan Kay
3173	"In Times Of Change Learners Inherit The Earth; While The Learned Find Themselves Beautifully Equipped To Deal With A World That No Longer Exists." - Eric Hoffer
3174	"I Value The Friend Who For Me Finds Time On His Calendar, But I Cherish The Friend Who For Me Does Not Consult His Calendar." - Robert Brault
3175	"The Genius Of A Good Leader Is To Leave Behind Him A Situation Which Common Sense, Without The Grace Of Genius, Can Deal With Successfully." - Walter Lippmann
3176	"If You Set Goals And Go After Them With All The Determination You Can Muster, Your Gifts Will Take You Places That Will Amaze You." - Les Brown

3177	"Every Day I Get Up And Look Through The Forbes List Of The Richest People In America. If I'm Not There, I Go To Work." - Robert Orben
3178	"If There Are No Stupid Questions, Then What Kind Of Questions Do Stupid People Ask? Do They Get Smart Just In Time To Ask Questions?" - Scott Adams
3179	"All Who Call On God In True Faith, Earnestly From The Heart, Will Certainly Be Heard, And Will Receive What They Have Asked And Desired." - Martin Luther
3180	"It Is Not In The Nature Of Politics That The Best Men Should Be Elected. The Best Men Do Not Want To Govern Their Fellowmen." - George Macdonald
3181	"There Are Those Who Look At Things The Way They Are, And Ask Why... I Dream Of Things That Never Were, And Ask Why Not?" - Robert Kennedy
3182	"It May Not Always Be Profitable At First For Businesses To Be Online, But It Is Certainly Going To Be Unprofitable Not To Be Online." - Esther Dyson
3183	"Success In Almost Any Field Depends More On Energy And Drive Than It Does On Intelligence. This Explains Why We Have So Many Stupid Leaders." - Sloan Wilson
3184	"Forgiveness Is The Remission Of Sins. For It Is By This That What Has Been Lost, And Was Found, Is Saved From Being Lost Again." - Saint Augustine
3185	"Life Is A Series Of Collisions With The Future; It Is Not The Sum Of What We Have Been, But What We Yearn To Be." - Jose Ortega Y Gasset
3186	"Today The World Changes So Quickly That In Growing Up We Take Leave Not Just Of Youth But Of The World We Were Young In." - Peter Medawar
3187	"Do You Know The Difference Between Education And Experience? Education Is When You Read The Fine Print; Experience Is What You Get When You Don't." - Pete Seeger
3188	"The Fleet Sailed To Its War Base In The North Sea, Headed Not So Much For Some Rendezvous With Glory As For Rendezvous With Discretion." - Barbara Tuchman
3189	"As Athletes, We're Used To Reacting Quickly. Here, It's 'Come, Stop, Come, Stop.' There's A Lot Of Downtime. That's The Toughest Part Of The Day." - Michael Jordan
3190	"The Modern Conservative Is Engaged In One Of Man's Oldest Exercises In Moral Philosophy; That Is, The Search For A Superior Moral Justification For Selfishness." - John Kenneth Galbraith

3191	"The Person Who Gets The Farthest Is Generally The One Who Is Willing To Do And Dare. The Sure-Thing Boat Never Gets Far From Shore." - Dale Carnegie
3192	"I Love America More Than Any Other Country In This World, And, Exactly For This Reason, I Insist On The Right To Criticize Her Perpetually." - James A. Baldwin
3193	"Upon The Plains Of Hesitation Bleach The Bones Of Countless Millions, Who When On The Dawn Of Victory Paused To Rest, And There Resting Died." - John Dretschmer
3194	"Be Careful To Leave Your Sons Well Instructed Rather Than Rich, For The Hopes Of The Instructed Are Better Than The Wealth Of The Ignorant." - Epictetus
3195	"Love Is The Word Used To Label The Sexual Excitement Of The Young, The Habituation Of The Middle-Aged, And The Mutual Dependence Of The Old." - John Ciardi
3196	"Don't You Stay At Home Of Evenings? Don You Love A Cushioned Seat In A Corner, By The Fireside, With Your Slippers On Your Feet?" - Oliver Wendell Holmes
3197	"Perseverance Is More Prevailing Than Violence And Many Things Which Cannot Be Overcome When They Are Together Yield Themselves Up When Taken Little By Little." - Plutarch
3198	"Even When Poetry Has A Meaning, As It Usually Has, It May Be Inadvisable To Draw It Out... Perfect Understanding Will Sometimes Almost Extinguish Pleasure." - A. E. Housman
3199	"The Majority Of Men Meet With Failure Because Of Their Lack Of Persistence In Creating New Plans To Take The Place Of Those Which Fail." - Napoleon Hill
3200	"Anger Is An Acid That Can Do More Harm To The Vessel In Which It Is Stored Than To Anything On Which It Is Poured." - Mark Twain
3201	"He Hits It Long. His Shoulders Are Impressively Quick Through The Ball. That's Where He's Getting His Power From. He's Young And Has Great Elasticity." - Nick Faldo
3202	"Posterity: You Will Never Know How Much It Has Cost My Generation To Preserve Your Freedom. I Hope You Will Make Good Use Of It." - John Quincy Adams
3203	"We Will Create A Civilization Of The Mind In Cyberspace. May It Be More Humane And Fair Than The World Your Governments Have Made Before." - John Perry Barlow
3204	"It Is A Common Experience That A Problem Difficult At Night Is Resolved In The Morning After The Committee Of Sleep Has Worked On It." - John Steinbeck

3205	"A Diplomat Is A Person Who Can Tell You To Go To Hell In Such A Way That You Actually Look Forward To The Trip." - Caskie Stinnett
3206	" It Is Common Sense To Take A Method And Try It. If It Fails, Admit It Frankly And Try Another. But Above All, Try Something." - Franklin D. Roosevelt
3207	"You Can Learn To Acquire Vast Amounts Of Wealth By Learning To Think Like The Men And Women Who Have Already Achieved Wealth And Success" - Napoleon Hill
3208	"Everybody Needs Beauty As Well As Bread, Places To Play In And Pray In, Where Nature May Heal And Give Strength To Body And Soul." - John Muir
3209	"A Cardinal Principle Of Total Quality Escapes Too Many Managers: You Cannot Continuously Improve Interdependent Systems And Processes Until You Progressively Perfect Interdependent, Interpersonal Relationships." - Stephen Covey
3210	"Experience Shows That Success Is Due Less To Ability Than To Zeal. The Winner Is He Who Gives Himself To His Work, Body And Soul." - Sir Thomas Fowell Buxton
3211	"To Make Us Feel Small In The Right Way Is A Function Of Art; Men Can Only Make Us Feel Small In The Wrong Way." - E. M. Forster
3212	" The Entrepreneur Is Essentially A Visualized And Actualized... He Can Visualize Something, And When He Visualizes It He Sees Exactly How To Make It Happen." - Robert L. Schwartz
3213	"To Hear Some Men Talk Of The Government, You Would Suppose That Congress Was The Law Of Gravitation, And Kept The Planets In Their Places." - Wendell Phillips
3214	"Hockey Is A Sport For White Men. Basketball Is A Sport For Black Men. Golf Is A Sport For White Men Dressed Like Black Pimps." - Tiger Woods
3215	"If The Grandfather Of The Grandfather Of Jesus Had Known What Was Hidden Within Him, He Would Have Stood Humble And Awe-Struck Before His Soul." - Kahlil Gibran
3216	"What Is A Scientist After All? It Is A Curious Man Looking Through A Keyhole, The Keyhole Of Nature, Trying To Know What's Going On." - Jacques Yves Cousteau
3217	"Success Is To Be Measured Not So Much By The Position That One Has Reached In Life As By The Obstacles Which He Has Overcome." - Booker T. Washington
3218	"New Yorkers Love It When You Spill Your Guts Out There. Spill Your Guts At Wimbledon And They Make You Stop And Clean It Up." - Jimmy Carter

3219	"All Of Us Failed To Match Our Dreams Of Perfection. So I Rate Us On The Basis Of Our Splendid Failure To Do The Impossible." - William Faulkner
3220	"To Live Anywhere In The World Today And Be Against Equality Because Of Race Or Color Is Like Living In Alaska And Being Against Snow." - William Faulkner
3221	"From The Equality Of Rights Springs Identity Of Our Highest Interests; You Cannot Subvert Your Neighbor's Rights Without Striking A Dangerous Blow At Your Own." - Carl Schurz
3222	"The Most Important Quality In A Leader Is That Of Being Acknowledged As Such. All Leaders Whose Fitness Is Questioned Are Clearly Lacking In Force." - Andre Maurois
3223	"Dad, I'm In Some Trouble. There's Been An Accident And You're Going To Hear All Sorts Of Things About Me From Now On. Terrible Things." - Edward Kennedy
3224	"It Is Easier To Lead Men To Combat, Stirring Up Their Passion, Than To Restrain Them And Direct Them Toward The Patient Labors Of Peace." - Andre Gide
3225	"The Greater The State, The More Wrong And Cruel Its Patriotism, And The Greater Is The Sum Of Suffering Upon Which Its Power Is Founded." - Leo Tolstoy
3226	"All That We Are Is The Result Of What We Have Thought. If A Man Speaks Or Acts With An Evil Thought, Pain Follows Him." - The Buddha
3227	"In Every Marriage More Than A Week Old, There Are Grounds For Divorce. The Trick Is To Find, And Continue To Find, Grounds For Marriage." - Robert Anderson
3228	"You Can Safely Assume That You've Created God In Your Own Image When It Turns Out That God Hates All The Same People You Do." - Anne Lamott
3229	"God Has Cared For These Trees, Saved Them From Drought, Disease, Avalanches, And A Thousand Tempests And Floods. But He Cannot Save Them From Fools." - John Muir
3230	"In Science, The Forces Are The Fundamental Energies Of The Universe. In Speculation, The Forces Are The Billion-Dollar Tides And Currents Of The Market Place." - Eugene M. Schwartz
3231	"It Is Art That Makes Life, Makes Interest, Makes Importance... And I Know Of No Substitute Whatever For The Force And Beauty Of Its Process." - Henry James
3232	"Lying In Bed Would Be An Altogether Perfect And Supreme Experience If Only One Had A Colored Pencil Long Enough To Draw On The Ceiling." - Gilbert K. Chesterton

3233	"A Man To Carry On A Successful Business Must Have Imagination. He Must See Things As In A Vision, A Dream Of The Whole Thing." - Charles M. Schwab
3234	"Man Does Not Weave This Web Of Life. He Is Merely A Strand Of It. Whatever He Does To The Web, He Does To Himself." - Chief Seattle
3235	"What We Think, Or What We Know, Or What We Believe Is, In The End, Of Little Consequence. The Only Consequence Is What We Do." - John Ruskin
3236	"It Isn't Enough To Talk About Peace. One Must Believe In It. And It Isn't Enough To Believe In It. One Must Work At It." - Eleanor Roosevelt
3237	"I Love To Think Of Nature As An Unlimited Broadcasting Station, Through Which God Speaks To Us Every Hour, If We Will Only Tune In." - George Washington Carver
3238	"The World Is Governed More By Appearance Than Realities So That It Is Fully As Necessary To Seem To Know Something As To Know It." - Daniel Webster
3239	"You Must Have Been Warned Against Letting The Golden Hours Slip By; But Some Of Them Are Golden Only Because We Let Them Slip By." - James M. Barrie
3240	"Art Produces Ugly Things Which Frequently Become More Beautiful With Time. Fashion, On The Other Hand, Produces Beautiful Things Which Always Become Ugly With Time." - Jean Cocteau
3241	"I Think We Dream So We Don't Have To Be Apart So Long. If We're In Each Other's Dreams, We Can Play Together All Night." - Bill Watterson
3242	"It's Better To Hang Out With People Better Than You. Pick Out Associ-ates Whose Behavior Is Better Than Yours And You'll Drift In That Direction." - Warren Buffett
3243	"The Concept Of Two People Living Together For 25 Years Without A Serious Dispute Suggests A Lack Of Spirit Only To Be Admired In Sheep." - A. P. Herbert
3244	"Just In Terms Of Allocation Of Time Resources, Religion Is Not Very Efficient. There's A Lot More I Could Be Doing On A Sunday Morning." - Bill Gates
3245	"Society Is One Vast Conspiracy For Carving One Into The Kind Of Statue Likes, And Then Placing It In The Most Convenient Niche It Has." - Randolph Bourne
3246	"When A Friend Is In Trouble, Don't Annoy Him By Asking If There Is Anything You Can Do. Think Up Something Appropriate And Do It." - Edward W. Howe

3247	"The Human Race's Prospects Of Survival Were Considerably Better When We Were Defenseless Against Tigers Than They Are Today When We Have Become Defenseless Against Ourselves." - Arnold J. Toynbee
3248	"Something As Curious As The Monarchy Won't Survive Unless You Take Account Of People's Attitudes. After All, If People Don't Want It, They Won't Have It." - Prince Charles
3249	"They Died Hard, Those Savage Men - Like Wounded Wolves At Bay. They Were Filthy, And They Were Lousy, And They Stunk. And I Loved Them." - Douglas Macarthur
3250	"Holding On To Anger Is Like Grasping A Hot Coal With The Intent Of Throwing It At Someone Else; You Are The One Who Gets Burned." - The Buddha
3251	"Every Few Seconds It Changes - Up An Eighth, Down An Eighth -It's Like Playing A Slot Machine. I Lose $20 Million, I Gain $20 Million." - Ted Turner
3252	"Our Greatest Lack Is Not Money For Any Undertaking, But Rather Ideas. If The Ideas Are Good, Cash Will Somehow Flow To Where It Is Needed." - Robert Schuller
3253	"When I See A Bird That Walks Like A Duck And Swims Like A Duck And Quacks Like A Duck, I Call That Bird A Duck." - James Whitcomb Riley
3254	"Faith Indeed Tells What The Senses Do Not Tell, But Not The Contrary Of What They See. It Is Above Them And Not Contrary To Them." - Blaise Pascal
3255	"When I Find Myself In The Company Of Scientists, I Feel Like A Shabby Curate Who Has Strayed By Mistake Into A Room Full Of Dukes." - W. H. Auden
3256	"All Men Whilst They Are Awake Are In One Common World: But Each Of Them, When He Is Asleep, Is In A World Of His Own." - Plutarch
3257	"The Real Test Of Friendship Is: Can You Literally Do Nothing With The Other Person? Can You Enjoy Those Moments Of Life That Are Utterly Simple?" - Eugene Kennedy
3258	"In Modern Business It Is Not The Crook Who Is To Be Feared Most, It Is The Honest Man Who Doesn't Know What He Is Doing." - William Wordsworth
3259	"The Sculptor Produces The Beautiful Statue By Chipping Away Such Parts Of The Marble Block As Are Not Needed - It Is A Process Of Elimination." - Elbert Hubbard

3260	"Government Is An Unnecessary Evil. Human Beings, When Accustomed To Taking Responsibility For Their Own Behavior, Can Cooperate On A Basis Of Mutual Trust And Helpfulness." - Fred Woodworth
3261	"Sorrows Gather Around Great Souls As Storms Do Around Mountains; But, Like Them, They Break The Storm And Purify The Air Of The Plain Beneath Them." - Jean Paul
3262	"The Difference Between A Successful Person And Others Is Not A Lack Of Strength, Not A Lack Of Knowledge, But Rather In A Lack Of Will." - Vincent T. Lombardi
3263	"I Hate Facts. I Always Say The Chief End Of Man Is To Form General Propositions - Adding That No General Proposition Is Worth A Damn." - Oliver Wendell Holmes
3264	"He Hoped And Prayed That There Wasn't An Afterlife. Then He Realized There Was A Contradiction Involved Here And Merely Hoped That There Wasn't An Afterlife." - Douglas Adams
3265	" If You Want To Be Successful, Find Someone Who Has Achieved The Results You Want And Copy What They Do And You'll Achieve The Same Results." - Anthony Robbins
3266	"It Is Not Light That We Need, But Fire; It Is Not The Gentle Shower, But Thunder. We Need The Storm, The Whirlwind, And The Earthquake." - Frederick Douglass
3267	"If You Live To Be A Hundred, I Want To Live To Be A Hundred Minus One Day So I Never Have To Live Without You." - A. A. Milne
3268	"Wars And Elections Are Both Too Big And Too Small To Matter In The Long Run. The Daily Work - That Goes On, It Adds Up." - Barbara Kingsolver
3269	"Carry Out A Random Act Of Kindness, With No Expectation Of Reward, Safe In The Knowledge That One Day Someone Might Do The Same For You." - Princess Diana
3270	"In The Sky, There Is No Distinction Of East And West; People Create Distinctions Out Of Their Own Minds And Then Believe Them To Be True." - The Buddha
3271	"We Live In A Moment Of History Where Change Is So Speeded Up That We Begin To See The Present Only When It Is Already Disappearing." - R. D. Laing
3272	"You Must Not Lose Faith In Humanity. Humanity Is An Ocean; If A Few Drops Of The Ocean Are Dirty, The Ocean Does Not Become Dirty." - Mohandas Gandhi
3273	"You Can Make A Lot Of Money In This Game. Just Ask My Ex-Wives. Both Of Them Are So Rich That Neither Of Their Husbands Work." - Lee Trevino

3274	"All Who Have Accomplished Great Things Have Had A Great Aim, Have Fixed Their Gaze On A Goal Which Was High, One Which Sometimes Seemed Impossible." - Orison Swett Marden
3275	"Ohio Claims They Are Due A President As They Haven't Had One Since Taft. Look At The United States, They Have Not Had One Since Lincoln." - Will Rogers
3276	"What The Mass Media Offers Is Not Popular Art, But Entertainment Which Is Intended To Be Consumed Like Food, Forgotten, And Replaced By A New Dish." - W. H. Auden
3277	"Golf Appeals To The Idiot In Us And The Child. Just How Childlike Golf Players Become Is Proven By Their Frequent Inability To Count Past Five." - John Updike
3278	"Nor Shall Derision Prove Powerful Against Those Who Listen To Humanity Or Those Who Follow In The Footsteps Of Divinity, For They Shall Live Forever. Forever." - Kahlil Gibran
3279	"To Be Idle Is A Short Road To Death And To Be Diligent Is A Way Of Life; Foolish People Are Idle, Wise People Are Diligent." - The Buddha
3280	"Nature Teaches More Than She Preaches. There Are No Sermons In Stones. It Is Easier To Get A Spark Out Of A Stone Than A Moral." - John Burroughs
3281	"There Are Two Kinds Of Companies, Those That Work To Try To Charge More And Those That Work To Charge Less. We Will Be The Second." - Jeff Bezos
3282	"Banks Have A New Image. Now You Have 'A Friend,' Your Friendly Banker. If The Banks Are So Friendly, How Come They Chain Down The Pens?" - Alan King
3283	"The Best Things In Life Have Little To Do With Money Or Success. They Are Based On Heart, Compassion, And Allowing Others To Express Their Passions." - Declan Dunn
3284	"The Measure Of Success Is Not Whether You Have A Tough Problem To Deal With, But Whether It Is The Same Problem You Had Last Year." - John Foster Dulles
3285	"If Human Beings Are Fundamentally Good, No Government Is Necessary; If They Are Fundamentally Bad, Any Government, Being Composed Of Human Beings, Would Be Bad Also." - Fred Woodworth
3286	"I Think That People Want Peace So Much That One Of These Days Government Had Better Get Out Of Their Way And Let Them Have It." - Dwight D. Eisenhower
3287	"Formerly, When Religion Was Strong And Science Weak, Men Mistook Magic For Medicine; Now, When Science Is Strong And Religion Weak, Men Mistake Medicine For Magic." - Thomas Szasz

3288	"In The Democracy Of The Dead All Men At Last Are Equal. There Is Neither Rank Nor Station Nor Prerogative In The Republic Of The Grave." - John James Ingalls
3289	"Imagination Has Brought Mankind Through The Dark Ages To Its Present State Of Civilization. Imagination Led Columbus To Discover America. Imagination Led Franklin To Discover Electricity." - L. Frank Baum
3290	"I've Been Called Many Names Like Perfectionist, Difficult And Obsessive. I Think It Takes Obsession, Takes Searching For The Details For Any Artist To Be Good." - Barbra Streisand
3291	" Instead Of Thinking About Where You Are, Think About Where You Want To Be. It Takes Twenty Years Of Hard Work To Become An Overnight Success." - Diana Rankin
3292	"If You Can't Sleep, Then Get Up And Do Something Instead Of Lying There Worrying. It's The Worry That Gets You, Not The Lack Of Sleep" - Dale Carnegie
3293	"Fear Is The Path To The Dark Side. Fear Leads To Anger, Anger Leads To Hate; Hate Leads To Suffering. I Sense Much Fear In You." - Yoda
3294	"Society Is One Vast Conspiracy For Carving One Into The Kind Of Statue It Likes, And Then Placing It In The Most Convenient Niche It Has." - Randolph Bourne
3295	"Nature Will Bear The Closest Inspection. She Invites Us To Lay Our Eye Level With Her Smallest Leaf, And Take An Insect View Of Its Plain." - Henry David Thoreau
3296	"A Poet's Work Is To Name The Unnamable, To Point At Frauds, To Take Sides, Start Arguments, Shape The World, And Stop It Going To Sleep." - Salman Rushdie
3297	"Open Markets Offer The Only Realistic Hope Of Pulling Billions Of People In Developing Countries Out Of Abject Poverty, While Sustaining Prosperity In The Industrialized World." - Kofi Annan
3298	"It Is A Mistake For A Sculptor Or A Painter To Speak Or Write Very Often About His Job. It Releases Tension Needed For His Work." - Henry Moore
3299	"Television Is Not So Much Interested In The Business Of Communications As In The Business Of Delivering Audiences To Advertisers. The Shows Are Merely The Bait." - Les Brown
3300	"Economists Report That A College Education Adds Many Thousands Of Dollars To A Man's Lifetime Income - Which He Then Spends Sending His Son To College." - Bill Vaughan

3301	"Bush Reiterated His Stand To Conservatives Opposing His Decision On Stem Cell Research. He Said Today He Believes Life Begins At Conception And Ends At Execution." - Jay Leno
3302	"Anthropology Demands The Open-Mindedness With Which One Must Look And Listen, Record In Astonishment And Wonder That Which One Would Not Have Been Able To Guess." - Margaret Mead
3303	"Nothing Can Stop The Man With The Right Mental Attitude From Achieving His Goal: Nothing On Earth Can Help The Man With The Wrong Mental Attitude." - Thomas Jefferson
3304	"I Find That A Man Is As Old As His Work. If His Work Keeps Him From Moving Forward, He Will Look Forward With The Work." - William Ernest Hocking
3305	"I Don't Believe One Grows Older. I Think That What Happens Early On In Life Is That At A Certain Age One Stands Still And Stagnates." - T. S. Eliot
3306	"Before Marriage, A Girl Has To Make Love To A Man To Hold Him. After Marriage, She Has To Hold Him To Make Love To Him." - Marilyn Monroe
3307	"Men Fear Death As Children Fear To Go In The Dark; And As That Natural Fear In Children Is Increased By Tales, So Is The Other." - Francis Bacon
3308	"If Patience Is Worth Anything, It Must Endure To The End Of Time. And A Living Faith Will Last In The Midst Of The Blackest Storm." - Mohandas Gandhi
3309	"It Is Time For Us All To Stand And Cheer For The Doer, The Achiever The One Who Recognizes The Challenge And Does Something About It." - Vince Lombardi
3310	"How Can A Woman Be Expected To Be Happy With A Man Who Insists On Treating Her As If She Were A Perfectly Normal Human Being." - Oscar Wilde
3311	"Sir, You Will Either Die On The Gallows Or Of Some Unspeakable Disease. That Depends, Sir, Said Disraeli, Whether I Embrace Your Policies Or Your Mistress." - Member Of Parliament To Disraeli
3312	"I Believe In Christianity As I Believe That The Sun Has Risen: Not Only Because I See It, But Because By It I See Everything Else." - C. S. Lewis
3313	"When You Go Into Court You Are Putting Your Fate Into The Hands Of Twelve People Who Weren't Smart Enough To Get Out Of Jury Duty." - Norm Crosby
3314	"Do Not Waste Your Time On Social Questions. What Is The Matter With The Poor Is Poverty; What Is The Matter With The Rich Is Uselessness." - George Bernard Shaw

3315	" You May Have A Fresh Start Any Moment You Choose, For This Thing That We Call Failure Is Not The Falling Down, But The Staying Down." - Mary Pickford
3316	"A Winner Is Someone Who Recognizes His God-Given Talents, Works His Tail Off To Develop Them Into Skills, And Uses These Skills To Accomplish His Goals." - Larry Bird
3317	"You May Have A Fresh Start Any Moment You Choose, For This Thing That We Call 'Failure' Is Not The Falling Down, But The Staying Down." - Mary Pickford
3318	"For Every Person Who Has Ever Lived There Has Come, At Last, A Spring He Will Never See. Glory Then In The Springs That Are Yours." - Pam Brown
3319	"Just Don't Give Up Trying To Do What You Really Want To Do. Where There Is Love And Inspiration, I Don't Think You Can Go Wrong." - Ella Fitzgerald
3320	"The Artist's World Is Limitless. It Can Be Found Anywhere, Far From Where He Lives Or A Few Feet Away. It Is Always On His Doorstep." - Paul Strand
3321	"Majority Rule Only Works If You're Also Considering Individual Rights. Because You Can't Have Five Wolves And One Sheep Voting On What To Have For Supper." - Larry Flynt
3322	" There Is No Failure Except In No Longer Trying. There Is No Defeat Except From Within, No Insurmountable Barrier Except Our Own Inherent Weakness Of Purpose." - Elbert Hubbard
3323	"How Can They Say My Life Is Not A Success? Have I Not For More Than Sixty Years Got Enough To Eat And Escaped Being Eaten?" - Logan P. Smith
3324	"Marriage Is An Alliance Entered Into By A Man Who Can't Sleep With The Window Shut, And A Woman Who Can't Sleep With The Window Open." - George Bernard Shaw
3325	"Time Is The Most Precious Element Of Human Existence. The Successful Person Knows How To Put Energy Into Time And How To Draw Success From Time." - Denis Waitley
3326	"You End Up As You Deserve. In Old Age You Must Put Up With The Face, The Friends, The Health, And The Children You Have Earned." - Judith Viorst
3327	"There Is No Scarcity Of Opportunity To Make A Living At What You Love To Do, There Is Only Scarcity Of Resolve To Make It Happen." - Wayne Dyer
3328	"The Robot Is Going To Lose. Not By Much. But When The Final Score Is Tallied, Flesh And Blood Is Going To Beat The Damn Monster." - Adam Smith

167

3329	"'Tis The Business Of Little Minds To Shrink; But He Whose Heart Is Firm, And Whose Conscience Approves His Conduct, Will Pursue His Principles Unto Death." - Thomas Paine
3330	"History Is A Relentless Master. It Has No Present, Only The Past Rushing Into The Future. To Try To Hold Fast Is To Be Swept Aside." - John F. Kennedy
3331	"Holding On To Anger Is Like Grasping A Hot Coal With The Intent Of Throwing It At Someone Else; You Are The One Who Gets Burned." - The Buddha
3332	"What's The Subject Of Life - To Get Rich? All Of Those Fellows Out There Getting Rich Could Be Dancing Around The Real Subject Of Life." - Paul A. Volcker
3333	"Computers Make It Easier To Do A Lot Of Things, But Most Of The Things They Make It Easier To Do Don't Need To Be Done." - Andy Rooney
3334	" To Make Our Way, We Must Have Firm Resolve, Persistence, Tenacity. We Must Gear Ourselves To Work Hard All The Way. We Can Never Let Up." - Ralph Bunche
3335	"Free Speech Is Not To Be Regulated Like Diseased Cattle And Impure Butter. The Audience That Hissed Yesterday May Applaud Today, Even For The Same Performance." - William O. Douglas
3336	"In This World Of Sin And Sorrow There Is Always Something To Be Thankful For; As For Me, I Rejoice That I Am Not A Republican." - H. L. Mencken
3337	"A Man's Country Is Not A Certain Area Of Land, Of Mountains, Rivers, And Woods, But It Is A Principle And Patriotism Is Loyalty To That Principle." - George William Curtis
3338	"The Proper Function Of Man Is To Live, Not To Exist. I Shall Not Waste My Days In Trying To Prolong Them. I Shall Use My Time." - Jack London
3339	"Checking The Results Of A Decision Against Its Expectations Shows Executives What Their Strengths Are, Where They Need To Improve, And Where They Lack Knowledge Or Information." - Peter Drucker
3340	"A Man Is A Success If He Gets Up In The Morning And Goes To Bed At Night And In Between Does What He Wants To Do." - Bob Dylan
3341	"I Cried On My 18th Birthday. I Thought 17 Was Such A Nice Age. You're Young Enough To Get Away With Things, But You're Old Enough, Too." - Liv Tyler
3342	"You Can't Operate A Company By Fear, Because The Way To Eliminate Fear Is To Avoid Criticism. And The Way To Avoid Criticism Is To Do Nothing." - Steve Ross

3343	"Clocks Slay Time... Time Is Dead As Long As It Is Being Clicked Off By Little Wheels; Only When The Clock Stops Does Time Come To Life." - William Faulkner
3344	"Why Should We Honor Those That Die Upon The Field Of Battle? A Man May Show As Reckless A Courage In Entering Into The Abyss Of Himself." - William Butler Yeats
3345	"I Think I Don't Regret A Single 'Excess' Of My Responsive Youth – I Only Regret, In My Chilled Age, Certain Occasions And Possibilities I Didn't Embrace." - Henry James
3346	"Human Beings, Who Are Almost Unique In Having The Ability To Learn From The Experience Of Others, Are Also Remarkable For Their Apparent Disinclination To Do So." - Douglas Adams
3347	"Imagination Was Given To Man To Compensate Him For What He Is Not, And A Sense Of Humor Was Provided To Console Him For What He Is." - Oscar Wilde
3348	"Humor Is Something That Thrives Between Man's Aspirations And His Limitations. There Is More Logic In Humor Than In Anything Else. Because, You See, Humor Is Truth." - Victor Borge
3349	"All The Breaks You Need In Life Wait Within Your Imagination, Imagination Is The Workshop Of Your Mind, Capable Of Turning Mind Energy Into Accomplishment And Wealth." - Napoleon Hill
3350	"A Liberal Is A Man Or A Woman Or A Child Who Looks Forward To A Better Day, A More Tranquil Night, And A Bright, Infinite Future." - Leonard Bernstein
3351	"I Do Not Feel Obliged To Believe That The Same God Who Has Endowed Us With Sense, Reason, And Intellect Has Intended Us To Forgo Their Use." - Galileo Galilei
3352	"The Strongest Reason For The People To Retain The Right To Keep And Bear Arms Is, As A Last Resort, To Protect Themselves Against Tyranny In Government." - Thomas Jefferson
3353	"I Have Tried To Lift France Out Of The Mud. But She Will Return To Her Errors And Vomitings. I Cannot Prevent The French From Being French." - Charles De Gaulle
3354	"The Doctor Has Been Taught To Be Interested Not In Health But In Disease. What The Public Is Taught Is That Health Is The Cure For Disease." - Ashley Montagu
3355	"Much Education Today Is Monumentally Ineffective. All Too Often We Are Giving Young People Cut Flowers When We Should Be Teaching Them To Grow Their Own Plants." - John W. Gardner
3356	"Most Of Us Are About As Eager To Be Changed As We Were To Be Born, And Go Through Our Changes In A Similar State Of Shock." - James Baldwin

3357	"There Is Only One Boss. The Customer. And He Can Fire Everybody In The Company From The Chairman On Down, Simply By Spending His Money Somewhere Else." - Sam Walton
3358	"In Every Community, There Is Work To Be Done. In Every Nation, There Are Wounds To Heal. In Every Heart, There Is The Power To Do It." - Marianne Williamson
3359	"I Predict Future Happiness For Americans If They Can Prevent The Government From Wasting The Labors Of The People Under The Pretense Of Taking Care Of Them." - Thomas Jefferson
3360	"There Are Three Roads To Ruin; Women, Gambling And Technicians. The Most Pleasant Is With Women, The Quickest Is With Gambling, But The Surest Is With Technicians." - Georges Pompidou
3361	"I Am Imagination. I Can See What The Eyes Cannot See. I Can Hear What The Ears Cannot Hear. I Can Feel What The Heart Cannot Feel." - Peter Nivio Zarlenga
3362	"It Is Enough That The People Know There Was An Election. The People Who Cast The Votes Decide Nothing. The People Who Count The Votes Decide Everything." - Joseph Stalin
3363	"The Way People In Democracies Think Of The Government As Something Different From Themselves Is A Real Handicap. And, Of Course, Sometimes The Government Confirms Their Opinion." - Lewis Mumford
3364	"A Taste For Irony Has Kept More Hearts From Breaking Than A Sense Of Humor, For It Takes Irony To Appreciate The Joke Which Is On Oneself." - Jessamyn West
3365	"Love Does Not Begin And End The Way We Seem To Think It Does. Love Is A Battle, Love Is A War; Love Is A Growing Up." - James A. Baldwin
3366	"It Is Not From The Benevolence Of The Butcher, The Brewer, Or The Baker That We Expect Our Dinner, But From Their Regard To Their Own Interest." - Adam Smith
3367	"If You Are To Be, You Must Begin By Assuming Responsibility. You Alone Are Responsible For Every Moment Of Your Life, For Every One Of Your Acts." - Antoine De Saint-Exupery
3368	"I Never Saw A Discontented Tree. They Grip The Ground As Though They Liked It, And Though Fast Rooted They Travel About As Far As We Do." - John Muir
3369	"Most Of The Important Things In The World Have Been Accomplished By People Who Have Kept On Trying When There Seemed To Be No Hope At All." - Dale Carnegie

3370	"Science May Have Found A Cure For Most Evils; But Is Has Found No Remedy For The Worst Of Them All - The Apathy Of Human Beings." - Helen Keller
3371	"Accept Yourself As You Are. Otherwise You Will Never See Opportunity. You Will Not Feel Free To Move Toward It; You Will Feel You Are Not Deserving." - Maxwell Maltz
3372	"The Test Of A First-Rate Intelligence Is The Ability To Hold Two Opposed Ideas In Mind At The Same Time And Still Retain The Ability To Function." - F. Scott Fitzgerald
3373	" Any Coward Can Fight A Battle When He's Sure Of Winning; But Give Me The Man Who Has The Pluck To Fight When He's Sure Of Losing." - George Eliot
3374	"The Triple Is The Most Exciting Play In Baseball. Home Runs Win A Lot Of Games, But I Never Understood Why Fans Are So Obsessed With Them." - Hank Aaron
3375	"Love Is The Ability And Willingness To Allow Those That You Care For To Be What They Choose For Themselves Without Any Insistence That They Satisfy You." - Wayne Dyer
3376	"Most Successful Men Have Not Achieved Their Distinction By Having Some New Talent Or Opportunity Presented To Them. They Have Developed The Opportunity That Was At Hand." - Dale Carnegie
3377	"A Nap, My Friend, Is A Brief Period Of Sleep Which Overtakes Superannuated Persons When They Endeavor To Entertain Unwelcome Visitors Or To Listen To Scientific Lectures." - George Bernard Shaw
3378	"Knowledge Is Power. The More Knowledge, Expertise, And Connections You Have, The Easier It Is For You To Make A Profit At The Game Of Your Choice." - Stuart Wilde
3379	"For In The True Nature Of Things, If We Rightly Consider, Every Green Tree Is Far More Glorious Than If It Were Made Of Gold And Silver." - Martin Luther
3380	"Every Creature Is Better Alive Than Dead, Men And Moose And Pine Trees, And He Who Understands It Aright Will Rather Preserve Its Life Than Destroy It." - Henry David Thoreau
3381	"I Do Not Think There Is Any Other Quality So Essential To Success Of Any Kind As The Quality Of Perseverance. It Overcomes Almost Everything, Even Nature." - John D. Rockefeller
3382	"Nothing Is More Memorable Than A Smell. One Scent Can Be Unexpected, Momentary And Fleeting, Yet Conjure Up A Childhood Summer Beside A Lake In The Mountains." - Diane Ackerman
3383	"I Haven't, In The 23 Years That I Have Been In The Uniformed Services Of The United States Of America, Ever Violated An Order - Not One." - Oliver North

3384	"By Three Methods We May Learn Wisdom: First, By Reflection, Which Is Noblest; Second, By Imitation, Which Is Easiest; And Third By Experience, Which Is The Bitterest." - Confucius
3385	"You Do Not Merely Want To Be Considered Just The Best Of The Best. You Want To Be Considered The Only One Who Does What You Do." - Jerry Garcia
3386	"Radical Changes In World Politics Leave America With A Heightened Responsibility To Be, For The World, An Example Of A Genuinely Free, Democratic, Just And Humane Society." - Pope John Paul II
3387	"There Is One Thing Even More Vital To Science Than Intelligent Methods; And That Is, The Sincere Desire To Find Out The Truth, Whatever It May Be." - Charles Pierce
3388	"They Say That We Are Better Educated Than Our Parents' Generation. What They Mean Is That We Go To School Longer. It Is Not The Same Thing." - Richard Yates
3389	"Let Us Learn To Appreciate There Will Be Times When The Trees Will Be Bare, And Look Forward To The Time When We May Pick The Fruit." - Anton Chekhov
3390	"People Ask Me What I Do In Winter When There's No Baseball. I'll Tell You What I Do. I Stare Out The Window And Wait For Spring." - Rogers Hornsby
3391	"Happiness Does Not Come From Doing Easy Work But From The Afterglow Of Satisfaction That Comes After The Achievement Of A Difficult Task That Demanded Our Best." - Theodore Isaac Rubin
3392	"Strong Managers Who Make Tough Decisions To Cut Jobs Provide The Only True Job Security In Today's World. Weak Managers Are The Problem. Weak Managers Destroy Jobs." - Jack Welch
3393	"Humor Is Richly Rewarding To The Person Who Employs It. It Has Some Value In Gaining And Holding Attention, But It Has No Persuasive Value At All." - John Kenneth Galbraith
3394	"Time Has Been Transformed, And We Have Changed; It Has Advanced And Set Us In Motion; It Has Unveiled Its Face, Inspiring Us With Bewilderment And Exhilaration." - Kahlil Gibran
3395	"Forgiveness Is The Answer To The Child's Dream Of A Miracle By Which What Is Broken Is Made Whole Again, What Is Soiled Is Made Clean Again." - Dag Hammarskjold
3396	"Being Divorced Is Like Being Hit By A Mack Truck. If You Live Through It, You Start Looking Very Carefully To The Right And To The Left." - Jean Kerr
3397	"Theology Is Never Any Help; It Is Searching In A Dark Cellar At Midnight For A Black Cat That Isn't There. Theologians Can Persuade Themselves Of Anything." - Robert A. Heinlein

3398	"Being Unwanted, Unloved, Uncared For, Forgotten By Everybody, I Think That Is A Much Greater Hunger, A Much Greater Poverty Than The Person Who Has Nothing To Eat." - Mother Teresa
3399	"It Is Now Quite Lawful For A Catholic Woman To Avoid Pregnancy By A Resort To Mathematics, Though She Is Still Forbidden To Resort To Physics Or Chemistry." - H. L. Mencken
3400	"The Wise Man Bridges The Gap By Laying Out The Path By Means Of Which He Can Get From Where He Is To Where He Wants To Go." - John Morgan And Ewing Webb
3401	"He Should Sweep Streets So Well That All The Host Of Heaven And Earth Will Pause To Say, 'Here Lives A Great Street-Sweeper Who Did His Job Well'." - Martin Luther King Jr.
3402	"These Flowers, Which Were Splendid And Sprightly, Waking In The Dawn Of The Morning, In The Evening Will Be A Pitiful Frivolity, Sleeping In The Cold Night's Arms." - Pedro Calderon De La Barca
3403	"Reverse Every Natural Instinct And Do The Opposite Of What You Are Inclined To Do, And You Will Probably Come Very Close To Having A Perfect Golf Swing." - Ben Hogan
3404	"There Is Nothing In Which The Birds Differ More From Man Than The Way In Which They Can Build And Yet Leave A Landscape As It Was Before." - Robert Wilson Lynd
3405	"You Do Not Know Our Culture, Our Ethics, Or The Unwritten Codes That Already Provide Our Society More Order Than Could Be Obtained By Any Of Your Impositions." - John Perry Barlow
3406	"The Good News About Computers Is That They Do What You Tell Them To Do. The Bad News Is That They Do What You Tell Them To Do." - Ted Nelson
3407	"A Picture Must Possess A Real Power To Generate Light And For A Long Time Now I've Been Conscious Of Expressing Myself Through Light Or Rather In Light." - Henri Matisse
3408	"When You Are Courting A Nice Girl An Hour Seems Like A Second. When You Sit On A Red-Hot Cinder A Second Seems Like An Hour. That's Relativity." - Albert Einstein
3409	"Effective Leadership Is Not About Making Speeches Or Being Liked; Leadership Is Defined By Results Not Attributes. Efficiency Is Doing Things Right; Effectiveness Is Doing The Right Things." - Peter Drucker
3410	"For Myself I Hold No Preferences Among Flowers, So Long As They Are Wild, Free, Spontaneous. Bricks To All Greenhouses! Black Thumb And Cutworm To The Potted Plant!" - Edward Abbey

3411	"Question With Boldness Even The Existence Of A God; Because, If There Be One, He Must More Approve Of The Homage Of Reason, Than That Of Blind-Folded Fear." - Thomas Jefferson
3412	"The Ability To Discipline Yourself To Delay Gratification In The Short Term In Order To Enjoy Greater Rewards In The Long Term Is The Indispensable Prerequisite For Success." - Brian Tracy
3413	"Adventure Upon All The Tickets In The Lottery, And You Lose For Certain; And The Greater The Number Of Your Tickets The Nearer Your Approach To This Certainty." - Adam Smith
3414	"A Prose Writer Gets Tired Of Writing Prose, And Wants To Be A Poet. So He Begins Every Line With A Capital Letter, And Keeps On Writing Prose." - Samuel Mcchord Crothers
3415	"Like Everybody Who Is Not In Love, He Thought One Chose The Person To Be Loved After Endless Deliberations And On The Basis Of Particular Qualities Or Advantages." - Marcel Proust
3416	"The Only Thing That I'd Rather Own Than Windows Is English, Because Then I Could Charge You Two Hundred And Forty-Nine Dollars For The Right To Speak It." - Scott Mcnealy
3417	"Sunshine Is Delicious, Rain Is Refreshing, Wind Braces Us Up, Snow Is Exhilarating; There Is Really No Such Thing As Bad Weather, Only Different Kinds Of Good Weather." - John Ruskin
3418	"All Of The Top Achievers I Know Are Life-Long Learners... Looking For New Skills, Insights, And Ideas. If They're Not Learning, They're Not Growing... Not Moving Toward Excellence." - Denis Waitley
3419	"Ours Is A World Of Nuclear Giants And Ethical Infants. We Know More About War That We Know About Peace, More About Killing That We Know About Living." - Omar N. Bradley
3420	"I Do Not Believe In A Fate That Falls On Men However They Act; But I Do Believe In A Fate That Falls On Them Unless They Act." - The Buddha
3421	"Not For Nothing Is Their Motto TGIF - 'Thank God It's Friday.' They Live For The Weekends, When They Can Go Do What They Really Want To Do." - Richard Nelso Bolles
3422	"Could I Have But A Line A Century Hence Crediting A Contribution To The Advance Of Peace, I Would Yield Every Honor Which Has Been Accorded By War." - Douglas Macarthur
3423	"What Then Is Time? If No One Asks Me, I Know What It Is. If I Wish To Explain It To Him Who Asks, I Do Not Know." - Saint Augustine
3424	"Baseball Is Almost The Only Orderly Thing In A Very Unorderly World. If You Get Three Strikes, Even The Best Lawyer In The World Can't Get You Off." - Bill Veeck

3425	"I Don't Know Why People Question The Academic Training Of An Athlete. Fifty Percent Of The Doctors In This Country Graduated In The Bottom Half Of Their Classes." - Al Mcguire
3426	"A Dying Man Needs To Die, As A Sleepy Man Needs To Sleep, And There Comes A Time When It Is Wrong, As Well As Useless, To Resist." - Stewart Alsop
3427	"We Now Accept The Fact That Learning Is A Lifelong Process Of Keeping Abreast Of Change. And The Most Pressing Task Is To Teach People How To Learn." - Peter Drucker
3428	"You Spend A Good Piece Of Your Life Gripping A Baseball And In The End It Turns Out That It Was The Other Way Around All The Time." - Jim Bouton
3429	"It Is Only After Years Of Preparation That The Young Artist Should Touch Color - Not Color Used Descriptively, That Is, But As A Means Of Personal Expression." - Henri Matisse
3430	"When I Can Look Life In The Eyes, Grown Calm And Very Coldly Wise, Life Will Have Given Me The Truth, And Taken In Exchange - My Youth." - Sara Teasdale
3431	"I Arise In The Morning Torn Between A Desire To Improve The World And A Desire To Enjoy The World. This Makes It Hard To Plan The Day." - E. B. White
3432	"The Hardest Thing To Believe About The Fan Is Not That Robert De Niro Is Stalking Somebody Again But That Anyone Cares That Much About A Baseball Player." - Bernie Lincicome
3433	"I'd Marry Again If I Found A Man Who Had Fifteen Million Dollars, Would Sign Over Half To Me, And Guarantee That He'd Be Dead Within A Year." - Bette Davis
3434	"The Superior Man, When Resting In Safety, Does Not Forget That Danger May Come. When In A State Of Security He Does Not Forget The Possibility Of Ruin." - Confucius
3435	"The Moment A Little Boy Is Concerned With Which Is A Jay And Which Is A Sparrow, He Can No Longer See The Birds Or Hear Them Sing." - Eric Berne
3436	"We've Heard That A Million Monkeys At A Million Keyboards Could Produce The Complete Works Of Shakespeare; Now, Thanks To The Internet, We Know That Is Not True." - Robert Wilensky
3437	"In The Long Run, We Shape Our Lives, And We Shape Ourselves. The Process Never Ends Until We Die. And The Choices We Make Are Ultimately Our Responsibility." - Eleanor Roosevelt
3438	"Music Is A Moral Law. It Gives Soul To The Universe, Wings To The Mind, Flight To The Imagination, And Charm And Gaiety To Life And To Everything." - Plato

3439	"But Friendship Is Precious, Not Only In The Shade, But In The Sunshine Of Life, And Thanks To A Benevolent Arrangement The Greater Part Of Life Is Sunshine." - Thomas Jefferson
3440	"The Challenge Of Statesmanship Is To Have The Vision To Dream Of A Better, Safer World And The Courage, Persistence, And Patience To Turn That Dream Into Reality." - Ronald Reagan
3441	" Real Success Comes In Small Portions Day By Day. You Need To Take Pleasure In Life's Daily Little Treasures. It Is The Most Important Thing In Measuring Success." - Denis Waitley
3442	"You Must Pursue This Investigation Of Watergate Even If It Leads To The President. I'm Innocent. You've Got To Believe I'm Innocent. If You Don't, Take My Job." - Richard M. Nixon
3443	"You Will Never Be Happy If You Continue To Search For What Happiness Consists Of. You Will Never Live If You Are Looking For The Meaning Of Life." - Albert Camus
3444	"The World Is Very Different Now. For Man Holds In His Mortal Hands The Power To Abolish All Forms Of Human Poverty, And All Forms Of Human Life." - John F. Kennedy
3445	"Success Is Not Measured By What You Accomplish, But By The Opposition You Have Encountered, And The Courage With Which You Have Maintained The Struggle Against Overwhelming Odds." - Orison Swett Marden
3446	"Anyone Who Stops Learning Is Old, Whether At Twenty Or Eighty. Anyone Who Keeps Learning Stays Young. The Greatest Thing In Life Is To Keep Your Mind Young." - Henry Ford
3447	"If I Weren't Earning $3 Million A Year To Dunk A Basketball, Most People On The Street Would Run In The Other Direction If They Saw Me Coming." - Charles Barkley
3448	"An Ordinary Man Can Surround Himself With Two Thousand Books And Thenceforward Have At Least One Place In The World In Which It Is Possible To Be Happy." - Augustine Birrell
3449	"When A Man Feels Throbbing Within Him The Power To Do What He Undertakes As Well As It Can Possibly Be Done, This Is Happiness, This Is Success." - Orison Swett Marden
3450	"The Opposite Of Play Isn't Work It's Depression. To Play Is To Act Out And Be Willful, Exultant And Committed As If One Is Assured Of One's Prospects" - Brian Sutton Smith
3451	"Anger Is A Killing Thing: It Kills The Man Who Angers, For Each Rage Leaves Him Less Than He Had Been Before - It Takes Something From Him." - Louis L'amour

3452	"Style Used To Be An Interaction Between The Human Soul And Tools That Were Limiting. In The Digital Era, It Will Have To Come From The Soul Alone." - Jaron Lanier
3453	"Keep Away From People Who Try To Belittle Your Ambitions. Small People Always Do That, But The Really Great Make You Feel That You, Too, Can Become Great." - Mark Twain
3454	"Play Will Be To The 21st Century What Work Was To The Last 300 Years Of Industrial Society - Our Dominant Way Of knowing Doing And Creating Value" - Pat Kane
3455	"Gates Is The Ultimate Programming Machine. He Believes Everything Can Be Defined, Examined, Reduced To Essentials, And Rearranged Into A Logical Sequence That Will Achieve A Particular Goal." - Stewart Alsop
3456	"You Must Have Courage To Bet On Your Ideals, To Take Calculated Risk, And Act.. Everyday Living Requires Courage If Life Is To Be Effective And Bring Happiness." - Maxwell Maltz
3457	"O Sleep, O Gentle Sleep, Nature's Soft Nurse, How Have I Frighted Thee, That Thou No More Wilt Weigh My Eyelids Down And Steep My Sense In Forgetfulness?" - William Shakespeare
3458	"Every Human Has Four Endowments- Self Awareness, Conscience, Independent Will And Creative Imagination. These Give Us The Ultimate Human Freedom... The Power To Choose, To Respond, To Change." - Stephen Covey
3459	"Advice In Old Age Is Foolish; For What Can Be More Absurd Than To Increase Our Provisions For The Road The Nearer We Approach To Our Journey's End." - Marcus Tullius Cicero
3460	"Lots Of People Want To Ride With You In The Limo, But What You Want Is Someone Who Will Take The Bus With You When The Limo Breaks Down." - Oprah Winfrey
3461	"My Hope Is That 10 Years From Now, After I've Been Across The Street At Work For A While, They'll All Be Glad They Gave Me That Wonderful Vote." - Sandra Day O'Connor
3462	"An Insincere And Evil Friend Is More To Be Feared Than A Wild Beast; A Wild Beast May Wound Your Body, But An Evil Friend Will Wound Your Mind." - The Buddha
3463	"Love Begins By Taking Care Of The Closest Ones - The Ones At Home. Love Is A Fruit In Season At All Times, And Within Reach Of Every Hand." - Mother Teresa
3464	"I Do Not Believe That The Men Who Served In Uniform In Vietnam Have Been Given The Credit They Deserve. It Was A Difficult War Against An Unorthodox Enemy." - William Westmoreland

3465	"When I Judge Art, I Take My Painting And Put It Next To A God Made Object Like A Tree Or Flower. If It Clashes, It Is Not Art." - Paul Cezanne
3466	"An Education Isn't How Much You Have Committed To Memory, Or Even How Much You Know. It's Being Able To Differentiate Between What You Know And What You Don't." - Anatole France
3467	"I Want To Rip Out His Heart And Feed It To Lennox Lewis. I Want To Kill People. I Want To Rip Their Stomachs Out And Eat Their Children." - Mike Tyson
3468	"I Am Sorry To Say That There Is Too Much Point To The Wisecrack That Life Is Extinct On Other Planets Because Their Scientists Were More Advanced Than Ours." - John F. Kennedy
3469	"Do More Than Is Required. What Is The Distance Between Someone Who Achieves Their Goals Consistently And Those Who Spend Their Lives And Careers Merely Following? The Extra Mile." - Gary Ryan Blair
3470	"Fourscore And Seven Years Ago Our Fathers Brought Forth On This Continent, A New Nation, Conceived In Liberty, And Dedicated To The Proposition That All Men Are Created Equal." - Abraham Lincoln
3471	"Inaction Breeds Doubt And Fear. Action Breeds Confidence And Courage. If You Want To Conquer Fear, Do Not Sit Home And Think About It. Go Out And Get Busy." - Dale Carnegie
3472	"If One Advances Confidently In The Direction Of His Dreams, And Endeavors To Live The Life Which He Has Imagined, He Will Meet With Success Unexpected In Common Hours." - Henry David Thoreau
3473	"This Is My Simple Religion. There Is No Need For Temples; No Need For Complicated Philosophy. Our Own Brain, Our Own Heart Is Our Temple; The Philosophy Is Kindness." - Dalai Lama
3474	"There Seems To Be A Terrible Misunderstanding On The Part Of A Great Many People To The Effect That When You Cease To Believe You May Cease To Behave." - Louis Kronenberger
3475	"When I Investigate And When I Discover That The Forces Of The Heavens And The Planets Are Within Ourselves, Then Truly I Seem To Be Living Among The Gods." - Leon Battista Alberti
3476	"My Formula For Living Is Quite Simple. I Get Up In The Morning And I Go To Bed At Night. In Between, I Occupy Myself As Best I Can." - Cary Grant
3477	"We Are Not The Same Persons This Year As Last; Nor Are Those We Love. It Is A Happy Chance If We, Changing, Continue To Love A Changed Person." - W. Somerset Maugham

3478	"Our Identities Have No Bodies, So, Unlike You, We Cannot Obtain Order By Physical Coercion. We Believe That From Ethics, Enlightened Self-Interest, And The Commonweal, Our Governance Will Emerge." - John Perry Barlow
3479	"We Have Petitioned And Our Petitions Have Been Disregarded, We Have Entreated And Our Entreaties Have Been Scorned. We Beg No More, We Petition No Longer, We Now Defy." - William Jennings Bryan
3480	" What's Money? A Man Is A Success If He Gets Up In The Morning And Goes To Bed At Night And In Between Does What He Wants To Do." - Bob Dylan
3481	"A Few Can Touch The Magic String, And Noisy Fame Is Proud To Win Them: Alas For Those That Never Sing, But Die With All Their Music In Them!" - Oliver Wendell Holmes
3482	"There Is One Quality That One Must Possess To Win, And That Is Definiteness Of Purpose, The Knowledge Of What One Wants, And A Burning Desire To Possess It." - Napoleon Hill
3483	"Don't Gamble; Take All Your Savings And Buy Some Good Stock And Hold It Till It Goes Up, Then Sell It. If It Don't Go Up, Don't Buy It." - Will Rogers
3484	"Poetry Is Ordinary Language Raised To The Nth Power. Poetry Is Boned With Ideas, Nerved And Blooded With Emotions, All Held Together By The Delicate, Tough Skin Of Words." - Paul Engle
3485	"Only After We Can Learn To Forgive Ourselves Can We Accept Others As They Are Because We Don't Feel Threatened By Anything About Them Which Is Better Than Us." - Stephen Covey
3486	"We All Know That Art Is Not Truth. Art Is A Lie That Makes Us Realize The Truth, At Least The Truth That Is Given To Us To Understand." - Pablo Picasso
3487	"If Any Foreign Minister Begins To Defend To The Death A Peace Conference, You Can Be Sure His Government Has Already Placed Its Orders For New Battleships And Airplanes." - Joseph Stalin
3488	"Punishment Is Now Unfashionable... Because It Creates Moral Distinctions Among Men, Which, To The Democratic Mind, Are Odious. We Prefer A Meaningless Collective Guilt To A Meaningful Individual Responsibility." - Thomas Szasz
3489	"First Comes Thought; Then Organization Of That Thought, Into Ideas And Plans; Then Transformation Of Those Plans Into Reality. The Beginning, As You Will Observe, Is In Your Imagination." - Napoleon Hill

3490	"John Dalton's Records, Carefully Preserved For A Century, Were Destroyed During The World War Ii Bombing Of Manchester. It Is Not Only The Living Who Are Killed In War." - Isaac Asimov
3491	" It Is The Height Of Absurdity To Sow Little But Weeds In The First Half Of One's Lifetime And Expect To Harvest A Valuable Crop In The Second Half." - Percy H. Johnston
3492	"Time Extracts Various Values From A Painter's Work. When These Values Are Exhausted The Pictures Are Forgotten, And The More A Picture Has To Give, The Greater It Is." - Henri Matisse
3493	"I Have Learned That Only Two Things Are Necessary To Keep One's Wife Happy. First, Let Her Think She's Having Her Own Way. And Second, Let Her Have It." - Lyndon B. Johnson
3494	"If You Want A Love Message To Be Heard, It Has Got To Be Sent Out. To Keep A Lamp Burning, We Have To Keep Putting Oil In It." - Mother Teresa
3495	"If An Elderly But Distinguished Scientist Says That Something Is Possible, He Is Almost Certainly Right; But If He Says That It Is Impossible, He Is Very Probably Wrong." - Arthur C. Clarke
3496	"If The United States Of America Or Britain Is Having Elections, They Don't Ask For Observers From Africa Or From Asia. But When We Have Elections, They Want Observers." - Nelson Mandela
3497	"Anyone Who Has Lost Track Of Time When Using A Computer Knows The Propensity To Dream, The Urge To Make Dreams Come True And The Tendency To Miss Lunch." - Tim Berners-Lee
3498	"And, For An Instant, She Stared Directly Into Those Soft Blue Eyes And Knew, With An Instinctive Mammalian Certainty, That The Exceedingly Rich Were No Longer Even Remotely Human." - William Gibson
3499	"Congress Will Pass A Law Restricting Public Comment On The Internet To Individuals Who Have Spent A Minimum Of One Hour Actually Accomplishing A Specific Task While On Line." - Andy Grove
3500	"The Test Of Our Progress Is Not Whether We Add More To The Abundance Of Those Who Have Much It Is Whether We Provide Enough For Those Who Have Little." - Franklin D. Roosevelt
3501	"Perhaps The Single Most Important Element In Mastering The Techniques And Tactics Of Racing Is Experience. But Once You Have The Fundamentals, Acquiring The Experience Is A Matter Of Time." - Greg Lemond
3502	"It Isn't What You Have, Or Who You Are, Or Where You Are, Or What You Are Doing That Makes You Happy Or Unhappy. It Is What You Think About." - Dale Carnegie

3503	" If Your Success Is Not On Your Own Terms, If It Looks Good To The World But Does Not Feel Good In Your Heart, It Is Not Success At All." - Anna Quindlen
3504	"It's Not Always About How Much Money We Earn, But How Much We Are Able To Keep, Expand. And Ultimately Use Wisely In Order To Avoid Slipping Into Financial Slavery. " - Richard Marvin Voigt
3505	"It Is A Measure Of The Framers' Fear That A Passing Majority Might Find It Expedient To Compromise 4th Amendment Values That These Values Were Embodied In The Constitution Itself." - Sandra Day O'connor
3506	"To Resist The Frigidity Of Old Age, One Must Combine The Body, The Mind, And The Heart. And To Keep These In Parallel Vigor One Must Exercise, Study, And Love." - Alan Bleasdale
3507	"An Educated Person Is One Who Has Learned That Information Almost Always Turns Out To Be At Best Incomplete And Very Often False, Misleading, Fictitious, Mendacious - Just Dead Wrong." - Russell Baker
3508	"Humor Is Perhaps A Sense Of Intellectual Perspective: An Awareness That Some Things Are Really Important, Others Not; And That The Two Kinds Are Most Oddly Jumbled In Everyday Affairs." - Christopher Morley
3509	"And While The Law Of Competition May Be Sometimes Hard For The Individual, It Is Best For The Race, Because It Ensures The Survival Of The Fittest In Every Department." - Andrew Carnegie
3510	"To Think That The New Economy Is Over Is Like Somebody In London In 1830 Saying The Entire Industrial Revolution Is Over Because Some Textile Manufacturers In Manchester Went Broke." - Alvin Toffler
3511	"The Common Idea That Success Spoils People By Making Them Vain, Egotistic And Self-Complacent Is Erroneous; On The Contrary It Makes Them, For The Most Part, Humble, Tolerant And Kind." - W. Somerset Maugham
3512	"Eskimo: If I Did Not Know About God And Sin, Would I Go To Hell? Priest: No, Not If You Did Not Know. Eskimo: Then Why Did You Tell Me?" - Annie Dillard
3513	"Each Player Must Accept The Cards That Life Deals Him Or Her. But Once In Hand One Must Decide How To Play The Cards In Order To Win The Game." - Voltaire
3514	"I'm Not A Crazy Conspiracy Theorist, Or On The Crack Pipe. Read This Entire Message And It Will All Make Perfect Sense. Keep This Picture In Mind When You Do." - Mike Dillard

3515	"Nobody Grows Old Merely By Living A Number Of Years. We Grow Old By Deserting Our Ideals. Years May Wrinkle The Skin, But To Give Up Enthusiasm Wrinkles The Soul." - Samuel Ullman
3516	"When Marrying, Ask Yourself This Question: Do You Believe That You Will Be Able To Converse Well With This Person Into Your Old Age? Everything Else In Marriage Is Transitory." - Friedrich Nietzsche
3517	"A Woodland In Full Color Is Awesome As A Forest Fire, In Magnitude At Least, But A Single Tree Is Like A Dancing Tongue Of Flame To Warm The Heart." - Hal Borland
3518	"If You Do Not Breathe Through Writing, If You Do Not Cry Out In Writing, Or Sing In Writing, Then Don't Write, Because Our Culture Has No Use For It." - Anais Nin
3519	"My Main Job Was Developing Talent. I Was A Gardener Providing Water And Other Nourishment To Our Top 750 People. Of Course, I Had To Pull Out Some Weeds, Too." - Jack Welch
3520	"If You Pick The Right People And Give Them The Opportunity To Spread Their Wings And Put Compensation As A Carrier Behind It You Almost Don't Have To Manage Them." - Jack Welch
3521	"We Are The Creative Force Of Our Life, And Through Our Own Decisions Rather Than Our Conditions, If We Carefully Learn To Do Certain Things, We Can Accomplish Those Goals." - Stephen Covey
3522	"The Next Major Explosion Is Going To Be When Genetics And Computers Come Together. I'm Talking About An Organic Computer - About Biological Substances That Can Function Like A Semiconductor." - Alvin Toffler
3523	"France Is Delighted At This New Opportunity To Show The World That When One Has The Will One Can Succeed In Joining Peoples Who Have Been Brought Close By History." - Francois Mitterrand
3524	"If You Made A List Of Reasons Why Any Couple Got Married, And Another List Of The Reasons For Their Divorce, You'd Have A Hell Of A Lot Of Overlapping." - Mignon Mclaughlin
3525	"Terrorism Takes Us Back To Ages We Thought Were Long Gone If We Allow It A Free Hand To Corrupt Democratic Societies And Destroy The Basic Rules Of International Life." - Jacques Chirac
3526	"Ninety Eight Percent Of The Adults In This Country Are Decent, Hardworking, Honest Americans. It's The Other Lousy Two Percent That Get All The Publicity. But Then, We Elected Them." - Lily Tomlin
3527	"Almost No One Is Foolish Enough To Imagine That He Automatically Deserves Great Success In Any Field Of Activity; Yet Almost Everyone Believes That He Automatically Deserves Success In Marriage." - Sydney J. Harris

3528	"I Wouldn't Attach Too Much Importance To These Student Riots. I Remember When I Was A Student At The Sorbonne In Paris, I Used To Go Out And Riot Occasionally." - John Foster Dulles
3529	"One Of The Things About Equality Is Not Just That You Be Treated Equally To A Man, But That You Treat Yourself Equally To The Way You Treat A Man." - Marlo Thomas
3530	"Death Is No More Than Passing From One Room Into Another. But There's A Difference For Me, You Know. Because In That Other Room I Shall Be Able To See." - Helen Keller
3531	"I Am Not Bound To Win, I Am Bound To Be True. I Am Not Bound To Succeed, But I Am Bound To Live Up To The Light I Have." - Abraham Lincoln
3532	"My Motto Was Always To Keep Swinging. Whether I Was In A Slump Or Feeling Badly Or Having Trouble Off The Field, The Only Thing To Do Was Keep Swinging." - Hank Aaron
3533	"I Was Once Asked If A Big Business Man Ever Reached His Objectives. I Replied That If A Man Ever Reached His Objective He Was Not A Big Business Man." - Charles M. Schwab
3534	"Earth And Sky, Woods And Fields, Lakes And Rivers, The Mountain And The Sea, Are Excellent Schoolmasters, And Teach Some Of Us More Than We Can Ever Learn From Books." - John Lubbock
3535	"He That Would Make His Own Liberty Secure Must Guard Even His Enemy From Oppression; For If He Violates This Duty He Establishes A Precedent That Will Reach To Himself." - Thomas Paine
3536	"I Have Known Strong Minds With Imposing Undoubting Cobbett-Like Manner But I Have Never Met A Great Mind Of This Sort. The Truth Is A Great Mind Must Be Androgynous." - Samuel Taylor Coleridge
3537	"We Must Respect The Other Fellow's Religion, But Only In The Sense And To The Extent That We Respect His Theory That His Wife Is Beautiful And His Children Smart." - H. L. Mencken
3538	"Man Has No Right To Kill His Brother. It Is No Excuse That He Does So In Uniform: He Only Adds The Infamy Of Servitude To The Crime Of Murder." - Percy Bysshe Shelley
3539	"The Toughest Thing About Success Is That You've Got To Keep On Being A Success. Talent Is Only A Starting Point In Business. You've Got To Keep Working That Talent." - Irving Berlin
3540	"No Matter What You've Done For Yourself Or For Humanity, If You Can't Look Back On Having Given Love And Attention To Your Own Family, What Have You Really Accomplished? " - Lee Iacocca
3541	"Technology Is A Gift Of God. After The Gift Of Life It Is Perhaps The Greatest Of God's Gifts. It Is The Mother Of Civilizations, Of Arts And Of Sciences." - Freeman Dyson

3542	"I Would Remind You That Extremism In The Defense Of Liberty Is No Vice! And Let Me Remind You Also That Moderation In The Pursuit Of Justice Is No Virtue." - Barry Goldwater
3543	"A Dream Is Your Creative Vision For Your Life In The Future. You Must Break Out Of Your Current Comfort Zone And Become Comfortable With The Unfamiliar And The Unknown." - Denis Waitley
3544	"Like Dogs In A Wheel, Birds In A Cage, Or Squirrels In A Chain, Ambitious Men Still Climb And Climb, With Great Labor, And Incessant Anxiety, But Never Reach The Top." - Robert Browing
3545	"All The President Is, Is A Glorified Public Relations Man Who Spends His Time Flattering, Kissing, And Kicking People To Get Them To Do What They Are Supposed To Do Anyway." - Harry S. Truman
3546	"If You Aren't Playing Well, The Game Isn't As Much Fun. When That Happens I Tell Myself Just To Go Out And Play As I Did When I Was A Kid." - Thomas J. Watson
3547	"You Will Find As You Look Back Upon Your Life That The Moments When You Have Truly Lived Are The Moments When You Have Done Things In The Spirit Of Love." - Henry Drummond
3548	"The Only Thing That Stands Between A Man And What He Wants From Life Is Often Merely The Will To Try It And The Faith To Believe That It Is Possible." - Richard M. Devos
3549	"Watch Your Thoughts; They Become Words. Watch Your Words; They Become Actions. Watch Your Actions; They Become Habits. Watch Your Habits; They Become Character. Watch Your Character; It Becomes Your Destiny." - Lao-Tze
3550	"I Think The Environment Should Be Put In The Category Of Our National Security. Defense Of Our Resources Is Just As Important As Defense Abroad. Otherwise What Is There To Defend?" - Robert Redford
3551	"Yesterday, December Seventh, 1941, A Date Which Will Live In Infamy, The United States Of America Was Suddenly And Deliberately Attacked By Naval And Air Forces Of The Empire Of Japan." - Franklin D. Roosevelt
3552	"For Years I Have Been Mourning And Not For My Dead, It Is For This Boy For Whatever Corner In My Heart Died When His Childhood Slid Out Of My Arms." - William Gibson
3553	"As Long As Any Adult Thinks That He, Like The Parents And Teachers Of Old, Can Become Introspective, Invoking His Own Youth To Understand The Youth Before Him, He Is Lost." - Margaret Mead

3554	"You Don't Need An Explanation For Everything. Recognize That There Are Such Things As Miracles, Events For Which There Are No Ready Explanations. Later Knowledge May Explain Those Events Quite Easily." - Harry Browne
3555	"In June As Many As A Dozen Species May Burst Their Buds On A Single Day. No Man Can Heed All Of These Anniversaries; No Man Can Ignore All Of Them." - Aldo Leopold
3556	"If There Is Anything That We Wish To Change In The Child, We Should First Examine It And See Whether It Is Not Something That Could Better Be Changed In Ourselves." - Carl Jung
3557	"Cut If You Will With Sleep's Dull Knife The Years From Off Your Life, My Friend! The Years That Death Takes Off My Life, He'll Take From Off The Other End!" - Edna St. Vincent Millay
3558	"I Think Everyone Should Go To College And Get A Degree And Then Spend Six Months As A Bartender And Six Months As A Cabdriver. Then They Would Really Be Educated." - Al Mcguire
3559	"If Liberty And Equality, As Is Thought By Some, Are Chiefly To Be Found In Democracy, They Will Be Best Attained When All Persons Alike Share In Government To The Utmost." - Aristotle
3560	"The Sun, With All Those Planets Revolving Around It And Dependent On It, Can Still Ripen A Bunch Of Grapes As If It Had Nothing Else In The Universe To Do." - Galileo Galilei
3561	"There Are No Extra Pieces In The Universe. Everyone Is Here Because He Or She Has A Place To Fill, And Every Piece Must Fit Itself Into The Big Jigsaw Puzzle." - Deepak Chopra
3562	"I Never Attempt To Make Money On The Stock Market. I Buy On The Assumption That They Could Close The Market The Next Day And Not Reopen It For Five Years." - Warren Buffett
3563	"If A Man Would Follow, Today, The Teachings Of The Old Testament, He Would Be A Criminal. If He Would Follow Strictly The Teachings Of The New, He Would Be Insane." - Robert Green Ingersoll
3564	"Whales Only Get Harpooned When They Come To The Surface, And Turtles Can Only Move Forward When They Stick Their Neck Out, But Investors Face Risk No Matter What They Do." - Charles A. Jaffe
3565	"Christmas Is The Time When Kids Tell Santa What They Want And Adults Pay For It. Deficits Are When Adults Tell Government What They Want And Their Kids Pay For It." - Richard Lamm
3566	"Stock Prices Have Been Quoted In Fractions For Two Centuries, Based On A System Descended From Spanish Pieces Of Eight. Each Dollar Was Cut Into Eight Bits Worth 12.5 Cents Each." - Charles A. Jaffe

3567	"I Love Power. But It Is As An Artist That I Love It. I Love It As A Musician Loves His Violin, To Draw Out Its Sounds And Chords And Harmonies." - Napoleon Bonaparte
3568	"The History Of Modern Art Is Also The History Of The Progressive Loss Of Art's Audience. Art Has Increasingly Become The Concern Of The Artist And The Bafflement Of The Public." - Paul Gauguin
3569	"A Life Lived With Integrity - Even If It Lacks The Trappings Of Fame And Fortune Is A Shinning Star In Whose Light Others May Follow In The Years To Come." - Denis Waitley
3570	"In Some Mysterious Way Woods Have Never Seemed To Me To Be Static Things. In Physical Terms, I Move Through Them; Yet In Metaphysical Ones, They Seem To Move Through Me." - John Fowles
3571	"The Only Thing That Stands Between A Person And What They Want From Life Is Often Merely The Will To TRY It And The Faith To BELIEVE That It Is Possible." - Anthony Robbins
3572	"Just Because Fate Doesn't Deal You The Right Cards, It Doesn't Mean You Should Give Up. It Just Means You Have To Play The Cards You Get To Their Maximum Potential." - Les Brown
3573	"It Is Incumbent On Every Generation To Pay Its Own Debts As It Goes. A Principle Which If Acted On Would Save One-Half The Wars Of The World. -- Thomas Jefferson" - Thomas Jefferson
3574	"I Love You When You Bow In Your Mosque, Kneel In Your Temple, Pray In Your Church. For You And I Are Sons Of One Religion, And It Is The Spirit." - Kahlil Gibran
3575	"Don't Flatter Yourself That Friendship Authorizes You To Say Disagreeable Things To Your Intimates. The Nearer You Come Into Relation With A Person, The More Necessary Do Tact And Courtesy Become." - Oliver Wendell Holmes
3576	"Forests, Lakes, And Rivers, Clouds And Winds, Stars And Flowers, Stupendous Glaciers And Crystal Snowflakes - Every Form Of Animate Or Inanimate Existence, Leaves Its Impress Upon The Soul Of Man." - Orison Swett Marden
3577	"The Essence Of Competitiveness Is Liberated When We Make People Believe That What They Think And Do Is Important - And Then Get Out Of Their Way While They Do It." - Jack Welch
3578	"Why Shouldn't We Give Our Teachers A License To Obtain Software, All Software, Any Software, For Nothing? Does Anyone Demand A Licensing Fee, Each Time A Child Is Taught The Alphabet?" - William Gibson
3579	"One Advantage Of Marriage Is That, When You Fall Out Of Love With Him Or He Falls Out Of Love With You, It Keeps You Together Until You Fall In Again." - Judith Viorst

3580	"For Imagination Sets The Goal Picture Which Our Automatic Mechanism Works On. We Act, Or Fail To Act, Not Because Of Will, As Is So Commonly Believed, But Because Of Imagination." - Maxwell Maltz
3581	"Sleep That Knits Up The Raveled Sleeve Of Care The Death Of Each Day's Life, Sore Labor's Bath Balm Of Hurt Minds, Great Nature's Second Course, Chief Nourisher In Life's Feast." - William Shakespeare
3582	"Don't Ever Dare To Take Your College As A Matter Of Course – Because, Like Democracy And Freedom, Many People You'll Never Know Have Broken Their Hearts To Get It For You." - Alice Duer Miller
3583	"The Basic Fact About Human Existence Is Not That It Is A Tragedy, But That It Is A Bore. It Is Not So Much A War As An Endless Standing In Line." - H. L. Mencken
3584	"It Is Better To Conquer Yourself Than To Win A Thousand Battles. Then The Victory Is Yours. It Cannot Be Taken From You, Not By Angels Or By Demons, Heaven Or Hell." - The Buddha
3585	"To Be Satisfied With A Little, Is The Greatest Wisdom; And He That Increaseth His Riches, Increaseth His Cares; But A Contented Mind Is A Hidden Treasure, And Trouble Findeth It Not." - Akhenaton
3586	"If It's Very Painful For You To Criticize Your Friends - You're Safe In Doing It. But If You Take The Slightest Pleasure In It, That's The Time To Hold Your Tongue." - Alice Duer Miller
3587	"Economic Depression Cannot Be Cured By Legislative Action Or Executive Pronouncement. Economic Wounds Must Be Healed By The Action Of The Cells Of The Economic Body - The Producers And Consumers Themselves." - Herbert Hoover
3588	"THE PROBLEMS OF THIS WORLD Cannot Possibly Be Solved By Skeptics Or Cynics Whose Horizons Are Limited By The Obvious Realities. We Need Men Who Can Dream Of Things That Never Were." - John F. Kennedy
3589	"The Real 1960s Began On The Afternoon Of November 22, 1963. It Came To Seem That Kennedy's Murder Opened Some Malign Trap Door In American Culture, And The Wild Bats Flapped Out." - Lance Morrow
3590	"Many A Person Has Held Close, Throughout Their Entire Lives, Two Friends That Always Remained Strange To One Another, Because One Of Them Attracted By Virtue Of Similarity, The Other By Difference." - Emil Ludwig

3591	"If Instead Of A Gem, Or Even A Flower, We Should Cast The Gift Of A Loving Thought Into The Heart Of A Friend, That Would Be Giving As The Angels Give." - George Macdonald
3592	"We Seem To Have A Compulsion These Days To Bury Time Capsules In Order To Give Those People Living In The Next Century Or So Some Idea Of What We Are Like." - Alfred Hitchcock
3593	"The Creative Act Lasts But A Brief Moment, A Lightning Instant Of Give-And-Take, Just Long Enough For You To Level The Camera And To Trap The Fleeting Prey In Your Little Box." - Henri Cartier-Bresson
3594	"He Who Joyfully Marches To Music In Rank And File Has Already Earned My Contempt. He Has Been Given A Large Brain By Mistake, Since For Him The Spinal Cord Would Suffice." - Albert Einstein
3595	"A Difficult Time Can Be More Readily Endured If We Retain The Conviction That Our Existence Holds A Purpose - A Cause To Pursue, A Person To Love, A Goal To Achieve." - John Maxwell
3596	"When A Woman Like That Whom I've Seen So Much, All Of A Sudden Drops Out Of Touch; Is Always Busy And Never Can, Spare You A Moment, It Means A Man." - Alice Duer Miller
3597	"No One Has Yet Realized The Wealth Of Sympathy, The Kindness And Generosity Hidden In The Soul Of A Child. The Effort Of Every True Education Should Be To Unlock That Treasure." - Emma Goldman
3598	"All Changes, Even The Most Longed For, Have Their Melancholy; For What We Leave Behind Us Is A Part Of Ourselves; We Must Die To One Life Before We Can Enter Another." - Anatole France
3599	"Let Us Not Be Satisfied With Just Giving Money. Money Is Not Enough, Money Can Be Got, But They Need Your Hearts To Love Them. So, Spread Your Love Everywhere You Go." - Mother Teresa
3600	"The Moment You Have In Your Heart This Extraordinary Thing Called Love And Feel The Depth, The Delight, The Ecstasy Of It, You Will Discover That For You The World Is Transformed." - Jiddu Krishnamurti
3601	"All Of The Books In The World Contain No More Information Than Is Broadcast As Video In A Single Large American City In A Single Year. Not All Bits Have Equal Value." - Carl Sagan
3602	"What Is The Use Of Physicians Like Myself Trying To Help Parents To Bring Up Children Healthy And Happy, To Have Them Killed In Such Numbers For A Cause That Is Ignoble?" - Benjamin Spock
3603	"No One Should Negotiate Their Dreams. Dreams Must Be Free To Fly High. No Government, No Legislature, Has A Right To Limit Your Dreams. You Should Never Agree To Surrender Your Dreams." - Jesse Jackson

3604	" Give Me A Stock Clerk With A Goal And I'll Give You A Man Who Will Make History. Give Me A Man With No Goals And I'll Give You A Stock Clerk." - J.C. Penney
3605	"But Whether It Be Dream Or Truth, To Do Well Is What Matters. If It Be Truth, For Truth's Sake. If Not, Then To Gain Friends For The Time When We Awaken." - Pedro Calderon De La Barca
3606	"I Advise You To Say Your Dream Is Possible And Then Overcome All Inconveniences, Ignore All The Hassles And Take A Running Leap Through The Hoop, Even If It Is In Flames." - Les Brown
3607	" In Any Moment Of Decision The Best Thing You Can Do Is The Right Thing, The Next Best Thing Is The Wrong Thing, And The Worst Thing You Can Do Is Nothing." - Theodore Roosevelt
3608	"I Come Into The Peace Of Wild Things Who Do Not Tax Their Lives With Forethought Of Grief... For A Time I Rest In The Grace Of The World, And Am Free." - Wendell Berry
3609	"The Marine Corps Is The Navy's Police Force And As Long As I Am President That Is What It Will Remain. They Have A Propaganda Machine That Is Almost Equal To Stalin's." - Harry S. Truman
3610	"As Both Capitalist And Communist States -- Not To Mention The Technological World --Have Evolved Under The Illusion That Men Purposefully Built Them, Ideological Optimism Seeps Into Every Niche Of Our Lives." - George Bernanos
3611	"We Are Told Never To Cross A Bridge Till We Come To It, But This World Is Owned By Men Who Have Crossed Bridges In Their Imagination Far Ahead Of The Crowd." - Speakers Library
3612	"To The Extent That The Judicial Profession Becomes The Daily Routine Of Deciding Cases On The Most Secure Precedents And The Narrowest Grounds Available, The Judicial Mind Atrophies And Its Perspective Shrinks." - Irving R. Kaufman
3613	"For My Confirmation, I Didn't Get A Watch And My First Pair Of Long Pants, Like Most Lutheran Boys. I Got A Telescope. My Mother Thought It Would Make The Best Gift." - Wernher Von Braun
3614	"The Radical Novelty Of Modern Science Lies Precisely In The Rejection Of The Belief... That The Forces Which Move The Stars And Atoms Are Contingent Upon The Preferences Of The Human Heart." - Walter Lippmann
3615	"Life Has Loveliness To Sell, All Beautiful And Splendid Things, Blue Waves Whitened On A Cliff, Soaring Fire That Sways And Sings, And Children's Faces Looking Up, Holding Wonder Like A Cup." - Sara Teasdale

3616	"A Sense Of Humor... Is Needed Armor. Joy In One's Heart And Some Laughter On One's Lips Is A Sign That The Person Down Deep Has A Pretty Good Grasp Of Life." - Hugh Sidey
3617	"The Mind Is The Limit. As Long As The Mind Can Envision The Fact That You Can Do Something, You Can Do It – As Long As You Really Believe A 100 Percent." - Arnold Schwarzenegger
3618	"The Artist Is A Receptacle For Emotions That Come From All Over The Place: From The Sky, From The Earth, From A Scrap Of Paper, From A Passing Shape, From A Spider's Web." - Pablo Picasso
3619	"The Great Secret Of Doctors, Known Only To Their Wives, But Still Hidden From The Public, Is That Most Things Get Better By Themselves; Most Things, In Fact, Are Better In The Morning." - Lewis Thomas
3620	"The Difference Between The Old Ballplayer And The New Ballplayer Is The Jersey. The Old Ballplayer Cared About The Name On The Front. The New Ballplayer Cares About The Name On The Back." - Steve Garvey
3621	"The Secret Of Health For Both Mind And Body Is Not To Mourn For The Past, Worry About The Future, Or Anticipate Troubles... But To Live In The Present Moment Wisely And Earnestly." - The Buddha
3622	"Dictionary Is The Only Place That Success Comes Before Work. Hard Work Is The Price We Must Pay For Success. I Think You Can Accomplish Anything If You're Willing To Pay The Price." - Vince Lombardi
3623	"A Comfortable Old Age Is The Reward Of A Well-Spent Youth. Instead Of Its Bringing Sad And Melancholy Prospects Of Decay, It Would Give Us Hopes Of Eternal Youth In A Better World." - Maurice Chevalier
3624	"The Successful Person Has The Habit Of Doing The Things Failures Don't Like To Do. They Don't Like Doing Them Either Necessarily. But Their Disliking Is Subordinated To The Strength Of Their Purpose." - E.M. Gray
3625	"The Idea That You Can Merchandise Candidates For High Office Like Breakfast Cereal - That You Can Gather Votes Like Box Tops - Is, I Think, The Ultimate Indignity To The Democratic Process." - Adlai E. Stevenson
3626	"Anybody Who Has Been Seriously Engaged Is Scientific Work Of Any Kind Realizes That Over The Entrance To The Gates Of The Temple Of Science Are Written The Words: 'Ye Must Have Faith.'" - Max Planck
3627	"It Seems Like Such A Terrible Shame That Innocent Civilians Have To Get Hurt In Wars, Otherwise Combat Would Be Such A Wonderfully Healthy Way To Rid The Human Race Of Unneeded Trash." - Fred Woodworth

3628	"The Days Are Cold, The Nights Are Long, The North Wind Sings A Doleful Song; Then Hush Again Upon My Breast; All Merry Things Are Now At Rest, Save Thee, My Pretty Love!" - Dorothy Wordsworth
3629	"The More I Study The Wealthy.. In An Effort To Learn How To Help More People Around The World Become One Of Them.. I'm Stunned By How Many People Are Actually Not Rich." - David Bach
3630	"The Difficulty Lies, Not In The New Ideas, But In Escaping From The Old Ones, Which Ramify, For Those Brought Up As Most Of Us Have Been, Into Every Corner Of Our Minds." - John Maynard Keynes
3631	"The Chief Condition On Which, Life, Health And Vigor Depend On, Is Action. It Is By Action That An Organism Develops Its Faculties, Increases Its Energy, And Attains The Fulfillment Of Its Destiny." - Colin Powell
3632	"The World Will Never Have Lasting Peace So Long As Men Reserve For War The Finest Human Qualities. Peace, No Less Than War, Requires Idealism And Self-Sacrifice And A Righteous And Dynamic Faith." - John Foster Dulles
3633	"We, Therefore, Here In Britain Stand Shoulder To Shoulder With Our American Friends In This Hour Of Tragedy, And We, Like Them, Will Not Rest Until This Evil Is Driven From Our World." - Tony Blair
3634	"A Man Should Live As He Pleases. This, They Say, Is The Mark Of Liberty, Since, On The Other Hand, Not To Live As A Man Wishes Is The Mark Of A Slave." - Aristotle
3635	"Most People Are Not Really Free. They Are Confined By The Niche In The World That They Carve Out For Themselves. They Limit Themselves To Fewer Possibilities By The Narrowness Of Their Vision." - V.S. Naipaul
3636	"In Motivating People, You've Got To Engage Their Minds And Their Hearts. I Motivate People, I Hope, By Example -- And Perhaps By Excitement, By Having Productive Ideas To Make Others Feel Involved." - Keith Rupert Murdoch
3637	"What Makes A River So Restful To People Is That It Doesn't Have Any Doubt - It Is Sure To Get Where It Is Going, And It Doesn't Want To Go Anywhere Else." - Hal Boyle
3638	"The Folly Of Mistaking A Paradox For A Discovery, A Metaphor For A Proof, A Torrent Of Verbiage For A Spring Of Capital Truths, And Oneself For An Oracle, Is Inborn In Us." - Paul Valery
3639	"Let Me Not Pray To Be Sheltered From Dangers, But To Be Fearless In Facing Them. Let Me Not Beg For The Stilling Of My Pain, But For The Heart To Conquer It." - Rabindranath Tagore

3640	"I Found That The Men And Women Who Got To The Top Were Those Who Did The Jobs They Had In Hand, With Everything They Had Of Energy And Enthusiasm And Hard Work." - Harry S. Truman
3641	"He's Got Everything. He' Not A Great Player Yet Because He Hasn't Won Any Major Championships, But It's A Matter Of Time. He's An Outstanding Talent. I Didn't Realize How Tall He Is." - Nick Price
3642	"Think What A Better World It Would Be If We All, The Whole World, Had Cookies And Milk About Three O'clock Every Afternoon And Then Lay Down On Our Blankets For A Nap." - Barbara Jordan
3643	"Fixing Your Objective Is Like Identifying The North Star - You Sight Your Compass On It And Then Use It As The Means Of Getting Back On Track When You Tend To Stray." - Marshall Dimock
3644	"When I Was 40, My Doctor Advised Me That A Man In His 40s Shouldn't Play Tennis. I Heeded His Advice Carefully And Could Hardly Wait Until I Reached 50 To Start Again." - Hugo Black
3645	"Our Government... Teaches The Whole People By Its Example. If The Government Becomes The Lawbreaker, It Breeds Contempt For Law; It Invites Every Man To Become A Law Unto Himself; It Invites Anarchy." - Louis D. Brandeis
3646	"Humankind Has Not Woven The Web Of Life. We Are But One Thread Within It. Whatever We Do To The Web, We Do To Ourselves. All Things Are Bound Together. All Things Connect." - Chief Seattle
3647	"The United States Brags About Its Political System, But The President Says One Thing During The Election, Something Else When He Takes Office, Something Else At Midterm And Something Else When He Leaves." - Deng Xiaoping
3648	"Champagne, If You Are Seeking The Truth, Is Better Than A Lie Detector. It Encourages A Man To Be Expansive, Even Reckless, While Lie Detectors Are Only A Challenge To Tell Lies Successfully." - Graham Greene
3649	"Every Time A Student Walks Past A Really Urgent, Expressive Piece Of Architecture That Belongs To His College, It Can Help Reassure Him That He Does Have That Mind, Does Have That Soul." - Louis Kahn
3650	"I Wish My Name Was Brian Because Maybe Sometimes People Would Misspell My Name And Call Me Brain. That's Like A Free Compliment And You Don't Even Gotta Be Smart To Notice It." - Mitch Hedberg
3651	"The Whole Aim Of Practical Politics Is To Keep The Populace Alarmed (And Hence Clamorous To Be Led To Safety) By Menacing It With An Endless Series Of Hobgoblins, All Of Them Imaginary." - H. L. Mencken

3652	"If You Are Going To Throw A Club, It Is Important To Throw It Ahead Of You, Down The Fairway, So You Don't Have To Waste Energy Going Back To Pick It Up." - Tommy Bolt
3653	"A Fact Is A Simple Statement That Everyone Believes. It Is Innocent, Unless Found Guilty. A Hypothesis Is A Novel Suggestion That No One Wants To Believe. It Is Guilty, Until Found Effective." - Edward Teller
3654	"Time Is Too Slow For Those Who Wait, Too Swift For Those Who Fear, Too Long For Those Who Grieve, Too Short For Those Who Rejoice, But For Those Who Love, Time Is Eternity." - Henry Van Dyke
3655	"We Must Look For Ways To Be An Active Force In Our Own Lives. We Must Take Charge Of Our Own Destinies, Design A Life Of Substance And Truly Begin To Live Our Dreams." - Les Brown
3656	"If A Thing Can Be Done Adequately By Means Of One, It Is Superfluous To Do It By Means Of Several; For We Observe That Nature Does Not Employ Two Instruments Where One Suffices" - Thomas Aquinas
3657	"I Think It's Fair To Say That Personal Computers Have Become The Most Empowering Tool We've Ever Created. They're Tools Of Communication, They're Tools Of Creativity, And They Can Be Shaped By Their User." - Bill Gates
3658	"The Greatest Pleasure Of A Dog Is That You May Make A Fool Of Yourself With Him... And Not Only Will He Not Scold You, But He Will Make A Fool Of Himself, Too." - Samuel Butler
3659	"Each Blade Of Grass Has Its Spot On Earth Whence It Draws Its Life, Its Strength; And So Is Man Rooted To The Land From Which He Draws His Faith Together With His Life." - Joseph Conrad
3660	"The Government, Which Was Designed For The People, Has Got Into The Hands Of The Bosses And Their Employers, The Special Interests. An Invisible Empire Has Been Set Up Above The Forms Of Democracy." - Woodrow Wilson
3661	"To Be Successful You Have To Be Selfish, Or Else You Never Achieve. And Once You Get To Your Highest Level, Then You Have To Be Unselfish. Stay Reachable. Stay In Touch. Don't Isolate." - Michael Jordan
3662	"Fear Of Serious Injury Alone Cannot Justify Oppression Of Free Speech And Assembly. Men Feared Witches And Burnt Women. It Is The Function Of Speech To Free Men From The Bondage Of Irrational Fears." - Louis D. Brandeis
3663	"The Obstacles That Others Put In Our Path Can Be Pushed Aside In Any Number Of Ways. The Obstacles That You Put In Your Own Way Can Be Removed Only By The Same Hands." - Sophia Bedford-Pierce

3664	"When I Stand Before God At The End Of My Life, I Would Hope That I Would Not Have A Single Bit Of Talent Left, And Could Say, I Used Everything You Gave Me." - Erma Bombeck
3665	"Fame Will Go By And, So Long, I've Had You, Fame. If It Goes By, I've Always Known It Was Fickle. So At Least It's Something I Experience, But That's Not Where I Live." - Marilyn Monroe
3666	"I Really Had A Lot Of Dreams When I Was A Kid, And I Think A Great Deal Of That Grew Out Of The Fact That I Had A Chance To Read A Lot." - Bill Gates
3667	"Strike An Average Between What A Woman Thinks Of Her Husband A Month Before She Marries Him And What She Thinks Of Him A Year Afterward, And You Will Have The Truth About Him." - H. L. Mencken
3668	"The Man Who Will Use His Skill And Constructive Imagination To See How Much He Can Give For A Dollar, Instead Of How Little He Can Give For A Dollar, Is Bound To Succeed." - Henry Ford
3669	"I Would Rather Live My Life As If There Is A God And Die To Find Out There Isn't, Than Live My Life As If There Isn't And Die To Find Out There Is." - Albert Camus
3670	"The Cloning Of Humans Is On Most Of The Lists Of Things To Worry About From Science, Along With Behavior Control, Genetic Engineering, Transplanted Heads, Computer Poetry And The Unrestrained Growth Of Plastic Flowers." - Lewis Thomas
3671	"A Scientific Truth Does Not Triumph By Convincing Its Opponents And Making Them See The Light, But Rather Because Its Opponents Eventually Die And A New Generation Grows Up That Is Familiar With It." - Max Planck
3672	"Every Gun That Is Made, Every Warship Launched, Every Rocket Fired, Signifies In The Final Sense A Theft From Those Who Hunger And Are Not Fed, Those Who Are Cold And Are Not Clothed." - Dwight D. Eisenhower
3673	"Aim For Success Not Perfection. Remember That Fear Always Lurks Behind Perfectionism. Confronting Your Fears And Allowing Yourself The Right To Be Human Can, Paradoxically, Make You A Far Happier And More Productive Person." - Dr. David Burns
3674	"Aim For Success Not Perfection... Remember That Fear Always Lurks Behind Perfectionism. Confronting Your Fears And Allowing Yourself The Right To Be Human Can, Paradoxically, Make You A Far Happier And More Productive Person." - Dr. David Burns

3675	"It Is Not Easy To See How The More Extreme Forms Of Nationalism Can Long Survive When Men Have Seen The Earth In Its True Perspective As A Single Small Globe Against The Stars." - Arthur C. Clarke
3676	"Most People Give Up Just When They're About To Achieve Success. They Quit On The One Yard Line. They Give Up At The Last Minute Of The Game One Foot From A Winning Touchdown." - Ross Perot
3677	"I've Made An Odd Discovery. Every Time I Talk To A Savant I Feel Quite Sure That Happiness Is No Longer A Possibility. Yet When I Talk With My Gardener, I'm Convinced Of The Opposite." - Bertrand Russell
3678	"The Secret To Productive Goal Setting Is In Establishing Clearly Defined Goals, Writing Them Down And Then Focusing On Them Several Times A Day With Words, Pictures And Emotions As If We've Already Achieved Them." - Denis Waitley
3679	"When I Was A Kid I Used To Pray Every Night For A New Bicycle. Then I Realized That The Lord Doesn't Work That Way So I Stole One And Asked Him To Forgive Me." - Emo Philips
3680	"I Thank You God For This Most Amazing Day, For The Leaping Greenly Spirits Of Trees, And For The Blue Dream Of Sky And For Everything Which Is Natural, Which Is Infinite, Which Is Yes." - E. E. Cummings
3681	"Anyone Can Become Angry--That Is Easy. But To Be Angry With The Right Person, To The Right Degree, At The Right Time, For The Right Purpose, And In The Right Way-- That Is Not Easy." - Aristotle
3682	"A Film Is - Or Should Be - More Like Music Than Like Fiction. It Should Be A Progression Of Moods And Feelings. The Theme, What's Behind The Emotion, The Meaning, All That Comes Later." - Stanley Kubrick
3683	"A Man Reserves His True And Deepest Love Not For The Species Of Woman In Whose Company He Finds Himself Electrified And Enkindled, But For That One In Whose Company He May Feel Tenderly Drowsy." - George Jean Nathan
3684	"Let Us Not Seek The Republican Answer Or The Democratic Answer, But The Right Answer. Let Us Not Seek To Fix The Blame For The Past. Let Us Accept Our Own Responsibility For The Future." - John F. Kennedy
3685	"In The Long Term We Can Hope That Religion Will Change The Nature Of Man And Reduce Conflict. But History Is Not Encouraging In This Respect. The Bloodiest Wars In History Have Been Religious Wars." - Richard M. Nixon

3686	"I Have A Dream That My Four Little Children Will One Day Live In A Nation Where They Will Not Be Judged By The Color Of Their Skin, But By The Content Of Their Character." - Martin Luther King, Jr.
3687	"Time Is The Coin Of Your Life. It Is The Only Coin You Have, And Only You Can Determine How It Will Be Spent. Be Careful Lest You Let Other People Spend It For You." - Carl Sandburg
3688	"Dreaming In Public Is An Important Part Of Our Job Description, As Science Writers, But There Are Bad Dreams As Well As Good Dreams. We're Dreamers, You See, But We're Also Realists, Of A Sort." - William Gibson
3689	"Action And Reaction, Ebb And Flow, Trial And Error, Change - This Is The Rhythm Of Living. Out Of Our Over-Confidence, Fear; Out Of Our Fear, Clearer Vision, Fresh Hope. And Out Of Hope, Progress." - Bruce Barton
3690	" We Learn Wisdom From Failure Much More Than From Success. We Often Discover What Will Do, By Finding Out What Will Not Do; And Probably He Who Never Made A Mistake Never Made A Discovery." - Samuel Smiles
3691	"Soon Silence Will Have Passed Into Legend. Man Has Turned His Back On Silence. Day After Day He Invents Machines And Devices That Increase Noise And Distract Humanity From The Essence Of Life, Contemplation, Meditation." - Jean Arp
3692	"Tradition Means Giving Votes To The Most Obscure Of All Classes, Our Ancestors. It Is The Democracy Of The Dead. Tradition Refuses To Submit To That Arrogant Oligarchy Who Merely Happen To Be Walking Around." - Gilbert K. Chesterton
3693	"The Establishment Center... Has Led Us Into The Stupidest And Cruelest War In All History. That War Is A Moral And Political Disaster - A Terrible Cancer Eating Away At The Soul Of Our Nation." - George Mcgovern
3694	"Do Not Wait; The Time Will Never Be 'Just Right'. Start Where You Stand, And Work With Whatever Tools You May Have At Your Command, And Better Tools Will Be Found As You Go Along." - Napoleon Hill
3695	"Man Is The Animal That Intends To Shoot Himself Out Into Interplanetary Space, After Having Given Up On The Problem Of An Efficient Way To Get Himself Five Miles To Work And Back Each Day." - Bill Vaughan
3696	"Our Attitudes Control Our Lives. Attitudes Are A Secret Power Working 24 Hours A Day, For Good Or Bad. It Is Of Paramount Importance That We Know How To Harness And Control This Great Force." - Tom Blandi

3697	"And If Tonight My Soul May Find Her Peace In Sleep, And Sink In Good Oblivion, And In The Morning Wake Like A New-Opened Flower Then I Have Been Dipped Again In God, And New-Created." - D.H. Lawrence
3698	"In My View, Far From Deserving Condemnation For Their Courageous Reporting, The New York Times, The Washington Post And Other Newspapers Should Be Commended For Serving The Purpose That The Founding Fathers Saw So Clearly." - Hugo Black
3699	"My Recollection Of A Hundred Lovely Lakes Has Given Me Blessed Release From Care And Worry And The Troubled Thinking Of Our Modern Day. It Has Been A Return To The Primitive And The Peaceful." - Hamlin Garland
3700	"There's No Website, Marketing System, Lead Source, Or Product That Will Save You. If You Don't Get Your Head Where It Needs To Be, Everything Else Is Just A Waste Of Time, Money, And Efforts." - Mike Dillard
3701	"Do Not Wait; The Time Will Never Be "Just Right." Start Where You Stand, And Work With Whatever Tools You May Have At Your Command, And Better Tools Will Be Found As You Go Along." - Napoleon Hill
3702	"Who Will Tell Whether One Happy Moment Of Love Or The Joy Of Breathing Or Walking On A Bright Morning And Smelling The Fresh Air, Is Not Worth All The Suffering And Effort Which Life Implies." - Erich Fromm
3703	"There Are Things That Have To Be Done And You Do Them And You Don't Talk About Them. You Don't Try To Justify Them. They Can't Be Justified. You Just Do Them. Then You Forget Them." - Mario Puzo
3704	"Without Accepting The Fact That Everything Changes, We Cannot Find Perfect Composure. But Unfortunately, Although It Is True, It Is Difficult For Us To Accept It. Because We Cannot Accept The Truth Of Transience, We Suffer." - Shunryu Suzuki
3705	"He Who Has Faith Has... An Inward Reservoir Of Courage, Hope, Confidence, Calmness, And Assuring Trust That All Will Come Out Well - Even Though To The World It May Appear To Come Out Most Badly." - B. C. Forbes
3706	"Everything That Is New Or Uncommon Raises A Pleasure In The Imagination, Because It Fills The Soul With An Agreeable Surprise, Gratifies Its Curiosity, And Gives It An Idea Of Which It Was Not Before Possessed." - Joseph Addison

3707	"I Could End The Deficit In 5 Minutes, You Just Pass A Law That Says, That Anytime There Is A Deficit Of More Than 3% Of GDP, All Sitting Members Of Congress Are Ineligible For Re-Election." - Warren Buffet
3708	"Serious Sport Has Nothing To Do With Fair Play. It Is Bound Up With Hatred, Jealousy, Boastfulness, Disregard Of All Rules And Sadistic Pleasure In Witnessing Violence. In Other Words, It Is War Minus The Shooting." - George Orwell
3709	"Sensible And Responsible Women Do Not Want To Vote. The Relative Positions To Be Assumed By Man And Woman In The Working Out Of Our Civilization Were Assigned Long Ago By A Higher Intelligence Than Ours." - Grover Cleveland
3710	"I Have A Dream That One Day On The Red Hills Of Georgia, The Sons Of Former Slaves And The Sons Of Former Slave Owners Will Be Able To Sit Together At The Table Of Brotherhood." - Martin Luther King, Jr.
3711	"Don't Spend Your Precious Time Asking 'Why Isn't The World A Better Place?' It Will Only Be Time Wasted. The Question To Ask Is 'How Can I Make It Better?' To That There Is An Answer." - Leo F. Buscaglia
3712	" To Follow Without Halt, One Aim; There Is The Secret Of Success. And Success? What Is It? I Do Not Find It In The Applause Of The Theater; It Lies Rather In The Satisfaction Of Accomplishment." - Anna Pavlova
3713	"He's Got An Overall Flair For The Game. It Looks To Me Like He Really Loves What He Does And He Can't Wait To Get Up In The Morning, Go Hit Some Balls And Go Play." - Gary Mccord
3714	"On Rare Occasions One Does Hear Of A Miraculous Case Of A Married Couple Falling In Love After Marriage, But On Close Examination It Will Be Found That It Is A Mere Adjustment To The Inevitable." - Emma Goldman
3715	"The Greatest Form Of Maturity Is At Harvest Time. That Is When We Must Learn How To Reap Without Complaint If The Amounts Are Small And How To Reap Without Apology If The Amounts Are Big." - Jim Rohn
3716	"In The End, We Do Battle Only With Ourselves. Once We Understand This And Focus Our Energy On What We Can Do To Control Our Lives... We Begin To Gain Important Insights Into How Life Works." - J. Stanley Judd
3717	"But Now I Have Come To Believe That The Whole World Is An Enigma, A Harmless Enigma That Is Made Terrible By Our Own Mad Attempt To Interpret It As Though It Had An Underlying Truth." - Umberto Eco

3718	"The Fact That Political Ideologies Are Tangible Realities Is Not A Proof Of Their Vitally Necessary Character. The Bubonic Plague Was An Extraordinarily Powerful Social Reality, But No One Would Have Regarded It As Vitally Necessary." - Wilhelm Reich
3719	"We Are The Children Of A Technological Age. We Have Found Streamlined Ways Of Doing Much Of Our Routine Work. Printing Is No Longer The Only Way Of Reproducing Books. Reading Them, However, Has Not Changed." - Lawrence Clark Powell
3720	"No One Ever Attains Very Eminent Success By Simply Doing What Is Required Of Him; It Is The Amount And Excellence Of What Is Over And Above The Required That Determines The Greatness Of Ultimate Distinction." - Charles Kendall Adams
3721	"Often The Difference Between A Successful Man And A Failure Is Not One's Better Abilities Or Ideas, But The Courage That One Has To Bet On His Ideas, To Take A Calculated Risk, And To Act." - Maxwell Maltz
3722	"The First Rule Of Any Technology Used In A Business Is That Automation Applied To An Efficient Operation Will Magnify The Efficiency. The Second Is That Automation Applied To An Inefficient Operation Will Magnify The Inefficiency." - Bill Gates
3723	"I'm A Great Believer That Any Tool That Enhances Communication Has Profound Effects In Terms Of How People Can Learn From Each Other, And How They Can Achieve The Kind Of Freedoms That They're Interested In." - Bill Gates
3724	"It Is Wonderful How Much Time Good People Spend Fighting The Devil. If They Would Only Expend The Same Amount Of Energy Loving Their Fellow Men, The Devil Would Die In His Own Tracks Of Ennui." - Helen Keller
3725	" If Your Work Is Becoming Uninteresting, So Are You. Work Is An Inanimate Thing And Can Be Made Lively And Interesting Only By Injecting Yourself Into It. Your Job Is Only As Big As You Are." - George C. Hubbs
3726	"Time Is Always In Short Supply. There Is No Substitute For Time. Everything Requires Time. All Work Takes Place In, And Uses Up Time. Yet Most People Take For Granted This Unique, Irreplaceable And Necessary Resource." - Peter Drucker
3727	"Persistence Gives Confidence And Continued Right Mental Attitude Followed By Consistent Action Will Bring Success. When You Have That Knowing Inside Of You, Fear Has Vanished And The Obstruction To A Life Of All Good Removed." - Anonymous

3728	"We Live In Deeds, Not Years: In Thoughts Not Breaths; In Feelings, Not In Figures On A Dial. We Should Count Time By Heart Throbs. He Most Lives Who Thinks Most, Feels The Noblest, Acts The Best." - David Bailey
3729	"Marketing Is Like Playing The Stock Market Or Being An Atomic Scientist. Marketing, Speculation And Science Are All Alike- They All Deal With Immense Natural Forces, Thousands Of Times More Powerful Than The Men Who Use Them." - Eugene M. Schwartz
3730	"I Think Computer Viruses Should Count As Life. I Think It Says Something About Human Nature That The Only Form Of Life We Have Created So Far Is Purely Destructive. We've Created Life In Our Own Image." - Stephen Hawking
3731	"When The Missionaries Came To Africa They Had The Bible And We Had The Land. They Said Let Us Pray. We Closed Our Eyes. When We Opened Them We Had The Bible And They Had The Land." - Desmond Tutu
3732	"It's A Fact That More People Watch Television And Get Their Information That Way Than Read Books. I Find New Technology And New Ways Of Communication Very Exciting And Would Like To Do More In This Field." - Stephen Covey
3733	" Greatness Is Not In Where We Stand, But In What Direction We Are Moving. We Must Sail Sometimes With The Wind And Sometimes Against It -- But Sail We Must And Not Drift, Nor Lie At Anchor." - Oliver Wendell Holmes
3734	"I Still Find Each Day Too Short For All The Thoughts I Want To Think, All The Walks I Want To Take, All The Books I Want To Read, And All The Friends I Want To See." - John Burroughs
3735	"Are You Bored With Life? Then Throw Yourself Into Some Work You Believe In With All Your Heart, Live For It, Die For It, And You Will Find Happiness That You Had Thought Could Never Be Yours." - Dale Carnegie
3736	"There Can Be No Equality Or Opportunity If Men And Women And Children Be Not Shielded In Their Lives From The Consequences Of Great Industrial And Social Processes Which They Cannot Alter, Control, Or Singly Cope With." - Woodrow Wilson
3737	"Do You Know What It Means To Come Home At Night To A Woman Who'll Give You A Little Love, A Little Affection, A Little Tenderness? It Means You're In The Wrong House, That's What It Means." - Henny Youngman

3738	"No Institution Can Possibly Survive If It Needs Geniuses Or Supermen To Manage It. It Must Be Organized In Such A Way As To Be Able To Get Along Under A Leadership Composed Of Average Human Beings." - Peter Drucker
3739	"A Free America... Means Just This: Individual Freedom For All, Rich Or Poor, Or Else This System Of Government We Call Democracy Is Only An Expedient To Enslave Man To The Machine And Make Him Like It." - Frank Lloyd Wright
3740	"I Remember A Hundred Lovely Lakes, And Recall The Fragrant Breath Of Pine And Fir And Cedar And Poplar Trees. The Trail Has Strung Upon It, As Upon A Thread Of Silk, Opalescent Dawns And Saffron Sunsets." - Hamlin Garland
3741	"In Everyone's Life, At Some Time, Our Inner Fire Goes Out. It Is Then Burst Into Flame By An Encounter With Another Human Being. We Should All Be Thankful For Those People Who Rekindle The Inner Spirit." - Albert Schweitzer
3742	"If You Want To Live A New Life, A Free Life, The Life Of An Entrepreneur, You Must Seek Out People Who Live In The World You Want, Because The Bus You Ride Now Doesn't Stop There." - Mike Dillard
3743	"Try A Thing You Haven't Done Three Times. Once, To Get Over The Fear Of Doing It. Twice, To Learn How To Do It. And A Third Time, To Figure Out Whether You Like It Or Not." - Virgil Garnett Thomson
3744	"I Try To Give To The Poor People For Love What The Rich Could Get For Money. No, I Wouldn't Touch A Leper For A Thousand Pounds; Yet I Willingly Cure Him For The Love Of God." - Mother Teresa
3745	"A Human Being Is A Part Of The Whole, Called By Us 'The Universe.' Our Tasks Must Be To Widen Our Circle Of Compassion. To Embrace All Living Creatures And The Whole Of Nature In Its Beauty." - Albert Einstein
3746	"Ideas Are Like Stars, You Will Not Succeed In Touching Them With Your Hands, But Like The Seafaring Man On The Desert Of Waters, You Choose Them As Your Guides, And, Following Them, You Reach Your Destiny." - Carl Schurz
3747	"What A Curious Phenomenon It Is That You Can Get Men To Die For The Liberty Of The World Who Will Not Make The Little Sacrifice That Is Needed To Free Themselves From Their Own Individual Bondage." - Bruce Barton
3748	"The Most Important And Urgent Problems Of The Technology Of Today Are No Longer The Satisfactions Of The Primary Needs Or Of Archetypal Wishes, But The Reparation Of The Evils And Damages By The Technology Of Yesterday." - Dennis Gabor

3749	"The Advice I Am Giving Always To All My Students Is Above All To Study The Music Profoundly... Music Is Like The Ocean, And The Instruments Are Little Or Bigger Islands, Very Beautiful For The Flowers And Trees." - Andres Segovia
3750	"A Friendship Can Weather Most Things And Thrive In Thin Soil; But It Needs A Little Mulch Of Letters And Phone Calls And Small, Silly Presents Every So Often - Just To Save It From Drying Out Completely." - Pam Brown
3751	"Experience Is Never Limited, And It Is Never Complete; It Is An Immense Sensibility, A Kind Of Huge Spider-Web Of The Finest Silken Threads Suspended In The Chamber Of Consciousness, And Catching Every Air-Borne Particle In Its Tissue." - Henry James
3752	"I Have Learned Through Bitter Experience The One Supreme Lesson To Conserve My Anger, And As Heat Conserved Is Transmitted Into Energy, Even So Our Anger Controlled Can Be Transmitted Into A Power That Can Move The World." - Mahandas Gandhi
3753	"A Few Minutes Ago Every Tree Was Excited, Bowing To The Roaring Storm, Waving, Swirling, Tossing Their Branches In Glorious Enthusiasm Like Worship. But Though To The Outer Ear These Trees Are Now Silent, Their Songs Never Cease." - John Muir
3754	"Everything You Want In Life Has A Price Connected To It. There's A Price To Pay If You Want To Make Things Better, A Price To Pay Just For Leaving Things As They Are, A Price For Everything." - Harry Browne
3755	"The Aim Of Every Artist Is To Arrest Motion, Which Is Life, By Artificial Means And Hold It Fixed So That A Hundred Years Later, When A Stranger Looks At It, It Moves Again Since It Is Life." - William Faulkner
3756	"Works Of Art, In My Opinion, Are The Only Objects In The Material Universe To Possess Internal Order, And That Is Why, Though I Don't Believe That Only Art Matters, I Do Believe In Art For Art's Sake." - E. M. Forster
3757	"Few Tragedies Can Be More Extensive Than The Stunting Of Life, Few Injustices Deeper Than The Denial Of An Opportunity To Strive Or Even To Hope, By A Limit Imposed From Without, But Falsely Identified As Lying Within." - Stephen Jay Gould
3758	"I Am Not Bound For Any Public Place, But For Ground Of My Own Where I Have Planted Vines And Orchard Trees, And In The Heat Of The Day Climbed Up Into The Healing Shadow Of The Woods." - Wendell Berry

3759	" The Man Who Is Anybody And Who Does Anything Is Surely Going To Be Criticized, Vilified, And Misunderstood. This Is Part Of The Penalty For Greatness, And Every Man Understands, Too, That It Is No Proof Of Greatness." - Elbert Hubbard
3760	"Success In Business Implies Optimism, Mutual Confidence, And Fair Play. A Business Man Must Hold A High Opinion Of The Worth Of What He Has To Sell And He Must Feel That He Is A Useful Public Servant." - R.H. Cabell
3761	"If You Have An Apple, And I Have An Apple And We Exchange Apples, We Each Still Have One Apple. But, If You Have An Idea And I Have An Idea And We Exchange Ideas...We Each Have Two Ideas." - George Bernard Shaw
3762	"Baseball Is A Game Where A Curve Is An Optical Illusion, A Screwball Can Be A Pitch Or A Person, Stealing Is Legal And You Can Spit Any-where You Like Except In The Umpire's Eye Or On The Ball." - James Patrick Murray
3763	"Sleep Is The Interest We Have To Pay On The Capital Which Is Called In At Death; And The Higher The Rate Of Interest And The More Regu-larly It Is Paid, The Further The Date Of Redemption Is Postponed." - Arthur Schopenhauer
3764	"I Was A Woman In A Man's World. I Was A Democrat In A Republican Administration. I Was An Intellectual In A World Of Bureaucrats. I Talked Differently. This May Have Made Me A Bit Like An Ink Blot." - Jeane Kirkpatrick
3765	"The Newest Computer Can Merely Compound, At Speed, The Oldest Problem In The Relations Between Human Beings, And In The End The Communicator Will Be Confronted With The Old Problem, Of What To Say And How To Say It." - Edward R. Murrow
3766	"Go For The Moon. If You Don't Get It, You'll Still Be Heading For A Star. Happiness Lies Not In The Mere Possession Of Money; It Lies In The Joy Of Achievement, In The Thrill Of The Creative Effort." - Franklin D. Roosevelt
3767	"Nothing Is So Galling To A People Not Broken In From The Birth As A Paternal, Or In Other Words A Meddling Government, A Government Which Tells Them What To Read And Say And Eat And Drink And Wear." - Thomas W. Higginson
3768	"The Poem Is A Little Myth Of Man's Capacity Of Making Life Meaning-ful. And In The End, The Poem Is Not A Thing We See-It Is, Rather, A Light By Which We May See-And What We See Is Life." - Robert Penn Warren

3769	"Can Anything Be Stupider Than That A Man Has The Right To Kill Me Because He Lives On The Other Side Of A River And His Ruler Has A Quarrel With Mine, Though I Have Not Quarreled With Him?" - Blaise Pascal
3770	"The Society Which Scorns Excellence In Plumbing As A Humble Activity And Tolerates Shoddiness In Philosophy Because It Is An Exalted Activity Will Have Neither Good Plumbing Nor Good Philosophy: Neither Its Pipes Nor Its Theories Will Hold Water." - John W. Gardner
3771	"The Democrats Are The Party That Says Government Will Make You Smarter, Taller, Richer, And Remove The Crabgrass On Your Lawn. The Republicans Are The Party That Says Government Doesn't Work And Then They Get Elected And Prove It." - P. J. O'Rourke
3772	"We All Dream; We Do Not Understand Our Dreams, Yet We Act As If Nothing Strange Goes On In Our Sleep Minds, Strange At Least By Comparison With The Logical, Purposeful Doings Of Our Minds When We Are Awake." - Erich Fromm
3773	"The Genius Of Our Ruling Class Is That It Has Kept A Majority Of The People From Ever Questioning The Inequity Of A System Where Most People Drudge Along, Paying Heavy Taxes For Which They Get Nothing In Return." - Gore Vidal
3774	"The Dogmas Of The Quiet Past Are Inadequate To The Stormy Present. The Occasion Is Piled High With Difficulty, And We Must Rise With The Occasion. As Our Case Is New, So We Must Think Anew And Act Anew." - Abraham Lincoln
3775	"The Mind, In Proportion As It Is Cut Off From Free Communication With Nature, With Revelation, With God, With Itself, Loses Its Life, Just As The Body Droops When Debarred From The Air And The Cheering Light From Heaven." - William Ellery Channing
3776	"If You Really Examine Any Well-Managed Organization, You Will Find That The People Who Are Most Successful Are Those Who Are Positive And Helpful, People Who Always Find The Time To Offer Encouragement And Praise When It Is Deserved." - Napoleon Hill
3777	"No Idea Is So Antiquated That It Was Not Once Modern. No Idea Is So Modern That It Will Not Some Day Be Antiquated.... To Seize The Flying Thought Before It Escapes Us Is Our Only Touch With Reality." - Ellen Glasgow
3778	"What Is Sad For Women Of My Generation Is That They Weren't Supposed To Work If They Had Families. What Were They Going To Do When The Children Are Grown - Watch The Raindrops Coming Down The Window Pane?" - Jackie Kennedy

3779	"If You Think Of Yourselves As Helpless And Ineffectual, It Is Certain That You Will Create A Despotic Government To Be Your Master. The Wise Despot, Therefore, Maintains Among His Subjects A Popular Sense That They Are Helpless And Ineffectual." - Frank Herbert
3780	"I Had Pro Offers From The Detroit Lions And Green Bay Packers, Who Were Pretty Hard Up For Linemen In Those Days. If I Had Gone Into Professional Football The Name Jerry Ford Might Have Been A House-hold Word Today." - Gerald R. Ford
3781	"What Is Success? I Think It Is A Mixture Of Having A Flair For The Thing That You Are Doing; Knowing That It Is Not Enough, That You Have Got To Have Hard Work And A Certain Sense Of Purpose." - Margaret Thatcher
3782	"There Isn't A Flaw In His Golf Or His Makeup. He Will Win More Ma-jors Than Arnold Palmer And Me Combined. Somebody Is Going To Dust My Records. It Might As Well Be Tiger, Because He's Such A Great Kid." - Jack Nicklaus
3783	"A Goal Is Not The Same As A Desire, And This Is An Important Distinc-tion To Make. You Can Have A Desire You Don't Intend To Act On. But You Can't Have A Goal You Don't Intend To Act On." - Tom Morris
3784	"I Have Always Been Amazed At The Way An Ordinary Observer Lends So Much More Credence And Attaches So Much More Importance To Waking Events Than To Those Occurring In Dreams... Man... Is Above All The Plaything Of His Memory." - Andre Breton
3785	"It Is Cruel, You Know, That Music Should Be So Beautiful. It Has The Beauty Of Loneliness Of Pain: Of Strength And Freedom. The Beauty Of Disappointment And Never-Satisfied Love. The Cruel Beauty Of Nature And Everlasting Beauty Of Monotony." - Benjamin Britten
3786	"You Are Educated. Your Certification Is In Your Degree. You May Think Of It As The Ticket To The Good Life. Let Me Ask You To Think Of An Alternative. Think Of It As Your Ticket To Change The World." - Tom Brokaw
3787	"Sleep Is Perverse As Human Nature, Sleep Is Perverse As Legislature.... So People Who Go To Bed To Sleep Must Count French Premiers Or Sheep, And People Who Ought To Arise From Bed Yawn And Go Back To Sleep Instead." - Ogden Nash
3788	"Discipline Yourself To Do The Things You Need To Do The Things You Need To Do When You Need To Them, And The Day Will Come When You Will Be Able To Do The Things You Want To Do Them!" - Zig Ziglar

3789	"I Guess There Is Nothing That Will Get Your Mind Off Everything Like Golf. I Have Never Been Depressed Enough To Take Up The Game, But They Say You Get So Sore At Yourself You Forget To Hate Your Enemies." - Will Rogers
3790	"If We Have No Dreams, If We Have No Goals, If We Have No Faith In And Beyond Ourselves, The Life We Choose To Create Becomes Like That Of An Unsharpened Pencil - It Has No Point To Record Responsibility!" - Richard Marvin Voigt
3791	"In Science, Fact Can Only Mean Confirmed To Such A Degree That It Would Be Perverse To Withhold Provisional Assent. I Suppose That Apples Might Start To Rise Tomorrow, But The Possibility Does Not Merit Equal Time In Physics Classrooms." - Stephen Jay Gould
3792	"Enthusiasm Is The Yeast That Makes Your Hopes Shine To The Stars. Enthusiasm Is The Sparkle In Your Eyes, The Swing In Your Gait, The Grip Of Your Hand, The Irresistible Surge Of Will And Energy To Execute Your Ideas." - Henry Ford
3793	"We Used To Root For The Indians Against The Cavalry, Because We Didn't Think It Was Fair In The History Books That When The Cavalry Won It Was A Great Victory, And When The Indians Won It Was A Massacre." - Dick Gregory
3794	"These Are My New Shoes. They're Good Shoes. They Won't Make You Rich Like Me, They Won't Make You Rebound Like Me, They Definitely Won't Make You Handsome Like Me. They'll Only Make You Have Shoes Like Me. That's It." - Charles Barkley
3795	"The More That Learn To Read The Less Learn How To Make A Living. That's One Thing About A Little Education. It Spoils You For Actual Work. The More You Know The More You Think Somebody Owes You A Living." - Will Rogers
3796	"Globalization, As Defined By Rich People Like Us, Is A Very Nice Thing... You Are Talking About The Internet, You Are Talking About Cell Phones, You Are Talking About Computers. This Doesn't Affect Two-Thirds Of The People Of The World." - Jimmy Carter
3797	"It Is Not So Much For Its Beauty That The Forest Makes A Claim Upon Men's Hearts, As For That Subtle Something, That Quality Of Air That Emanation From Old Trees, That So Wonderfully Changes And Renews A Weary Spirit." - Robert Louis Stevenson
3798	"Rest Is Not Idleness, And To Lie Sometimes On The Grass Under Trees On A Summer's Day, Listening To The Murmur Of The Water, Or Watching The Clouds Float Across The Sky, Is By No Means A Waste Of Time." - John Lubbock

3799	"We Should So Provide For Old Age That It May Have No Urgent Wants Of This World To Absorb It From Meditation On The Next. It Is Awful To See The Lean Hands Of Dotage Making A Coffer Of The Grave." - Pearl S. Buck
3800	"Every Person Who Wins In Any Undertaking Must Be Willing To Cut All Sources Of Retreat. Only By Doing So Can One Be Sure Of Maintaining That State Of Mind Known As A Burning Desire To Win - Essential To Success." - Napoleon Hill
3801	"Whenever The Pressure Of Our Complex City Life Thins My Blood And Numbs My Brain, I Seek Relief In The Trail; And When I Hear The Coyote Wailing To The Yellow Dawn, My Cares Fall From Me - I Am Happy." - Hamlin Garland
3802	"If You Don't Like The President, It Costs You 90 Bucks To Fly To Washington To Picket. If You Don't Like The Governor, It Costs You 60 Bucks To Fly To Albany To Picket. If You Don't Like Me, 90 Cents." - Edward Koch
3803	"Teaching Is The Only Major Occupation Of Man For Which We Have Not Yet Developed Tools That Make An Average Person Capable Of Competence And Performance. In Teaching We Rely On The "Naturals," The Ones Who Somehow Know How To Teach." - Peter Drucker
3804	"There Isn't A Single Situation In Your Career, Your Relationships With Others, Or In Your Personal Life That Benefits From A Negative Attitude. All Will Be Greatly Improved If You Make It A Practice To Approach Life In A Positive Way" - Napoleon Hill
3805	"We Are Born At A Given Moment, In A Given Place And, Like Vintage Years Of Wine, We Have The Qualities Of The Year And Of The Season Of Which We Are Born. Astrology Does Not Lay Claim To Anything More." - Carl Jung
3806	"I Used To Think That Cyberspace Was Fifty Years Away. What I Thought Was Fifty Years Away, Was Only Ten Years Away. And What I Thought Was Ten Years Away... It Was Already Here. I Just Wasn't Aware Of It Yet." - Bruce Sterling
3807	"The Pursuit Of Peace And Progress Cannot End In A Few Years In Either Victory Or Defeat. The Pursuit Of Peace And Progress, With Its Trials And Its Errors, Its Successes And Its Setbacks, Can Never Be Relaxed And Never Abandoned." - Dag Hammarskjold
3808	"I Can Forgive, But I Cannot Forget, Is Only Another Way Of Saying, I Will Not Forgive. Forgiveness Ought To Be Like A Cancelled Note - Torn In Two, And Burned Up, So That It Never Can Be Shown Against One." - Henry Ward Beecher

3809	" How Far You Go In Life Depends On You Being Tender With The Young, Compassionate With The Aged, Sympathetic With The Striving And Tolerant Of The Weak And The Strong. Because Someday In Life You Will Have Been All Of These." - George Washington Carver
3810	"As Your Faith Is Strengthened You Will Find That There Is No Longer The Need To Have A Sense Of Control, That Things Will Flow As They Will, And That You Will Flow With Them, To Your Great Delight And Benefit." - Emmanuel Teney
3811	"Consult Not Your Fears But Your Hopes And Your Dreams. Think Not About Your Frustrations, But About Your Unfulfilled Potential. Concern Yourself Not With What You Tried And Failed In, But With What It Is Still Possible For You To Do." - Pope John XXIII
3812	"The Question That Will Decide Our Destiny Is Not Whether We Shall Expand Into Space. It Is: Shall We Be One Species Or A Million? A Million Species Will Not Exhaust The Ecological Niches That Are Awaiting The Arrival Of Intelligence." - Freeman Dyson
3813	"To Me Education Is A Leading Out Of What Is Already There In The Pupil's Soul. To Miss Mackay It Is A Putting In Of Something That Is Not There, And That Is Not What I Call Education. I Call It Intrusion." - Muriel Spark
3814	"Twenty YEARS From Now You Will Be More DISAPPOINTED By The Things You DIDN'T Do Then By The ONES You Did. So Throw Off The BOWLINES, Sail Away From This Safe HARBOR, Catch The Trade WINDS In Your SAILS. EXPLORE. DREAM. DISCOVER." - Mark Twain
3815	"The Stories Of Childhood Leave An Indelible Impression, And Their Author Always Has A Niche In The Temple Of Memory From Which The Image Is Never Cast Out To Be Thrown On The Rubbish Heap Of Things That Are Outgrown And Outlived." - Howard Pyle
3816	"He's Going To Be Around A Long, Long Time, If His Body Holds Up. That's Always A Concern With A Lot Of Players Because Of How Much They Play. A Lot Of Guys Can't Handle It. But It Looks Like He Can." - Jack Nicklaus
3817	"And Here Is The Key To All Of It... You Have The Power To Completely Create The Rules That Define Your Reality. And You Can Do It Instantly. What Was Impossible Today Can Be Possible Tomorrow If You Desire It To Be." - Mike Dillard
3818	"Very Few People Possess True Artistic Ability. It Is Therefore Both Unseemly And Unproductive To Irritate The Situation By Making An Effort. If You Have A Burning, Restless Urge To Write Or Paint, Simply Eat Something Sweet And The Feeling Will Pass." - Fran Lebowitz

3819	"If You Are Neutral In Situations Of Injustice, You Have Chosen The Side Of The Oppressor. If An Elephant Has Its Foot On The Tail Of A Mouse And You Say That You Are Neutral, The Mouse Will Not Appreciate Your Neutrality." - Desmond Tutu
3820	"Just The Fact That Some Geniuses Were Laughed At Does Not Imply That All Who Are Laughed At Are Geniuses. They Laughed At Columbus, They Laughed At Fulton, They Laughed At The Wright Brothers. But They Also Laughed At Bozo The Clown." - Carl Sagan
3821	"The Bed Is A Bundle Of Paradoxes: We Go To It With Reluctance, Yet We Quit It With Regret; We Make Up Our Minds Every Night To Leave It Early, But We Make Up Our Bodies Every Morning To Keep It Late." - Charles Caleb Colton
3822	"I Was About Half In Love With Her By The Time We Sat Down. That's The Thing About Girls. Every Time They Do Something Pretty... You Fall Half In Love With Them, And Then You Never Know Where The Hell You Are." - J. D. Salinger
3823	"The Artist One Day Falls Through A Hole In The Brambles, And From That Moment He Is Following The Dark Rapids Of An Underground River Which May Sometimes Flow So Near To The Surface That The Laughing Picnic Parties Are Heard Above." - Cyril Connolly
3824	" The Person Who Tries To Live Alone Will Not Succeed As A Human Being. His Heart Withers If It Does Not Answer Another Heart. His Mind Shrinks Away If He Hears Only The Echoes Of His Own Thoughts And Finds No Other Inspiration." - Pearl S. Buck
3825	"The Great Successful Men Of The World Have Used Their Imagination...They Think Ahead And Create Their Mental Picture In All Its Details, Filling In Here, Adding A Little There, Altering This A Bit And That A Bit, But Steadily Building - Steadily Building." - Robert Collier
3826	"Look At Growth, Look At How Much Time People Spend On The Net And Look At The Variety Of Things That They Are Doing. It's All Really Good, So I Am Actually Encouraged By The Fundamentals That Underlie Usage Growth On The Net." - Meg Whitman
3827	"Our Achievements Speak For Themselves. What We Have To Keep Track Of Are Our Failures, Discouragements And Doubts. We Tend To Forget The Past Difficulties, The Many False Starts, And The Painful Groping. We See Our Past Achievements As The End Results Of." - Eric Hoffer
3828	"We Shall Defend Our Island, Whatever The Cost May Be, We Shall Fight On The Beaches, We Shall Fight On The Landing Grounds, We Shall Fight In The Fields And In The Streets, We Shall Fight In The Hills; We Shall Never Surrender." - Winston Churchill

3829	"Be Assured Those Will Be Thy Worst Enemies, Not To Whom Thou Hast Done Evil, But Who Have Done Evil To Thee. And Those Will Be Thy Best Friends, Not To Whom Thou Hast Done Good, But Who Have Done Good To Thee." - Tacitus
3830	"Most People Go To Their Grave With Their Music Still In Them. (Actual Quote: A Few Can Touch The Magic String, and Noisy Fame Is Proud To Win Them: Alas For Those That Never Sing, But Die With All Their Music In Them." - Oliver Wendell Holmes
3831	"They Tell Us That Suicide Is The Greatest Piece Of Cowardice... That Suicide Is Wrong; When It Is Quite Obvious That There Is Nothing In The World To Which Every Man Has A More Unassailable Title Than To His Own Life And Person." - Arthur Schopenhauer
3832	"I Found That I Could Find The Energy... That I Could Find The Determination To Keep On Going. I Learned That Your Mind Can Amaze Your Body, If You Just Keep Telling Yourself, I Can Do It...I Can Do It...I Can Do It! " - Jon Erickson
3833	" If I Have Been Of Service, If I Have Glimpsed More Of The Nature And Essence Of Ultimate Good, If I Am Inspired To Reach Wider Horizons Of Thought And Action, If I Am At Peace With Myself, It Has Been A Successful Day." - Alex Noble
3834	"There Was Endless Action - Not Just Football, But Sailboats, Tennis And Other Things: Movement. There Was Endless Talk - The Ambassador At The Head Of The Table Laying Out The Prevailing Wisdom, But Everyone Else Weighing In With Their Opinions And Taking Part." - Charles Spalding
3835	"I've Missed More Than 9000 Shots In My Career. I've Lost Almost 300 Games. 26 Times, I've Been Trusted To Take The Game Winning Shot And Missed. I've Failed Over And Over And Over Again In My Life. And That Is Why I Succeed." - Michael Jordan
3836	"She Is A Friend Of Mind. She Gather Me, Man. The Pieces I Am, She Gather Them And Give Them Back To Me In All The Right Order. It's Good, You Know, When You Got A Woman Who Is A Friend Of Your Mind." - Toni Morrison
3837	"I Cannot Lead You Into Battle. I Do Not Give You Laws Or Administer Justice But I Can Do Something Else - I Can Give My Heart And My Devotion To These Old Islands And To All The Peoples Of Our Brotherhood Of Nations." - Elizabeth II
3838	"I Like Nonsense, It Wakes Up The Brain Cells. Fantasy Is A Necessary Ingredient In Living, It's A Way Of Looking At Life Through The Wrong End Of A Telescope. Which Is What I Do, And That Enables You To Laugh At Life's Realities." - Theodor Geisel

3839	"A Child Too, Can Never Grasp The Fact That The Same Mother Who Cooks So Well, Is So Concerned About His Cough, And Helps So Kindly With His Homework, In Some Circumstance Has No More Feeling Than A Wall Of His Hidden Inner World." - Alice Duer Miller
3840	"It's The Movies That Have Really Been Running Things In America Ever Since They Were Invented. They Show You What To Do, How To Do It, When To Do It, How To Feel About It, And How To Look How You Feel About It." - Andy Warhol
3841	"One Of The Most Tragic Things I Know About Human Nature Is That All Of Us Tend To Put Off Living. We Are All Dreaming Of Some Magical Rose Garden Over The Horizon Instead Of Enjoying The Roses That Are Blooming Outside Our Windows Today." - Dale Carnegie
3842	"The Man Is A Success Who Has Lived Well, Laughed Often, And Loved Much; Who Has Gained The Respect Of Intelligent Men And The Love Of Children; Who Has Filled His Niche And Accomplished His Task; Who Leaves The World Better Than He Found It." - Bessie Stanley
3843	"Given Pounds And Five Years, And An Ordinary Man Can In The Ordi-nary Course, Without Any Undue Haste Or Putting Any Pressure Upon His Taste, Surround Himself With Books, All In His Own Language, And Thence Forward Have At Least One Place In The World." - Augustine Birrell
3844	"Everyone Who Has Achieved Financial Independence Will Tell You That – At Least In The Early Days -- You Have To Work Smarter And Harder. The Price Of Success Must Be Paid In Full, And It Must Be Paid In Advance. There Are No Shortcuts." - John Cummuta
3845	"If Any Man Claims The Negro Should Be Content... Let Him Say He Would Willingly Change The Color Of His Skin And Go To Live In The Negro Section Of A Large City. Then And Only Then Has He A Right To Such A Claim." - Robert Kennedy
3846	"We Emphasize That We Believe In Change Because We Were Born Of It, We Have Lived By It, We Prospered And Grew Great By It. So The Status Quo Has Never Been Our God, And We Ask No One Else To Bow Down Before It." - Carl T. Rowan
3847	"Although... The Chief Magistrate Must Almost Of Necessity Be Chosen By A Party And Stand Pledged To Its Principles And Measures, Yet In His Official Action He Should Not Be The President Of A Party Only, But Of The Whole People Of The United States." - James Polk

3848	"I Was Told To Avoid The Business All Together Because Of The Rejection. People Would Say To Me, 'Don't You Want To Have A Normal Job And A Normal Family?' I Guess That Would Be Good Advice For Some People, But I Wanted To Act." - Jennifer Aniston
3849	"Death Is A Natural Part Of Life. Rejoice For Those Around You Who Transform Into The Force. Mourn Them Do Not. Miss Them Do Not. Attachment Leads To Jealousy. The Shadow Of Greed That Is. Train Yourself To Let Go Of Everything You Fear To Lose." - Yoda
3850	"There Are Two Big Forces At Work, External And Internal. We Have Very Little Control Over External Forces Such As Tornados, Earthquakes, Floods, Disasters, Illness And Pain. What Really Matters Is Internal Force. How Do I Respond To Those Disasters? Over That I Have Complete Control." - Leo Buscaglia
3851	"A Flock Of Sheep That Leisurely Pass By One After One; The Sound Of Rain, And Bees Murmuring; The Fall Of Rivers, Winds And Seas, Smooth Fields, White Sheets Of Water, And Pure Sky - I've Thought Of All By Turns, And Still I Lie Sleepless." - William Wordsworth
3852	"The Person Who Has Nothing For Which He Is Willing To Fight, Nothing Which Is More Important Than His Own Personal Safety, Is A Miserable Creature And Has No Chance Of Being Free Unless Made And Kept So By The Exertions Of Better Men Than Himself." - John Stuart Mill
3853	"Poetry Is Not A Turning Loose Of Emotion, But An Escape From Emotion; It Is Not The Expression Of Personality, But An Escape From Personality. But, Of Course, Only Those Who Have Personality And Emotions Know What It Means To Want To Escape From These Things." - T. S. Eliot
3854	"Thus So Wretched Is Man That He Would Weary Even Without Any Cause For Weariness... And So Frivolous Is He That, Though Full Of A Thousand Reasons For Weariness, The Least Thing, Such As Playing Billiards Or Hitting A Ball, Is Sufficient Enough To Amuse Him." - Blaise Pascal
3855	"The Strongest Oak Of The Forest Is Not The One That Is Protected From The Storm And Hidden From The Sun. It's The One That Stands In The Open Where It Is Compelled To Struggle For Its Existence Against The Winds And Rains And The Scorching Sun." - Napoleon Hill
3856	"You Always Do What You Want To Do. This Is True With Every Act. You May Say That You Had To Do Something, Or That You Were Forced To, But Actually, Whatever You Do, You Do By Choice. Only You Have The Power To Choose For Yourself." - W. Clement Stone

3857	"The Difference Between Great People And Everyone Else Is That Great People Create Their Lives Actively, While Everyone Else Is Created By Their Lives, Passively Waiting To See Where Life Takes Them Next. The Difference Between The Two Is The Difference Between Living Fully And Just Existing." - Michael E. Gerber
3858	"When We Honestly Ask Ourselves Which Person In Our Lives Means The Most To Us, We Often Find That It Is Those Who, Instead Of Giving Advice, Solutions, Or Cures, Have Chosen Rather To Share Our Pain And Touch Our Wounds With A Warm And Tender Hand." - Henri Nouwen
3859	"Whatever Task You Undertake, Do It With All Your Heart And Soul. Always Be Courteous, Never Be Discouraged. Beware Of Him Who Promises Something For Nothing. Do Not Blame Anybody For Your Mistakes And Failures. Do Not Look For Approval Except The Consciousness Of Doing Your Best." " - Bernard Mannes Baruch
3860	"If You're Trying To Achieve, There Will Be Roadblocks. I've Had Them; Everybody Has Had Them. But Obstacles Don't Have To Stop You. If You Run Into A Wall, Don't Turn Around And Give Up. Figure Out How To Climb It, Go Through It, Or Work Around It." - Michael Jordan
3861	"If A Politician Murders His Mother, The First Response Of The Press Or Of His Opponents Will Likely Be Not That It Was A Terrible Thing To Do, But Rather That In A Statement Made Six Years Before He Had Gone On Record As Being Opposed To Matricide." - Meg Greenfield
3862	"When You're In Love You Never Really Know Whether Your Elation Comes From The Qualities Of The One You Love, Or If It Attributes Them To Her; Whether The Light Which Surrounds Her Like A Halo Comes From You, From Her, Or From The Meeting Of Your Sparks." - Natalie Clifford Barney
3863	"Your Memory Is A Monster; You Forget - It Doesn't. It Simply Files Things Away. It Keeps Things For You, Or Hides Things From You - And Summons Them To Your Recall With A Will Of Its Own. You Think You Have A Memory; But It Has You!" - John Irving
3864	"When We Forgive Evil We Do Not Excuse It, We Do Not Tolerate It, We Do Not Smother It. We Look The Evil Full In The Face, Call It What It Is, Let Its Horror Shock And Stun And Enrage Us, And Only Then Do We Forgive It." - Lewis B. Smedes
3865	"As I Approve Of A Youth That Has Something Of The Old Man In Him, So I Am No Less Pleased With An Old Man That Has Something Of The Youth. He That Follows This Rule May Be Old In Body, But Can Never Be So In Mind." - Marcus Tullius Cicero

3866	"The People Who Occupy The Top Positions Are Almost Always Happy, Enthusiastic People Who Encourage Others To Behave In The Same Way. Yet There Are Always A Few Individuals Who Never Seem To Get The Message And Behave As Though They Can Complain Their Way To The Top." - Napoleon Hill
3867	"In America Everybody Is Of The Opinion That He Has No Social Superiors, Since All Men Are Equal, But He Does Not Admit That He Has No Social Inferiors, For, From The Time Of Jefferson Onward, The Doctrine That All Men Are Equal Applies Only Upwards, Not Downwards." - Bertrand Russell
3868	"How Do People Go To Sleep? I'm Afraid I've Lost The Knack. I Might Try Busting Myself Smartly Over The Temple With The Night-Light. I Might Repeat To Myself, Slowly And Soothingly, A List Of Quotations Beautiful From Minds Profound; If I Can Remember Any Of The Damn Things." - Dorothy Parker
3869	"Set The Course Of Your Lives By The Three Stars- Sincerity, Courage, Unselfishness. From These Flow A Host Of Other Virtues... He Who Follows Them And Does Not Seek Success, Will Attain The Highest Type Of Success. That Which Lies In The Esteem Of Those Among Whom He Dwells." - Dr. Monroe E. Deutsch
3870	"You Build On Failure. You Use It As A Stepping Stone. Close The Door On The Past. You Don't Try To Forget The Mistakes, But You Don't Dwell On It. You Don't Let It Have Any Of Your Energy, Or Any Of Your Time, Or Any Of Your Space." - Johnny Cash
3871	"My Illusions Didn't Have Anything To Do With Being A Fine Actress. I Knew How Third Rate I Was. I Could Actually Feel My Lack Of Talent, As If It Were Cheap Clothes I Was Wearing Inside. But, My God, How I Wanted To Learn, To Change, To Improve!" - Marilyn Monroe
3872	"Poetry Is The Journal Of The Sea Animal Living On Land, Wanting To Fly In The Air. Poetry Is A Search For Syllables To Shoot At The Barriers Of The Unknown And The Unknowable. Poetry Is A Phantom Script Telling How Rainbows Are Made And Why They Go Away." - Carl Sandburg
3873	"You Are Not Here Merely To Make A Living. You Are Here In Order To Enable The World To Live More Amply, With Greater Vision, With A Finer Spirit Of Hope And Achievement. You Are Here To Enrich The World, And You Impoverish Yourself If You Forget The Errand." - Woodrow Wilson

3874	"Many People Think That If They Were Only In Some Other Place, Or Had Some Other Job, They Would Be Happy. Well, That Is Doubtful. So Get As Much Happiness Out Of What You Are Doing As You Can And Don't Put Off Being Happy Until Some Future Date." - Dale Carnegie
3875	"Failure Seems To Be Regarded As The One Unpardonable Crime, Success As The All Redeeming Virtue, The Acquisition Of Wealth As The Single Worthy Aim Of Life. The Hair-4 -Raising Revelations Of Skullduggery And Grand-Scale Thievery Merely Incite Others To Surpass By Yet Bolder Outrages And More Corrupt Combinations." - Charles Francis Adams II
3876	"I Know My Country Has Not Perfected Itself. At Times, We've Struggled To Keep The Promise Of Liberty And Equality For All Of Our People. We've Made Our Share Of Mistakes, And There Are Times When Our Actions Around The World Have Not Lived Up To Our Best Intentions." - Barack Obama
3877	"The World We See That Seems So Insane Is The Result Of A Belief System That Is Not Working. To Perceive The World Differently, We Must Be Willing To Change Our Belief System, Let The Past Slip Away, Expand Our Sense Of Now, And Dissolve The Fear In Our Minds." - William James
3878	"Giving People Self-Confidence Is By Far The Most Important Thing That I Can Do. Because Then They Will Act. Globalization Has Changed Us Into A Company That Searches The World, Not Just To Sell Or To Source, But To Find Intellectual Capital - The World's Best Talents And Greatest Ideas." - Jack Welch
3879	"Even Thus Last Night, And Two Nights More I Lay, And Could Not Win Thee, Sleep, By Any Stealth: So Do Not Let Me Wear To-Night Away. Without Thee What Is All The Morning's Wealth? Come, Blessed Barrier Between Day And Day, Dear Mother Of Fresh Thoughts And Joyous Health!" - William Wordsworth
3880	"The Repose Of Sleep Refreshes Only The Body. It Rarely Sets The Soul At Rest. The Repose Of The Night Does Not Belong To Us. It Is Not The Possession Of Our Being. Sleep Opens Within Us An Inn For Phantoms. In The Morning We Must Sweep Out The Shadows." - Gaston Bachelard
3881	"A Pun Does Not Commonly Justify A Blow In Return. But If A Blow Were Given For Such Cause, And Death Ensued, The Jury Would Be Judges Both Of The Facts And Of The Pun, And Might, If The Latter Were Of An Aggravated Character, Return A Verdict Of Justifiable Homicide." - Oliver Wendell Holmes

3882	"One Cannot Buy, Rent Or Hire More Time. The Supply Of Time Is Totally Inelastic. No Matter How High The Demand, The Supply Will Not Go Up. There Is No Price For It. Time Is Totally Perishable And Cannot Be Stored. Yesterday's Time Is Gone Forever, And Will Never Come Back." - Peter Drucker
3883	"Look At A Stone Cutter Hammering Away At His Rock, Perhaps A Hundred Times Without As Much As A Crack Showing In It. Yet At The Hundred-And-First Blow It Will Split In Two, And I Know It Was Not The Last Blow That Did It, But All That Had Gone Before." - Jacob A. Riis
3884	"Everyone Is A House With Four Rooms, A Physical, A Mental, An Emotional, And A Spiritual. Most Of Us Tend To Live In One Room Most Of The Time, But Unless We Go Into Every Room Every Day, Even If Only To Keep It Aired, We Are Not A Complete Person." - Rumer Godden
3885	"All Men Dream, But Not Equally. Those Who Dream By Night In The Dusty Recesses Of Their Minds, Wake In The Day To Find That It Was Vanity: But The Dreamers Of The Day Are Dangerous Men, For They May Act On Their Dreams With Open Eyes, To Make Them Possible." - Thomas E. Lawrence
3886	"Our Life's Journey Of Self-Discovery Is Not A Straight-Line Rise From One Level Of Consciousness To Another. Instead, It Is A Series Of Steep Climbs And Flat Plateaus, Then Further Climbs. Even Though We All Approach The Journey From Different Directions, Certain Of The Journey's Characteristics Are Common To All Of Us." - Stuart Wilde
3887	"By Reading The Scriptures I Am So Renewed That All Nature Seems Renewed Around Me And With Me. The Sky Seems To Be A Pure, A Cooler Blue, The Trees A Deeper Green. The Whole World Is Charged With The Glory Of God And I Feel Fire And Music Under My Feet." - Thomas Merton
3888	"Every State Has A Natural Right In Cases Not Within The Compact (Causes Non Faederis) To Nullify Of Their Own Authority All Assumptions Of Power By Others Within Their Limits. Without This Right, They Would Be Under The Dominion, Absolute And Unlimited, Of Whosoever Might Exercise This Right Of Judgment For Them." - Thomas Jefferson
3889	"We Call That Person Who Has Lost His Father, An Orphan; And A Widower That Man Who Has Lost His Wife. But That Man Who Has Known The Immense Unhappiness Of Losing A Friend, By What Name Do We Call Him? Here Every Language Is Silent And Holds Its Peace In Impotence." - Joseph Roux

3890	"Nothing Is As Difficult As To Achieve Results In This World If One Is Filled Full Of Great Tolerance And The Milk Of Human Kindness. The Person Who Achieves Must Generally Be A One-Idea Individual, Concentrated Entirely On That One Idea, And Ruthless In His Aspect Toward Other Men And Other Ideas." - Corinne Roosevelt Robinson
3891	"If You Know The Enemy And Know Yourself, You Need Not Fear The Result Of A Hundred Battles. If You Know Yourself But Not The Enemy, For Every Victory Gained You Will Also Suffer A Defeat. If You Know Neither The Enemy Nor Yourself, You Will Succumb In Every Battle." - Sun Tzu"
3892	"Look, I Don't Want To Wax Philosophic, But I Will Say That If You're Alive You've Got To Flap Your Arms And Legs, You've Got To Jump Around A Lot, For Life Is The Very Opposite Of Death, And Therefore You Must At Very Least Think Noisy And Colorfully, Or You're Not Alive." - Mel Brooks
3893	"Many Politicians Are In The Habit Of Laying It Down As A Self-Evident Proposition That No People Ought To Be Free Till They Are Fit To Use Their Freedom. The Maxim Is Worthy Of The Fool In The Old Story Who Resolved Not To Go Into The Water Till He Had Learned To Swim." - Thomas B. Macaulay
3894	"If A Man Walks In The Woods For Love Of Them Half Of Each Day, He Is In Danger Of Being Regarded As A Loafer. But If He Spends His Days As A Speculator, Shearing Off Those Woods And Making The Earth Bald Before Her Time, He Is Deemed An Industrious And Enterprising Citizen." - Henry David Thoreau
3895	"My Mother Drew A Distinction Between Achievement And Success. She Said That Achievement Is The Knowledge That You Have Studied And Worked Hard And Done The Best That Is In You. Success Is Being Praised By Others. That Is Nice But Not As Important Or Satisfying. Always Aim For Achievement And Forget About Success." - Helen Hayes
3896	"Where There Is A Will There Is A Way. Is An Old True Saying. He Who Resolves Upon Doing A Thing, By That Very Resolution Often Scales The Barriers To It, And Secures Its Achievement. To Think We Are Able, Is Almost To Be So -- To Determine Upon Attainment Is Frequently Attainment Itself." - Samuel Smiles
3897	"It May Be Hard For An Egg To Turn Into A Bird: It Would Be A Jolly Sight Harder For It To Learn To Fly While Remaining An Egg. We Are Like Eggs At Present. And You Cannot Go On Indefinitely Being Just An Ordinary, Decent Egg. We Must Be Hatched Or Go Bad." - Mignon Mclaughlin

3898	"You Gain Strength, Courage, And Confidence By Every Experience In Which You Really Stop To Look Fear In The Face... The Danger Lies In Refusing To Face The Fear, In Not Daring To Come To Grips With It... You Must Make Yourself Succeed Every Time. You Must Do The Thing You Think You Cannot Do." - Eleanor Roosevelt
3899	"The Only Time You Ever Have In Which To Learn Anything Or See Any-thing Or Feel Anything, Or Express Any Feeling Or Emotion, Or Respond To An Event, Or Grow, Or Heal, Is This Moment, Because This Is The Only Moment Any Of Us Ever Gets. You're Only Here Now; You're Only Alive In This Moment." - Jon Kabat-Zinn
3900	"The Only Time You Ever Have In Which To Learn Anything Or See Anything Or Feel Anything, Or Express Any Feeling Or Emotion, Or Respond To An Event, Or Grow, Or Heal, Is This Moment, Because This Is The Only Moment Any Of Us Ever Gets. You're Only Here Now; You're Only Alive In This Moment." - Marianne Williamson
3901	"A Business, Professional, Or Personal Relationship Built Upon A Lie Cannot Long Endure, But One That Is Founded On Truth And Equality Of Benefit For The Participants Is Unlimited. Make It A Practice To Tell The Truth In All That You Do-Even When It Doesn't Matter-And You Will Form A Habit Of Truthfulness. Of What Others Think." - Napoleon Hill
3902	"Normal Is Getting Dressed In Clothes That You Buy For Work And Driving Through Traffic In A Car That You Are Still Paying For - In Order To Get To The Job You Need To Pay For The Clothes And The Car, And The House You Leave Vacant All Day So You Can Afford To Live In It." - Ellen Goodman
3903	"In Marketing, The Forces Are The Hopes, Fears And Desires Of Millions Upon Millions Of Men And Women, All Over The World. The Men Who Use These Forces Did Not Create Them; They Can't Turn Them Or Shut Them Down; Neither Can They Diminish Them Or Add To Them In Any Way. All They Can Do Is Harness Them!" - Eugene M. Schwartz
3904	"The Mere Word Kindness Is Grateful To Our Ears; So Much Good Is Implied In It, So Much Lightening Of Loads, So Much Brightening Of Dark Lives. It Is Compounded Of So Many Warm, Noble Things: Once It Is A Manifestation Of Pity, Once Of Sympathy, Once Of Love, Once Of Justice -- It Can Flow From So Many Springs In Our Soul." - Ruhiyyah Rabbani

3905	"Innovation: Continuous, Repeated Innovation A Steady Stream Of New Ideas- Fresh New Solutions To New Problems. Created Above All Not By The Impossible Route Of Memory - But By Analysis. And What Is Analysis? As Gene Says, It's A Series Of Measuring Rods, Checkpoints, Benchmarks And Signposts That Show You Where A Particular Force Is Going, And Enable You To Get There First." - Eugene M. Schwartz
3906	"Freedom Is Never More Than One Generation Away From Extinction. We Didn't Pass It To Our Children In The Bloodstream. It Must Be Fought For, Protected, And Handed On For Them To Do The Same, Or One Day We Will Spend Our Sunset Years Telling Our Children And Our Children's Children What It Was Once Like In The United States Where Men Were Free." - Ronald Reagan
3907	"I Believe That Banking Institutions Are More Dangerous To Our Liberties Than Standing Armies. If The American People Ever Allow Private Banks To Control The Issue Of Their Currency, First By Inflation, Then By Deflation, The Banks And Corporations That Will Grow Up Around The Banks Will Deprive The People Of All Property - Until Their Children Wake-Up Homeless On The Continent Their Fathers Conquered." - Thomas Jefferson
3908	"Would You Like Me To Give You A Formula For Success? It's Quite Simple, Really. Double Your Rate Of Failure. You Are Thinking Of Failure As The Enemy Of Success. But It Isn't At All. You Can Be Discouraged By Failure Or You Can Learn From It, So Go Ahead And Make Mistakes. Make All You Can. Because Remember That's Where You Will Find Success." - Thomas J. Watson
3909	"The Key Word Is Flexibility, The Ability To Adapt Constantly. Darwin Said It Clearly. People Thought That He Mainly Talked About Survival Of The Fittest. What He Said Was That The Species That Survive Are Usually Not The Smartest Or The Strongest, But The Ones Most Responsive To Change. So Being Attentive To Customers And Potential Partners Is My Best Advice--After, Of Course, Perseverance And Patience." - Philippe Kahn
3910	"Somehow I Can't Believe That There Are Any Heights That Can't Be Scaled By A Man Who Knows The Secrets Of Making Dreams Come True. This Special Secret, It Seems To Me, Can Be Summarized In Four C's. They Are Curiosity, Confidence, Courage, And Constancy, And The Greatest Of All Is Confidence. When You Believe In A Thing, Believe In It All The Way, Implicitly And Unquestionable." - Walt Disney

3911	"Business Is A Great Teacher: It Makes You Take Risks, Go For Your Dreams, Face Fears, Handle Your Emotions, Deal With Difficult People, And Learn Balance. You Don't Have To Do Any Weird Workshops Or Sign Up For Any Therapy Sessions. Go Into Business And You'll Be Enrolled In The Greatest Seminar Of All Time. And It Happens Every Day, Every Where, To Every One. You Can't Avoid It." - Joe Vitale
3912	"Now, Blessings Light On Him That First Invented Sleep! It Covers A Man All Over, Thoughts And All, Like A Cloak; It Is Meat For The Hungry, Drink For The Thirsty, Heat For The Cold, And Cold For The Hot. It Is The Current Coin That Purchases All The Pleasures Of The World Cheap, And The Balance That Sets The King And The Shepherd, The Fool And The Wise Man, Even." - Miguel De Cervantes
3913	"The Most Successful Men In The End Are Those Whose Success Is The Result Of Steady Accretion. . . It Is The Man Who Carefully Advances Step By Step, With His Mind Becoming Wider And Wider — And Progressively Better Able To Grasp Any Theme Or Situation — Persevering In What He Knows To Be Practical, And Concentrating His Thought Upon It, Who Is Bound To Succeed In The Greatest Degree." " - Alexander Graham Bell
3914	"It Is From Numberless Diverse Acts Of Courage And Belief That Human History Is Shaped. Each Time A Man Stands Up For An Ideal, Or Acts To Improve The Lot Of Others, Or Strikes Out Against Injustice, He Sends A Tiny Ripple Of Hope, And Crossing Each Other From A Million Different Centers Of Energy And Daring Those Ripples Build A Current Which Can Sweep Down The Mightiest Walls Of Oppression And Resistance." - Robert F. Kennedy
3915	"I Would Rather Be Ashes Than Dust! I Would Rather That My Spark Would Burn Out In A Brilliant Blaze Than It Should Be Stifled Out By Dry Rot. I Would Rather Be A Superb Meteor, Every Atom Of Me In Magnificent Glow, Than A Sleepy And Permanent Planet. The Function Of Man Is To Live, Not To Exist. I Shall Not Waste My Days Trying To Prolong Them. I Shall Use My Time." - Robert Frost
3916	"Fight One More Round. When Your Arms Are So Tired That You Can Hardly Lift Your Hands To Come On Guard, Fight One More Round. When Your Nose Is Bleeding And Your Eyes Are Black And You Are So Tired That You Wish Your Opponent Would Crack You One On The Jaw And Put You To Sleep, Fight One More Round – Remembering That The Man Who Always Fights One More Round Is Never Whipped." - James Corbett

3917	"Even Famous Published Authors Will Find It Difficult To Make A Living With A Single Book. The First Question An Author Is Asked Upon Signing A Contract For A First Book Is, What Else Do You Have? To Make Any Real Money For Them Or The Author. It Takes Several Books, Within The Same Genre, To Build The Author's Presence In The Marketplace. In Other Words, It Takes Constant Innovation Of New Products And Ideas." - Eugene M. Schwartz
3918	"The Problem With Most Failing Businesses Is Not That Their Owners Don't Know Enough About Finance, Marketing, Management, And Operations -- They Don't, But Those Things Are Easy Enough To Learn -- But That They Spend Their Time And Energy Defending What They Think They Know. My Experience Has Shown Me That The People Who Are Exceptionally Good In Business Aren't So Because Of What They Know But Because Of Their Insatiable Need To Know More." - Michael Gerber
3919	"How Important Is "Marketing"... Really? You've Seen The Letters The Emails And The Products: Courses, Books, Ebooks And Teleseminars Showing You How Important 'Marketing' Is… You And I Have Tools Through The Internet Right Now. Just A Few Years Ago Would Give Their Eye Teeth For. These Are Incredible Time Savers And Money-Makers And They Will Allow You To Generate Tons Of Profits If You See The Opportunity In Front Of You." - Gabor Olah
3920	"Every Day, Think As You Wake Up, Today I Am Fortunate To Be Alive, I Have A Precious Human Life, I Am Not Going To Waste It. I Am Going To Use All My Energies To Develop Myself, To Expand My Heart Out To Others; To Achieve Enlightenment For The Benefit Of All Beings. I Am Going To Have Kind Thoughts Towards Others, I Am Not Going To Get Angry Or Think Badly About Others. I Am Going To Benefit Others As Much As I Can." - The Dalai Lama
3921	"Generosity Is Another Quality Which, Like Patience, Letting Go, Non-Judging, And Trust, Provides A Solid Foundation For Mindfulness Practice. You Might Experiment With Using The Cultivation Of Generosity As A Vehicle For Deep Self-Observation And Inquiry As Well As An Exercise In Giving. A Good Place To Start Is With Yourself. See If You Can Give Yourself Gifts That May Be True Blessings, Such As Self-Acceptance, Or Some Time Each Day With No Purpose. Practice Feeling Deserving Enough To Accept These Gifts Without Obligation-To Simply Receive From Yourself, And From The Universe." - Jon Kabat-Zinn

3922	"When Employees Come To You With Suggestions Or Ideas About How They Might Approach Something Differently, Do You Move Immediately To No? Do You Kill An Idea Before It Is Even Off The Tongue? We Hear That Employees Feel Put Down And Turned Down Far More Than Their Managers Are Aware. And That Makes Leaving Easier. Instead Try Listening To The Entire Idea, Try Playing With It As A What If. Ask For More Information. Sleep On It, Mull It Over. Think, Isn't That Interesting Before You Think, It Will Never Work." - Beverly Kay And Sharon Jordan-Evans
3923	"I Am An Irresistible Magnet, With The Power To Attract Unto Myself Everything That I Divinely Desire, According To The Thoughts, Feelings And Mental Pictures I Constantly Entertain And Radiate. I Am The Center Of My Universe! I Have The Power To Create Whatever I Wish. I Attract Whatever I Radiate. I Attract Whatever I Mentally Choose And Accept. I Begin Choosing And Mentally Accepting The Highest And Best In Life. I Now Choose And Accept Health, Success And Happiness. I Now Choose Lavish Abundance For Myself And For All Mankind. This Is A Rich, Friendly Universe And I Dare To Accept Its Riches, Its Hospitality, And To Enjoy Them Now!" - Catherine Ponde
3924	"What Chance Gathers She Easily Scatters. A Great Person Attracts Great People And Knows How To Hold Them Together." - Johann Wolfgang Von Goethe
3925	"Minds Are Like Parachutes - They Only Function When Open." - Thomas Dewar
3926	"A General Is Just As Good Or Just As Bad As The Troops Under His Command Make Him." - General Douglas Macarthur
3927	"The Real Leader Has No Need To Lead--He Is Content To Point The Way." - Henry Miller
3928	"A Leader Is A Dealer In Hope." - Napoleon Bonaparte
3929	"If Your Actions Inspire Others To Dream More, Learn More, Do More And Become More, You Are A Leader." - John Quincy Adams
3930	"He Who Has Never Learned To Obey Cannot Be A Good Commander." - Aristotle
3931	"The Ultimate Measure Of A Man Is Not Where He Stands In Moments Of Comfort, But Where He Stands At Times Of Challenge And Controversy." - Martin Luther King Jr., Jr.
3932	"Where There Is No Vision, The People Perish." - Proverbs 29:18
3933	"Misfortunes, Untoward Events, Lay Open, Disclose The Skill Of A General, While Success Conceals His Weakness, His Weak Points" - Horace

3934	"In This World A Man Must Either Be An Anvil Or Hammer." - Henry Wadsworth Longfellow
3935	"Leadership Does Not Always Wear The Harness Of Compromise." - Woodrow Wilson
3936	"The Greater A Man Is In Power Above Others, The More He Ought To Excel Them In Virtue. None Ought To Govern Who Is Not Better Than The Governed." - Publius Syrus
3937	"To Be A Great Leader And So Always Master Of The Situation, One Must Of Necessity Have Been A Great Thinker In Action. An Eagle Was Never Yet Hatched From A Goose's Egg." - James Thomas
3938	"When I Give A Minister An Order, I Leave It To Him To Find The Means To Carry It Out." - Napoleon Bonaparte
3939	"No Man Can Stand On Top Because He Is Put There." - H. H. Vreeland
3940	"A Ruler Should Be Slow To Punish And Swift To Reward." - Ovid
3941	"It Is Impossible To Imagine Anything Which Better Becomes A Ruler Than Mercy." - Seneca
3942	"No General Can Fight His Battles Alone. He Must Depend Upon His Lieutenants, And His Success Depends Upon His Ability To Select The Right Man For The Right Place." - Philip Armour
3943	"To Do Great Things Is Difficult; But To Command Great Things Is More Difficult." - Friedrich Nietzche
3944	"Let Him Who Would Be Moved To Convince Others, Be First Moved To Convince Himself." - Thomas Carlyle
3945	"Action May Not Always Bring Happiness, But There Is No Happiness Without Action." - Benjamin Disraeli
3946	"Nobody Made A Greater Mistake Than He Who Did Nothing Because He Could Do Only A Little." - Edmund Burke
3947	"You Can't Do Anything About The Length Of Your Life, But You Can Do Something About Its Width And Depth." - Shira Tehrani
3948	"Well Done Is Better Than Well Said." - Benjamin Franklin
3949	"If The World Seems Cold To You, Kindle Fires To Warm It." - Lucy Larcom
3950	"A Book Of Quotations, Can Never Be Complete." - Robert M. Hamilton
3951	"Life Itself Is A Quotation." - Jorge Luis Borges
3952	"One Must Be A Wise Reader To Quote Wisely And Well." - Amos Bronson Alcott
3953	"A Fine Quotation Is A Diamond On The Finger Of A Man Of Wit, And A Pebble In The Hand Of A Fool." - Joseph Roux

3954	"It Is A Good Thing For An Uneducated Man To Read Books Of Quotations...The Quotations When Engraved Upon The Memory Give You Good Thoughts... And Look For More." - Sir Winston Churchill
3955	"Life Is A Great Big Canvas, And You Should Throw All The Paint You Can On It." - Danny Kaye
3956	"Bite Off More Than You Can Chew, Then Chew It." - Ella Williams
3957	"Whether You Think You Can Or Whether You Think You Can't, You're Right." - Henry Ford
3958	"You See Things; And You Say 'Why?' But I Dream Things That Never Were; And I Say - Why Not?" - George Bernard Shaw
3959	"Within Each Of Us Lies The Power Of Our Consent To Health And Sickness, To Riches And Poverty, To Freedom And To Slavery. It Is We Who Control These, And Not Another." - Richard Bach
3960	"Never Look Down On Anybody Unless You're Helping Him Up." - Jesse Jackson
3961	"To Be Yourself In A World That Is Constantly Trying To Make You Something Else Is The Greatest Accomplishment." - Ralph Waldo Emerson
3962	"The Reasonable Man Adapts Himself To The World; The Unreasonable One Persists In Trying To Adapt The World To Himself. Therefore, All Progress Depends On The Unreasonable Man." - George Bernard Shaw
3963	"People Are Like Stained-Glass Windows. They Sparkle And Shine When The Sun Is Out, But When The Darkness Sets In, Their True Beauty Is Revealed Only If There Is A Light From Within." - Elizabeth Kubler Ross
3964	"If You Can't Make A Mistake, You Can't Make Anything." - Marva Collins
3965	"What The World Really Needs Is More Love And Less Paper Work." - Pearl Bailey
3966	"I Have Always Observed That To Succeed In The World One Should Appear Like A Fool But Be Wise." - Charles De Mantesquieu
3967	"The Easiest Way To Avoid Wrong Notes Is To Never Open Your Mouth And Sing. What A Mistake That Would Be." - Pete Seeger
3968	"It Is Surmounting Difficulties That Makes Heroes." - Lajos Kossuth
3969	"Thoughts Lead On To Purposes; Purposes Go Forth In Action; Actions Form Habits; Habits Decide Character; And Character Fixes Our Destiny" - Tyron Edwards
3970	"I Learned That It Is The Weak Who Are Cruel, And That Gentleness Is To Be Expected Only From The Strong." - Leo Rosten

3971	"Quality Is Remembered Long After The Price Is Forgotten." - Gucci Slogan
3972	"You Will Never Find Time For Anything. If You Want The Time, You Must Make It." - Charles Buxton
3973	"If We Wait For The Moment When Everything, Absolutely Everything Is Ready, We Shall Never Begin." - Ivan Turgenew
3974	"It Is Good To Have An End To Journey Toward; But It Is The Journey That Matters, In The End." - Ursual Le Guin
3975	"All Successful People Men And Women Are Big Dreamers. They Imagine What Their Future Could Be, Ideal In Every Respect, And Then They Work Every Day Toward Their Distant Vision, That Goal Or Purpose." - Brian Tracy
3976	"One Of The Best Uses Of Your Time Is To Increase Your Competence In Your Key Result Areas." - Brian Tracy
3977	"Go Confidently In The Direction Of Your Dreams. Live The Life You Have Imagined." - Henry David Thoreau
3978	"Whatever You Can Do, Or Dream You Can Do, Begin It. Boldness Has Genius, Power And Magic In It." - Johann Wolfgang Von Goethe
3979	"The More Difficulties One Has To Encounter, Within And Without, The More Significant And The Higher In Inspiration His Life Will Be." - Horace Bushnell
3980	"Three Rules Of Work: Out Of Clutter Find Simplicity; From Discord Find Harmony; In The Middle Of Difficulty Lies Opportunity." - Albert Einstein
3981	"There Are No Elevators In The House Of Success." - H. H. Vreeland
3982	"In The Confrontation Between The Stream And The Rock, The Stream Always Wins - Not Through Strength, But Through Persistence." - The Buddha
3983	"Twenty Years From Now You Will Be More Disappointed By The Things You Didn't Do Than By The Ones You Did." - Mark Twain
3984	"So Throw Off The Bowlines, Sail Away From The Safe Harbor. Catch The Trade Winds In Your Sails." - Mark Twain
3985	"Explore. Dream. Discover." - Mark Twain
3986	"There Is No Security In This Life. There Is Only Opportunity." - Douglas Macarthur
3987	"Keep Away From Those Who Try To Belittle Your Ambitions. Small People Always Do That, But The Really Great Make You Believe That You Too Can Become Great." - Mark Twain

3988	"When One Door Of Happiness Closes, Another Opens: But Often We Look So Long At The Closed Door That We Do Not See The One Which Has Been Opened For Us." - Helen Keller
3989	"Failure Is Only The Opportunity To Begin Again More Intelligently." - Henry Ford
3990	"Opportunities Multiply As They Are Seized." - Sun Tzu
3991	"The Greatest Discovery Of My Generation Is That A Human Being Can Alter His Life By Altering His Attitude." - William James
3992	"There Is Nothing Impossible To Him Who Will Try." - Alexander The Great
3993	"There Are Only Two Ways To Live Your Life. One Is As Though Nothing Is A Miracle. The Other Is As Though Everything Is A Miracle." - Albert Einstein
3994	"What We Think, We Become. All That We Are Arises With Our Thoughts. With Our Thoughts, We Make The World." - The Buddha
3995	"If You Cry Because The Sun Has Gone Out Of Your Life, Your Tears Will Prevent You From Seeing The Stars." - Rabindranath Tagore
3996	"Try Not To Become A Man Of Success But A Man Of Value." - Albert Einstein
3997	"If You Have Built Castles In The Air, Your Work Need Not Be Lost; That Is Where They Should Be. Now Put Foundations Under Them." - Henry David Thoreau
3998	"Inspiration And Genius--One And The Same." - Victor Hugo
3999	"To Find What You Seek In The Road Of Life, The Best Proverb Of All Is That Which Says: - Leave No Stone Unturned." - Edward Bulwer Lytton
4000	"If You Would Create Something, You Must Be Something." - Johann Wolfgang Von Goethe
4001	"Do We Not All Agree To Call Rapid Thought And Noble Impulse By The Name Of Inspiration?" - George Eliot
4002	"No Great Man Ever Complains Of Want Of Opportunities." - Ralph Waldo Emerson
4003	"Happy Are Those Who Dream Dreams And Are Ready To Pay The Price To Make Them Come True." - Lwon J. Suenes
4004	"The Power Of Imagination Makes Us Infinite." - John Muir
4005	"First Say To Yourself What You Would Be; And Then Do What You Have To Do." - Epictetus
4006	"Happiness Is When What You Think, What You Say, And What You Do Are In Harmony." - Anonymous

4007	"To Select Well Among Old Things, Is Almost Equal To Inventing New Ones." - Nicholas Charles Trublet
4008	"Proverbs Are Mental Gems Gathered In The Diamond Districts Of The Mind." - William R. Alger
4009	"What Gems Of Painting Or Statuary Are In The World Of Art, Or What Flowers Are In The World Of Nature, Are Gems Of Thought To The Cultivated And The Thinking." - Oliver Wendell Holmes
4010	"Stealing Someone Else's Words Frequently Spares The Embarrassment Of Eating Your Own." - Peter Anderson
4011	"It Often Happens That The Quotations Constitute The Most Valuable Part Of A Book." - Vicesimus Knox
4012	"A Collection Of Rare Thoughts Is Nothing Less Than A Cabinet Of Intellectual Gems." - William B. Sprague
4013	"It Is Delightful To Transport One's Self Into The Spirit Of The Past, To See How A Wise Man Has Thought Before Us." - Johann Wolfgang Von Goethe

"One Can Only Imagine All The Wisdom That Exists Within Your Mind, That You Have Yet To Record."
- Richard Marvin Voigt

Our Beginning Thoughts

This Golden Vault contains timeless wisdom from the greatest minds and inspired world leaders, sharing insightful thoughts of excellence, achievement, and solid core values throughout history.

The world certainly would not be the same if not for these wise and stimulating teachers for their timeless and inspirational words that continue to touch and motivate the hearts and minds of billions of people from around our planet.

May our collection of 4,000+ of the world's greatest motivational quotations from 1,600+ brilliant world leaders, philosophers, business leaders, writers, and artists inspire your followers and motivate them to live their lives to their fullest potential.

We hope you too will be inspired to always give your very best in all of your life's adventures!

Richard & Lynn Voigt

About The Authors:

Richard and Lynn have been serving their clients as Domain Acquisition & Internet Marketing Education Specialists and Business Consultants since 1997. They present a unique team approach with each of their clients, working side-by-side; they work as a unique team utilizing their skills as life & business coaches, teachers, inventors, artists, and authors. Teaching by example they address each client's specific goals by recommending success strategies based upon their experiences in managing over a hundred of premium keyword websites on behalf of their company, RIVO Inc.

Their life-long mission is to continually uncover new strategies, products, and services networking useful solutions for their clients, on & offline entrepreneurs, small business owners, writers, local artists, models, teachers, and students and marketing professionals.

Feel free to contact them if you have questions or would like to tap into their talents and expertise. They appreciate your feedback & success stories.

Richard & Lynn Voigt - RIVO
I. M. Education Specialists

RIVO INC - RIVO Marketing
13720 West Keefe Avenue
Brookfield, Wisconsin 53005 – USA

Email: support@RIVOinc.com

For additional information visit: www.RIVOinc.com
View Lynn's Garden: www.WisconsinGarden.net
View Richard Unique Artwork: www.RIVOart.com

Want To See What We've Been Up To:

Visit Lynn's Garden: www.WisconsinGarden.net
          view hundreds of great garden video blogs

See Richard's Unique Artwork: www.RIVOart.com
          view over 3,000 original compositions

Watch For Additional RIVO Titles:

The Golden Vault Of Motivational Quotations –
          Words of Wisdom From The Greatest Minds & Leaders

Action Headlines That Drive Emotions – Volumes 1- 6
          Paint Dreams, Sell Ideas & Market Your Message

Twittering – The Art of 140
          A Funny Collection of 5,825 Silly Tweets

8,000 Clichés – All For One & One For All – A Goldmine
          Of Information That Leaves A Lasting Impression

The Language Of Millionaires –
          What Internet Marketers Say That Earns Millions

600 Useful Strategies, Tips & Ideas For Your Business

5,000 Hot Trigger Keywords For Marketing Niches -
          Words That Sell Ideas, Products & Services

BABYNAME.me – 18,500+ Unique Names & Nicknames –
          For Your Baby, Pets, and Favorite Man-Toys

How 2 Draw –Doodling For Kids & Executives
          Who Simply Love To Draw

Garden Alphabet – A Delicious Mouth-Watering Harvest
          From Apples To Zucchinis

PERSONAL NOTES:

www.ingramcontent.com/pod-product-compliance
Lightning Source LLC
Chambersburg PA
CBHW051452170526
45166CB00001B/216